EXPR~~~~~~~~D
REPRESENTATIONALISM

Pragmatists have traditionally been enemies of representationalism but friends of naturalism, when naturalism is understood to pertain to human subjects, in the sense of Hume and Nietzsche. In this volume Huw Price presents his distinctive version of this traditional combination, as delivered in his René Descartes Lectures at Tilburg University in 2008. Price contrasts his view with other contemporary forms of philosophical naturalism, comparing it with other pragmatist and neo-pragmatist views such as those of Robert Brandom and Simon Blackburn. Linking their different 'expressivist' programmes, Price argues for a radical *global* expressivism that combines key elements from both. With Paul Horwich and Michael Williams, Brandom and Blackburn respond to Price in new essays. Price replies in the closing essay, emphasising links between his views and those of Wilfrid Sellars. The volume will be of great interest to advanced students of philosophy of language and metaphysics.

EXPRESSIVISM, PRAGMATISM AND REPRESENTATIONALISM

HUW PRICE

with

SIMON BLACKBURN
ROBERT BRANDOM
PAUL HORWICH
MICHAEL WILLIAMS

CAMBRIDGE
UNIVERSITY PRESS

1006914911

CAMBRIDGE UNIVERSITY PRESS
Cambridge, New York, Melbourne, Madrid, Cape Town,
Singapore, São Paulo, Delhi, Mexico City

Cambridge University Press
The Edinburgh Building, Cambridge CB2 8RU, UK

Published in the United States of America by Cambridge University Press, New York

www.cambridge.org
Information on this title: www.cambridge.org/9781107009844

© Cambridge University Press 2013

First published 2013

Printed and bound in the United Kingdom by the MPG Books Group

A catalogue record for this publication is available from the British Library

Library of Congress Cataloguing in Publication data
Price, Huw, 1953–
Expressivism, pragmatism and representationalism / Huw Price with Simon Blackburn,
Robert Brandom, Paul Horwich, Michael Williams.
pages cm
Includes bibliographical references and index.
ISBN 978-1-107-00984-4 (hardback) – ISBN 978-0-521-27906-2 (paperback)
1. Pragmatism.   2. Representation (Philosophy).
3. Expressivism (Ethics).   4. Naturalism.
I. Blackburn, Simon, 1944–   II. Brandom, Robert.   III. Horwich, Paul.
IV. Williams, Michael, 1947 July 6–   V. Title.
B832.P85 2013
144′.3–dc23   2012038086

ISBN 978-1-107-00984-4 Hardback
ISBN 978-0-521-27906-2 Paperback

For Ava and Aubrey Mungo

Contents

Contents

Contributors

HUW PRICE is Bertrand Russell Professor of Philosophy and Fellow of Trinity College at the University of Cambridge. His publications include *Facts and the Function of Truth* (1988), *Time's Arrow and Archimedes' Point* (1996) and *Naturalism Without Mirrors* (2011). He is also co-editor (with Richard Corry) of *Causation, Physics, and the Constitution of Reality: Russell's Republic Revisited* (2007).

SIMON BLACKBURN is a Fellow of Trinity College, Cambridge, where he was Bertrand Russell Professor of Philosophy until 2011. He is a Distinguished Research Professor at the University of North Carolina, Chapel Hill, and Professor at the New College of the Humanities. His recent books include *How to Read Hume* (2008), *Practical Tortoise Raising* (2011) and *What Do we Know: The Big Questions of Philosophy* (2012).

ROBERT BRANDOM is Distinguished Professor of Philosophy at the University of Pittsburgh, and Fellow of the American Academy of Arts and Sciences. His most recent books include *Between Saying and Doing: Towards an Analytic Pragmatism* (2008), *Reason in Philosophy: Animating Ideas* (2009) and *Perspectives on Pragmatism: Classical, Recent, and Contemporary* (2011).

PAUL HORWICH is Professor of Philosophy at New York University. His recent work includes *From a Deflationary Point of View* (2004), *Reflections on Meaning* (2005), *Truth-Meaning-Reality* (2010), and *Wittgenstein's Metaphilosophy* (2012).

MICHAEL WILLIAMS is a Krieger-Eisenhower Professor and Chair of the Department of Philosophy at Johns Hopkins University. He is the author of *Groundless Belief* (1977; 2nd edition 1999), *Unnatural Doubts* (1992; 2nd edition 1996) and *Problems of Knowledge* (2001).

Preface

The origins of this volume lie in a kind invitation from the Tilburg Center
for Logic and Philosophy of Science (TiLPS), to deliver their inaugural René
Descartes Lectures in May 2008. I was delighted to accept, and presented
the lectures under the title 'Three Themes in Contemporary Pragmatism'
(the themes in question being naturalism, representationalism and pluralism). The lecture series was held in conjunction with a research workshop
on pragmatism and naturalism, providing me with a remarkable opportunity to discuss some of my recent work with the best kind of philosophical
audience – broadly sympathetic to a considerable extent, yet challenging on
many points. I am very grateful indeed to Professor Stephan Hartmann and
his colleagues at TiLPS for their hospitality, and for doing me the honour
of inviting me in the first place. I am also greatly indebted to the workshop
speakers and participants, for their part in making it such a memorable and
educational experience, from my point of view.

With the promise of such an excellent audience, I tried to use the lectures
to do two things: first, to present what I felt to be the most interesting ideas
in my recent work at that time, and, second, to try to think through some
succeeding steps (very much work in progress, at that stage). Accordingly,
I used the first lecture to present some material that was then recently in
print, on the role and significance of representationalist presuppositions in
conventional forms of philosophical naturalism.[1] In the second and third
lectures, I went on to discuss my developing ideas about an alternative form
of naturalism that rejects these presuppositions in their standard form.

Some of the latter ideas have since found their way into print in other
places. One of the key themes of Lecture 2 involves an attempt to compare

---

[1] A substantial portion of the version that appears in this volume was originally published as 'Naturalism
Without Representationalism', in David Macarthur and Mario de Caro, eds., *Naturalism in Question*,
Cambridge, MA: Harvard University Press, pp. 71–88 (© 2004 by the President and Fellows of Harvard
College), and is reprinted here by kind permission of the publisher.

and combine the (seemingly distinct) 'expressivist' programmes of writers such as Simon Blackburn, on the one hand, and of Robert Brandom, on the other. I have since discussed that project at greater length in 'Expressivism for Two Voices' (Price 2011a), incorporating some material from the lecture printed here. Other portions of that lecture and the next made their way into the introduction to my recent collection *Naturalism Without Mirrors* (Price 2011b). But in preparing this volume I have tried to resist the temptation to update the lectures in the light of that later work, instead confining second thoughts to my new Postscript.

I am indebted to Stephan Hartmann not only for the initial invitation and his hospitality during the lectures but also for the proposal to try to turn them into a volume by inviting commentary essays, with which the lectures themselves would appear. Two of the commentators here, Paul Horwich and Michael Williams, were present at the original lecture series and workshop in Tilburg, while Simon Blackburn and Robert Brandom joined the project at a later stage. I am very grateful indeed to all four, and delighted to have the opportunity to respond to their essays in this volume. I am also much indebted to my editors at Cambridge University Press, Hilary Gaskin and Anna Lowe, for their encouragement, assistance and patience, through what – due to factors entirely on my side – turned out to be a much lengthier process than any of us had anticipated or intended.

The delay had a silver lining, in that it gave me an opportunity to present the lectures a second time (now under the title 'Rethinking Representationalism') as Nordic Pragmatism Lecturer in Helsinki in September 2011. I am grateful to Sami Pihlström, Henrik Rydenfelt and the Kotkasaari family for their kind hospitality on that occasion, and to the participants in an associated seminar series, which gave me an opportunity to discuss the four commentary essays in this volume. I had already had a similar opportunity in a graduate seminar at the University of Sydney earlier in 2011, in conjunction with a visit to the Pragmatic Foundations Project at the Centre for Time by Matthew Chrisman (to whom, as to other participants in that seminar, I am also greatly indebted).

Most recently, and another happy consequence of my own tardiness, a welcome incentive to discuss the relationship between my 'global expressivism' and the views of Wilfrid Sellars came from Jim O'Shea, of University College Dublin, in the form of an invitation to speak at his Sellars Centenary Conference in June 2012. I am conscious that my remarks on this subject in the Postscript are rather preliminary, but I am very grateful to have been given such a spur to begin to explore this fascinating topic (and indebted to Willem deVries for comments on an early version).

The research on which this volume is based has been generously supported by an Australian Research Council Federation Fellowship, with associated funding from the University of Sydney; I am greatly indebted to both organisations. Among other things, this support made possible a series of conferences and workshops related to these themes, with many fascinating speakers and participants (including, at various stages, all four of my commentators in this volume). While I'm acutely aware of the impossibility of acknowledging all debts in such a rich field, and the inevitable arbitrariness involved in falling short, I would like to express my gratitude to the following partial list – participants in workshops, visitors, colleagues and former colleagues – from all of whom I have learned a great deal over the past few years: Robert Dunn, Patrick Greenough, Jenann Ismael, Robert Kraut, Anton Leist, Michael Lynch, David Macarthur, Paul Redding, Michael Ridge, Kevin Scharp, Lionel Shapiro and Amie Thomasson. I am also grateful to John Cusbert, for much invaluable and characteristically good-humoured editorial assistance.

PART I

The Descartes Lectures 2008

CHAPTER I

Naturalism without representationalism

Huw Price

What is philosophical naturalism? Most fundamentally, presumably, it is the view that natural science properly constrains philosophy, in the following sense. The concerns of the two disciplines are not simply disjointed, and science takes the lead where the two overlap. At the very least, then, to be a philosophical naturalist is to believe that philosophy is not simply a different enterprise from science, and that philosophy should defer to science, where the concerns of the two disciplines coincide.

Naturalism as spare as this is by no means platitudinous. However, most opposition to naturalism in contemporary philosophy is not opposition to naturalism in this basic sense but to a more specific view of the relevance of science to philosophy. Similarly on the pro-naturalistic side. What most self-styled naturalists have in mind is the more specific view. As a result, I think, both sides of the contemporary debate pay insufficient attention to a different kind of philosophical naturalism – a different view of the impact of science on philosophy. This different view is certainly not new – it has been with us at least since Hume – but nor is it prominent in many contemporary debates.

In this lecture I try to do something to remedy this deficit. I begin by making good the claim that the position commonly called naturalism is not a necessary corollary of naturalism in the basic sense outlined above. There are two very different ways of taking science to be relevant to philosophy. And contrary, perhaps, to first appearances, the major implications of these two views for philosophy arise from a common starting point. There is a single kind of core problem to which the two kinds of naturalism recommend very different sorts of answer.

I'll argue that the less well known view is more fundamental than its rival, in a sense to be explained, and that in calling attention to the difference between the two we call attention to a deep structural difficulty for the latter. I'll thus be defending philosophical naturalism in what I take to

3

be its more fundamental form, while criticising its popular contemporary manifestation.

Both the difficulty for the popular view and the conceptual priority of its unpopular rival turn on the foundational role of certain 'semantic' or 'representationalist' presuppositions in naturalism of the popular sort. This role is not well understood, in my view, but of considerable interest in its own right. (I shall return to it in Lecture 2.) For present purposes, its importance lies in four facts. First, the presuppositions concerned are non-compulsory and represent a crucial choice point for naturalism; reject them and one thereby rejects naturalism of the popular variety. Second, the standpoint from which the choice is properly made is that of naturalism of the unpopular variety – this is the sense in which this kind of naturalism is conceptually prior to its more popular cousin. Third, the possibility of rejection of these suppositions is no mere idle threat; it is a corollary of some mainstream views in contemporary philosophy. And fourth, and potentially worst of all, the presuppositions concerned turn out to be doubtfully acceptable, by the standards of the kind of naturalism they themselves are supposed to underpin.

Concerning naturalism itself, then, my argument is something like this. To assess the prospects for philosophical naturalism, we need a clear sense of the task of philosophy, in the areas in which science might conceivably be relevant. Clarity about this matter reveals not only that the approach commonly called naturalism is not the only science-sensitive option for philosophy in these areas, but also that a different approach is the pre-eminent approach, in the various senses just outlined. As bad news for contemporary naturalists of the orthodox sort, this may sound like good news for contemporary non-naturalists. But I hope it will be clear that my intentions are much more even-handed. Many non-naturalists share the representationalist presuppositions of their naturalist opponents, and in questioning those presuppositions, we question both sides of the debate they underpin. So I oppose both naturalism and non-naturalism as popularly understood, and favour a different kind of naturalism – a naturalism without representationalism.

1 OBJECTS AND SUBJECTS

The popular kind of naturalism – the view often called simply 'naturalism' – exists in both ontological and epistemological keys. As an ontological doctrine, it is the view that in some important sense, all there *is* is the world studied by science. As an epistemological doctrine, it is the view that all genuine knowledge is scientific knowledge.[1]

I'll call this view *object naturalism*. Though it is widely endorsed in contemporary philosophy, many of its supporters agree with some of its critics in thinking that it leads to some profound difficulties. The view implies that in so far as philosophy is concerned with the nature of objects and properties of various kinds, its concern is with something in the natural world, or with nothing at all. For there simply is nothing else. Perhaps there are very different ways of talking about the world-as-studied-by-science – different 'modes of presentation' of aspects of the same natural reality. But the object of each kind of talk is an aspect of the world-as-studied-by-science, or else nothing at all. The difficulties stem from the fact that in many interesting cases it is hard to see what natural facts we could be talking about. Different people will offer different lists of these 'hard problems' – common candidates include meaning, value, mathematical truth, causation and physical modality, and various aspects of mentality, for example – but it is almost an orthodoxy of contemporary philosophy, on both sides of the issue between naturalists and their opponents, that the list is non-empty.

More in a moment on these issues – *placement problems*, as I'll call them. Before we turn to such issues, I want to distinguish object naturalism from a second view of the relevance of science to philosophy. According to this second view, philosophy needs to begin with what science tells us *about ourselves*. Science tells us that we humans are natural creatures, and if the claims and ambitions of philosophy conflict with this view, then philosophy needs to give way. This is naturalism in the sense of Hume, then, and arguably Nietzsche.[2] I'll call it *subject naturalism*.

What is the relationship between object naturalism and subject naturalism? At first sight, the latter may seem no more than an obvious corollary of the former. Contemporary 'naturalists' – object naturalists, in my terms – would surely insist that they are also subject naturalists. After all, if all real entities are natural entities, we humans are surely natural entities. But in my view the relationship between the two approaches is much more interesting than this. Subject naturalism comes first, in a very important sense.

---

[1] It is a nice issue whether there is any deep difference between these two versions of the view, but an issue I'll ignore for present purposes.

[2] Both attributions call for some qualification. As a parent of empiricism, for one thing, Hume certainly bears some responsibility for the object naturalist's conception of the nature of knowledge.

I want to defend the following claim:

Priority Thesis   Subject naturalism is theoretically prior to object naturalism, because the latter depends on validation from a subject naturalist perspective.

What do 'priority' and 'validation' mean in this context? As I noted earlier, subject naturalism directs our attention to the issue of the scientific 'respectability' of the claims and presuppositions of philosophy – in particular their compatibility with the recognition that we humans are natural creatures. If the presuppositions of object naturalism turn out to be suspect, from this self-reflective scientific standpoint, then subject naturalism gives us reason to reject object naturalism. Subject naturalism thus comes first and could conceivably 'invalidate' object naturalism.

In my view, this threat to object naturalism is very real. I'll also defend this claim:

Invalidity Thesis   There are strong reasons for doubting whether object naturalism deserves to be 'validated' – whether its presuppositions do survive subject naturalist scrutiny.

As advertised, my case for this claim will depend on the role of certain 'semantic' or 'representationalist' presuppositions in the foundations of object naturalism. The crucial role of such presuppositions is far from obvious, however. To make it visible, we need to examine the structure of the well-recognised hard cases for object naturalism, the cases I've termed placement problems.

2 THE PLACEMENT ISSUE

If all reality is ultimately natural reality, how are we to 'place' moral facts, mathematical facts, meaning facts, and so on? How are we to locate topics of these kinds within a naturalistic framework, thus conceived? In cases of this kind, we seem to be faced with a choice between forcing the topic concerned into a category which for one reason or another seems ill shaped to contain it, or regarding it as at best second-rate – not a genuine area of fact or knowledge.

One way to escape this dilemma is to reject the naturalism that produces it. If genuine knowledge need not be scientific knowledge, genuine facts not scientific facts, there is no need to try to squeeze the problem cases into naturalistic clothing. Thus, placement problems provide the motivation for much contemporary opposition to naturalism in philosophy. However, there are two very different ways to reject the kind of naturalism that gives rise to these problems. One way is to be non-naturalistic in the same ontological or epistemic keys – to be an object non-naturalist, so to speak. The other way is to be naturalistic in a different key – to reject *object* naturalism, in favour of a subject-naturalist approach to the same theoretical problems.

At first sight, there seems to be no conceptual space for the latter view, at least in general, and at least if we want to avoid a universal subjectivism about all the hard cases. For subject naturalism rests on the fact that we humans are natural creatures, whereas the placement problems arise for topics which are at least not obviously human in nature. This is too quick, however. The possibility of a distinctive subject-naturalist approach to the placement issues turns on the fact that, at least arguably, these problems *originate* as problems about human linguistic usage.

In fact, it turns out that there are two possible conceptions of the origins of placement problems – two conceptions of the 'raw data' with which philosophy begins in such cases. On one conception, the problem begins with linguistic (or perhaps psychological) data; on the other, it begins with the objects themselves. These two conceptions are not often clearly distinguished, but the distinction turns out to be very important. As I'll explain, the priority of subject naturalism, and hence the vulnerability of object naturalism, rests on the thesis that the linguistic conception is the right one.

2.1 Where do placement problems begin?

On the face of it, a typical placement problem seeks to understand how some object, property or fact can be a *natural* object, property or fact. Ignoring for present purposes the distinction between objects, properties and facts, the issue is thus how some thing, X, can be a *natural* thing – the sort of thing revealed by science (at least in principle).

How do such issues arise in philosophy? On one possible view, the starting point is the object itself. We are simply acquainted with X and hence – in the light of a commitment to object naturalism – come to wonder how this thing-with-which-we-are-acquainted could be the kind of thing studied by science. On the other possible view, the starting point lies in human linguistic practices, broadly construed. Roughly, we note that humans (ourselves or others) employ the term 'X' in language, or the concept *X*, in thought. In the light of a commitment to object naturalism, again, we come to wonder how what these speakers are thereby talking or thinking *about* could be the kind of thing studied by science.

Let us call these two views of the origin of the placement problem the *material conception* and the *linguistic conception*, respectively. In favour of the material conception, it might be argued that the placement problem for X is a problem about the *thing* X, not a problem about the *term* 'X'. In other words, it is the problem as to how to locate X itself in the natural world, not the problem about how to locate the term 'X'.

In favour of the linguistic conception, on the other hand, note that some familiar moves in the philosophical debates to which placement problems give rise simply don't make sense, if we assume a material construal of the problem. Consider non-cognitivism, which tries to avoid the placement problem by arguing that *talk* of Xs – i.e. standard *use* of the term 'X' – does not have a referential or descriptive function. Here the claim is that in the light of a correct understanding of the *language* concerned there is no *material* problem. Of course, non-cognitivism might be mistaken in any particular case, but if the material view of the placement problem is right, it is not so much wrong as completely wrong-headed – a view that simply starts in the wrong place. Perhaps non-cognitivism is wrong-headed in this way. But the fact that this is not a common view reveals widespread implicit acceptance of a linguistic conception of the placement issue.

This appeal to philosophical practice isn't meant to be conclusive, of course. Instead, I'm going to proceed as follows. For the moment, I'll simply assume that the linguistic conception is correct, and explore its consequences for object naturalism. (I'll remind readers at several points that my conclusions depend on this assumption.) At the end of the paper I'll come back to the question whether the assumption is compulsory – whether object naturalism can evade my critical conclusions by adopting the material conception. I'll argue, albeit somewhat tentatively, that this is not a live option, and hence that my earlier conclusions cannot be side-stepped in this way.

3 THE SEMANTIC LADDER

If the linguistic conception is correct, then placement problems are initially problems about human linguistic behaviour (or perhaps about human thought). What turns such a concern into an issue about something else – about value, mathematical reality, causation, or whatever? The answer to this question was implicit above, when our attention shifted from the *term* to what it is *about*. The shift relies on what we may call the *representationalist* assumption. Roughly, this is the assumption that the *linguistic* items in question 'stand for' or 'represent' something *non-linguistic* (at least in general – let's leave aside for present purposes the special case in which the subject matter is also linguistic). This assumption grounds our shift in focus from the *term* 'X' or *concept X*, to its assumed *object*, X.

At first sight, however, the required assumption may seem trivial. Isn't it a truism that 'X' refers to X? Isn't this merely the referential analogue of the fact that 'Snow is white' is true if and only if snow is white?

The familiarity of these principles masks a serious confusion, in my view. True, the move in question is in one sense a familiar semantic descent. A semantic relation – reference, if we are dealing with terms, or truth, if we are dealing with sentences – is providing the 'ladder' that leads us from an issue about language to an issue about non-linguistic reality. But it is vital to see that in the present case the move involves a real shift of theoretical focus, a real change of subject matter. So this is a *genuine* logical descent, then, and not a mere reversal of Quine's deflationary 'semantic ascent'. Quine's semantic ascent never really leaves the ground. Quine himself (1970: 12) puts it like this: 'By calling the sentence ["Snow is white"] true, we call snow white. The truth predicate is a device of disquotation.' So Quine's deflationary semantic ladder never really takes us 'up', whereas the present semantic ladder does need to take us 'down'.

If we begin with Quine's deflationary semantic notions, in other words, then talking about the *referent* of the term 'X', or the *truth* of the sentence 'X is F', is just another way of talking about the *object*, X. So if our original question was really about language, and we rephrase the issue in these semantic terms, we've simply changed the subject. We haven't traversed the semantic ladder but simply taken up *a different issue*, talking in what Carnap called the formal mode about objects, rather than talking about language. On this deflationary view, then, object naturalism commits a fallacy of equivocation – a kind of mention–use fallacy, in fact[3] – on the way to its formulation of what it takes to be the central issue.

---

3 The fallacy turns on the fact that on the disquotational view, an expression of the form '"Snow is white" is true' contains a use masquerading as a mention. If it were a genuine mention, to call 'Snow is white' true would not be 'to call snow white', as Quine puts it. If we term this disquotational mention a *formal* mention, then formal mention is effective use, and the fallacy here involves a confusion between genuine and formal mention, or true mention and effective use.

This point is easy to overlook because we run up and down these semantic ladders so easily. But, if Quine is right, the reason the climbs are so effortless is that the ladders lead us nowhere. In the present case, we do need to get somewhere. If we begin with a linguistic conception of the origins of the placement issues – if we see these issues as initially questions about linguistic usage – then it takes a genuine shift of theoretical focus to get us to an issue about the nature of non-linguistic objects. If the shift is to be mediated by semantic properties or relations of some kind, they must be substantial properties, in the following sense. They must be such that in ascribing such properties to a term or sentence we are making some theoretical claim about the linguistic items concerned rather than simply using those items to make a claim about something else.

True, these properties must also be such as to allow us to make the transition to an issue about objects. Our theoretical focus must be led from the issue about the terms and sentences to an issue about their assumed semantic objects or values. For the object naturalist's conception of the resulting programme, moreover, it is vital that this transition track the disquotational schema. (How else could a concern with the use of the term 'X' lead us to an interest in X itself?) My point is that unless there is more to the semantic notions than simply disquotation, the starting point is not genuinely linguistic and so there is no transition at all. (One might argue that this is good news because placement issue begins at the material level in any case. But for the moment we are assuming the linguistic conception of the origin of the problem, and this response is therefore excluded.)

Given a linguistic view of the placement issue, then, substantial, non-deflationary semantic notions turn out to play a critical theoretical role in the foundations of object naturalism. Without such notions, there can be no subsequent issue about the natural 'place' of entities such as meanings, causes, values and the like. Object naturalism thus rests on substantial theoretical assumptions about what we humans do with language – roughly, the assumption that substantial 'word–world' semantic relations are a part of the best scientific account of our use of the relevant terms.

However, these assumptions lie in the domain of subject naturalism. Moreover, as the conceptual possibility of deflationism already illustrates, they are non-compulsory; more on this in a moment. Hence my priority thesis: given a linguistic conception of the origin of placement problems, subject naturalism is theoretically prior to object naturalism and object naturalism depends on validation from a subject-naturalist perspective.

4 SHOULD OBJECT NATURALISM BE VALIDATED?

It is one thing to establish a need, another to show that there are serious grounds for doubting whether that need can be met. However, it seems to me that there are actually strong grounds for doubting whether object naturalism can be satisfactorily validated, in the above sense. These grounds are of three kinds: the first appeals to the attractions and consequences of semantic deflationism; the second exploits an argument due to Stephen Stich; and the third challenges the coherence of a linguistically grounded object naturalism about semantic notions themselves. I shall discuss these difficulties in turn.

4.1 The threat of semantic deflationism

I have already noted that deflationism about truth and reference blocks an object naturalist's access to the kind of semantic ladder needed to transform a theoretical question about terms into a question about their assumed objects. Given the attractions of deflationism, this is clearly grounds for concern, from an object naturalist's point of view.

It is worth emphasising two further points. First, deflationism itself is clearly of a subject-naturalist character. It offers a broadly scientific hypothesis about what linguistic creatures like us 'do' with terms such as 'true' and 'refers' – what role these terms play in our linguistic lives. Of course, the use of these terms itself comprises the basis of one particularly interesting placement problem. So semantic deflationism both *exemplifies* a subject-naturalist approach to a particular placement problem (an approach that seeks to explain the *use* of the semantic terms in question), and provides a general obstacle to an object naturalist construal of placement problems at large.

Second, it is worth noting in passing how the distinctions in play at this point enable semantic deflationism to avoid Paul Boghossian's charge that any such view is inconsistent. Boghossian (1989, 1990) argues that irrealism about semantic notions is incoherent, because irrealism involves, precisely, a *denial* that the term or sentence in question has semantic properties (a referent, or truth conditions). If this characterisation of irrealism is indeed mandatory, then Boghossian seems right. Irrealism *presupposes* semantic notions, and hence the denial in question is incoherent in the case of the semantic terms themselves.

However, the point turns on the fact that, so construed, irrealism relies on the kind of theoretical framework provided by the representational view of language. So long as a semantic deflationist simply *rejects* this theoretical framework, her position is not incoherent. Of course, one might insist that the resulting position no longer deserves to be called irrealism, but this is merely a terminological issue. The important point is that it is indisputably deflationary. A deflationist can consistently offer a use-explanatory account of semantic terms, while saying nothing of theoretical weight about whether these terms 'refer' or 'have truth-conditions'.

The answer to Boghossian's challenge to deflationism thus depends on a distinction between *denying in one's theoretical voice* that these terms refer or have truth conditions (which Boghossian is right to point out that a deflationist cannot do); and *being silent in one's theoretical voice* about whether these terms refer or have truth conditions. A deflationist can – indeed must – do the latter, having couched her theoretical claims about the terms concerned in other terms entirely – and having insisted, *qua* deflationist, that the semantic notions do no interesting causal-explanatory work.

I'll return to Boghossian's argument in a moment, for in my view it does comprise a problem for my object naturalist opponents. For the moment, what matters is that it does not provide an obstacle to a well-formulated deflationism.

4.2 Stich's problem

We have seen that in the light of a linguistic conception of the origins of the placement problem, semantic deflationism is incompatible with object naturalism. In so far as deflationism is an attractive view, in other words, the 'validation' of object naturalism must remain in doubt.

But rejecting deflationism does not necessarily solve the object naturalist's problems. One way to appreciate this is to adapt the considerations discussed by Stephen Stich in *Deconstructing the Mind* (1996). In effect, Stich argues that even a non-deflationary scientific account of reference is unlikely to be determinate enough to do the work that object naturalism requires. Stich's own immediate concern is with eliminativism, and thus (in linguistic mode) with issues as to whether terms such as 'belief' refer at all. He argues that so long as we retain a linguistic conception of our starting point in metaphysics, these questions inevitably become hostage to indeterminacies in our theory of reference. Evidently, if Stich is right, then the problem is not confined to eliminativism. It affects the issue 'What is belief?', for example, as much as it affects the issue 'Are there any beliefs?' So realist as well as anti-realist responses to the placement problem are equally afflicted.

Stich himself responds by disavowing the linguistic conception of the *explanandum*. We'll return below to the question as to whether this is really an option. For the moment, I simply help myself to Stich's useful discussion of these issues in support of the following tentative conclusion. Even setting aside the threat of deflationism, it is very far from clear that a 'scientific' account of semantic relations is going to provide what we need in order to turn an interesting theoretical issue about *terms* ('causation', 'belief', 'good' and so on) into an interesting issue about *objects*.

4.3 Is object naturalism coherent?

We have seen that if placement problems originate at the linguistic level, substantial semantic notions are needed to transform a question about linguistic usage into a question about non-linguistic objects. Object naturalism thus presupposes substantial semantic properties or relations of some kind. The two previous reasons for doubting whether object naturalism is entitled to this presupposition turned first on the possibility of deflationism, which denies that semantic properties are load-bearing in the appropriate sense, and, second, on the possibility that even a non-deflationary scientific account of reference might be too loosely constrained to be useful as the required semantic ladder.

Now to an even more serious difficulty. In view of the fact that object naturalism presupposes the semantic notions in this way, it is doubtful whether these notions themselves can consistently be investigated in an object naturalist spirit. Naturalism of this kind seems committed to the empirical contingency of semantic relations. For any given term or sentence, it must be to some extent an empirical matter whether, and if so to what, that term refers; whether, and if so where, it has a truthmaker. However, it seems impossible to make sense of this empirical attitude with respect to the semantic terms themselves.

The difficulty here is closely related to Boghossian's objection to semantic irrealism. In that context, the problem was that if semantic notions are presupposed in the issue between realists and irrealists – for example, if the realist/irrealist issue is taken to *be* that as to whether the terms and sentences of some domain refer, or have truth conditions – then irrealism about these notions themselves is incoherent. Here, the problem is as follows. The object naturalist's project requires in general that irrealism be treated as live empirical possibility, but Boghossian's point shows that the object naturalist cannot adopt this attitude to the semantic terms themselves.

Boghossian takes the point to amount to a transcendental argument for a non-naturalist realism about semantic content. In my view, however, it is better seen as a pro-naturalist – pro-*subject* naturalist – point, in that it exposes what is inevitably a non-naturalistic presupposition in the leading contemporary conception of what is involved in taking science seriously in philosophy. Of course, the possibility of this interpretation depends on the fact that there is a consistent alternative naturalism, which walks away from the usual semantically grounded conception of issue. (In a different way, it also depends on a linguistic conception of the starting point – a conception we are assuming at this point, and a conception to which Boghossian himself is obviously committed.)

It might seem implausible that there could be a problem here which is specific to object naturalism. After all, I have suggested that it is an empirical possibility that the subject-naturalist standpoint might not yield the kind of substantial semantic relations required for object naturalism. Isn't this same possibility all that object naturalism needs to make sense of the possibility of irrealism about semantics, in its sense?

No. The empirical possibility we have discussed is not that subject naturalism will discover that there are no semantic properties of the right sort but simply that it will find no reason to say that there are. This is the distinction I appealed to above in explaining how deflationism escapes Boghossian's trap. The subject naturalist's basic task is to account for the use of various terms – among them, the semantic terms themselves – in the lives of natural creatures in a natural environment. The distinction just mentioned turns on the possibility that in completing this task the subject naturalist might simply find no need for an explanatory category of semantic properties and relations. (At no point would she need to say that the term 'refer' does or does not refer to anything, for example, except in the deflationary, non-theoretical sense.) Of course, from the object naturalist's perspective, this looks like an investigation as to whether there are semantic properties, but the subject naturalist has no reason to construe it that way. Indeed, she has a very good reason *not* to construe it that way, if, as Boghossian has argued, that construal is simply incoherent.

The issue of the coherence of the object-naturalist approach to the semantic terms is subtle and difficult, and I don't pretend to have made a case that the difficulty is conclusive. What I hope to have established is something weaker. A naturalist has neither need nor automatic entitlement to a substantial account of semantic relations between words or thoughts and the rest of the natural world – no automatic entitlement because, by naturalism's own lights, it is at best an empirical matter; and no need because there are ways of being naturalist that don't depend on any such assumption. Nevertheless, the stronger thesis, the incoherency thesis, seems to me both fascinating and plausible, and I want briefly to mention another way of fleshing out the difficulty.

If there is a coherent object-naturalist account of the semantic relations, then, as we noted earlier, the object naturalist will want to say that the right account is not *a priori* – there is more than one coherent possibility, and the issue is in part an empirical matter. Let's consider just two of the coherent possibilities – two rival accounts of what reference is, for example. Account 1 says that reference is the natural relation R*, Account 2 that it is the natural relation R**. Thus, apparently, we have two incompatible views as to what reference actually is.

But do we? Let's think a little more closely about what each of these views claims. The first account claims that the ordinary term 'Reference' picks out, or refers to, the relation R* – in other words, by its own lights, that

'Reference' stands in the relation R* to the relation R*.

The second account claims that the ordinary term 'Reference' picks out, or refers to, the relation R** – in other words, by its own lights, that

'Reference' stands in the relation R** to the relation R**.

Are these claims incompatible? Not at all. The term 'Reference' might very well stand in these two different relations to two different things, even if we allow (as proponents of both views will want to insist), that in the case of each relation singly no term could stand in that relation to both.

Again, the problem stems from the fact that the object naturalist is trying to ask a question that renders its own presuppositions fluid. There is no fixed question, with a range of answers, but, so to speak, a different question for each answer. I leave as an exercise another puzzle of this kind (see Figure 1.1). It is multiple choice, and the problem is not that there is no right answer but that there are too many right answers.[4] Again, the upshot seems to be that in the light of the role of semantic notions in the object naturalist's conception of the task of philosophy, that task does not make sense with respect to the semantic terms themselves.

---

4 In a more detailed examination of these issues, it would be interesting to consider the connection between this kind of consideration (and indeed Boghossian's argument) and Putnam's 'just more theory' concerns about the metaphysical use of a theory of reference (see Putnam 1978, 1981).

The option selected below is:

A. Option A   ☐

B. Option B   ☐

C. Option C   ☐

D. None of the above   ☐

Figure 1.1. A multiple choice examination.

5 REJECTING THE LINGUISTIC CONCEPTION?

As I have emphasised, the above discussion has assumed a linguistic conception of the origins of the placement problem. Is this an optional assumption?
Can a material conception get object naturalism off the hook? I close with
two reasons for scepticism on this point.

5.1 The cat is out of the bag

It is clear that the linguistic conception of the placement issue is already
in play. I noted earlier that to treat non-cognitivism as an option in these
debates is to commit oneself to a linguistic conception of the origin of the
problem. The threat to object naturalism takes off from this point, noting
that the representationalist assumption is non-compulsory, that there are
other possible theoretical approaches to language in which semantic notions
play no significant role. We have thus been offered the prospect of a (subject)
naturalistic account of the relevant aspects of human talk and thought, from
the perspective of which the material question ('What are Xs?') simply
doesn't arise.[5] At this stage, the only way for object naturalists to regain
control of the ball is to *defend* the representationalist assumption (a project
fraught with difficulty, for the reasons noted above).

---

[5] That is to say, it doesn't arise as a question driven by naturalism. Such questions arise in many other
contexts, of course – 'What is justice?', 'What is irony?', 'What is choux pastry?', for example. If
more or less commonplace questions of these kinds do give rise to puzzles of an object-naturalist sort,
the subject naturalist recommends a dose of linguistic therapy: think carefully about what you are
assuming about language before you allow yourself to be convinced that there's a genuine ontological
puzzle.

Couldn't an object naturalism challenge the current conception of the starting point? What is wrong with Stich's proposal, that we simply begin at the material level and do metaphysics without semantic crutches? What is wrong with it, I think, is that it amounts to the proposal that we should simply *ignore* the possibility that philosophy might have something to learn from naturalistic – *subject* naturalistic – reflection on the things that we humans do with language. (If this seems controversial, note that it would be to ignore the possibility of non-cognitivism.) So it is a radically anti-naturalistic move. For someone who takes science seriously, the only route to object naturalism is the hard one: to concede that the problem begins at the linguistic level and to defend the representationalist view.

5.2 The semantic toolkit of modern metaphysics

The second consideration deserves a much more detailed discussion than I can give it here.[6] Briefly, however, it seems that semantic notions such as reference and truth have become instruments in the investigative programme of contemporary metaphysics. It has become common practice to identify one's objects of interest in semantic ways – as truth-makers or referents, say, or more generally as 'realisers' of semantic roles.

However, the relevance of this observation about philosophical practice is far from straightforward. One of the difficulties is to decide which of the many uses of such semantic notions are 'substantial' theoretical uses and which can be regarded in a merely Quinean fashion – convenient but theoretically uncommitted uses of deflationary semantic terms. For the reasons discussed earlier, the use of deflationary semantic notions in metaphysics is not incompatible with a material conception of the origins of the placement issue. But if more substantial notions are in play then the linguistic domain seems to play a correspondingly more significant role. Claims about language come to play a role analogous to that of observational data in science, with the semantic relations supporting inferences to an unobserved reality. The enterprise thus becomes committed to a linguistic conception of its starting point.

There are many strands in this linguistic retooling of contemporary metaphysics – the linguistic return, as we might call it. One significant strand runs as follows, I think. In David Lewis's influential conception of theoretical identification in science (1970, 1972), objects of interest are identified as occupiers of causal roles. If the theoretical term 'X' is defined in this way,

6 I discuss it further in Price (2009) and Menzies and Price (2009).

we know what to do to answer the question 'What is X?' We experiment in the laboratory of the world, adjusting this, twiddling that, until we discover just what it is that does the causal job our theory assigns to X.

In the view of many, however, Lewis's programme is fit not just for science but for metaphysics as well.[7] Indeed, some who think this would reject the suggestion, implicit in my formulation, that metaphysics is something different from science. But there is one difference at least. In metaphysics, there is no guarantee that our objects of interest will be the kinds of things which have *causal* roles. We might be interested in numbers, or values, or indeed in causation itself, and for all of these things it is at least controversial whether they can be identified as the cause of this, the effect of that.[8]

So, in the global programme, the place of causation must be taken by something else. What else could it be? It seems to me that there are two possibilities. One is that causal roles get replaced by semantic roles. In this case, the procedure for answering a question of the form 'What is X?' is analogous to the one described above, except that the aim of our fiddling and twiddling – conceptual, now, rather than experimental – is to discover, say, to what the term 'X' *refers*, or what *makes true* the claim that X is F.

That's the first possibility – that semantic relations play the same substantial role in the general programme as causal relations played in the original programme. If so, then the upshot is as we have seen. Language has become the starting point for metaphysics, and the resulting position is vulnerable in the ways described above.

The second possibility is that *nothing* specific replaces causation. It simply depends on the particular case, on what the Ramsey-Lewis method turns out to tell us about the X in question. Semantic terms may figure in the description of the task, but on this view they are no more than deflationary. We say, 'X is the thing that makes this Ramsey sentence true', but this is just a convenient way of doing what we could do by saying 'X is the thing such that …' and then *using* the Ramsey sentence in question.

---

[7] See, especially, Jackson (1998).

[8] The claim that metaphysics extends beyond the causal realm is perhaps more controversial than I here allow. Someone who rejects it will be inclined to say that where causation stops, non-metaphysical modes of philosophy begin: formalism, perhaps, in the case of mathematics, non-cognitivism in the case of value, and so on. For present purposes, it is enough to point out that such a view is thereby committed to a linguistic conception of the placement issue, for the latter views are linguistic in nature. However, it is worth noting that in a causally grounded metaphysics of this kind the notion of causation is likely to be problematic, in a way analogous to the semantic notions in a linguistically grounded object naturalism. It will be a primitive notion, inaccessible to the programme's own professed methods.

I think that this second version does avoid essential use of non-deflationary semantic notions, and is hence compatible with a material conception of our starting point in metaphysics. The problem is that it thereby cuts itself off from any general argument for (object) naturalism, of a kind that would parallel Lewis's famous argument for physicalism about the mental (Lewis 1966). Lewis's argument relies on a premise to the effect that all causation is physical causation – the assumption of 'the explanatory adequacy of physics', as Lewis puts it. Without such a premise, clearly, there is nothing to take us from the conclusion that a mental state M has a particular causal role to the conclusion that M is a physical state. The problem for the second of the two versions of the generalised Lewisean programme is that without any single thing to play the role that causation plays in the restricted programme, there can be no analogue of this crucial premise in support of a generalised argument for physicalism.

Thus it seems to me that object naturalists face a dilemma. If they appeal to substantial semantic relations they have some prospect of an argument for naturalism, couched in terms of those relations – for example, an argument that all truths have natural truth-makers. In this case, however, they are implicitly committed to a linguistic conception of the 'raw data' for these investigations and face the problems identified earlier. If they don't appeal to substantial semantic relations they avoid these difficulties but lose the theoretical resources with which to formulate a general argument for naturalism, conceived on the object-naturalist model.

Without the protection of such an argument, the difficult opponent is not someone who agrees to play the game in material mode but then bats for non-naturalism, defending a primitive plurality of ontological realms. The difficult opponent is the naturalist who takes advantage of a non-representationalist theoretical perspective to avoid the material mode altogether. If such an opponent can explain why natural creatures in a natural environment come to *talk* in these plural ways – of 'truth', 'value', 'meaning', 'causation' and all the rest – what puzzle remains? What debt does philosophy now owe to science?

Summing up, it is doubtful whether an object naturalist can avoid a linguistic conception of the placement issue and thereby escape the difficulties identified earlier. Some versions of object naturalism help themselves to the linguistic conception in any case, in order to put semantic relations to work in the service of metaphysics. In other cases, the inescapability of the linguistic conception turns on the fact that it is always available to the object naturalist's subject-naturalist opponent, as the basis of an alternative view of the task of philosophy in these cases. The object naturalist's instinct is always to appeal to the representational character of language to bring the issue back to the material level, but this, as we have seen, is a recipe for grave discomfort.

6 NATURAL PLURALITY

Linguistically construed, the placement problem stems from a striking multiplicity in ordinary language, a puzzling plurality of topics of talk. Given a naturalistic conception of speakers, the addition of a representationalist conception of speech makes the object naturalist's ontological interpretation of the placement problem almost irresistible. Term by term, sentence by sentence, topic by topic, the representationalist's semantic ladder leads us from language to the world, from words to their worldly objects. Somehow, the resulting multiplicity of kinds of entities – values, modalities, meanings and the rest – needs to be accommodated within the natural realm. To what else, after all, could natural speakers be related by natural semantic relations?

Without a representationalist conception of the talk, however, the puzzle takes a very different form. It remains in the linguistic realm, a puzzle about a plurality of *ways of talking*, of forms of human linguistic behaviour. The challenge is now simply to explain in naturalistic terms how creatures like us come to talk in these various ways. This is a matter of explaining what role the different language games play in our lives – what differences there are between the functions of talk of value and the functions of talk of electrons, for example.[9] This certainly requires plurality in the world, but of a familiar kind, in a familiar place. Nobody expects human behaviour to be anything other than highly complex. Without representationalism, the joints between topics remain joints between kinds of behaviour, and don't need to be mirrored in ontology of any other kind.

In the remaining lectures I want to try to give a sense of what this alternative programme looks like, especially by locating it with respect to familiar landmarks in the contemporary philosophical landscape. To conclude this lecture, I want to stress two things: first that this is a recognisably naturalistic project and, second, that it is a very different project from that of most

---

9 This kind of linguistic pluralism is very Wittgensteinian in spirit, of course. One of Wittgenstein's main themes in the early sections of the *Investigations* is that philosophy misses important distinctions about the uses of language, distinctions which are hidden from us by 'the uniform appearances of words' (Wittgenstein 1953 §11). The view proposed here may be too naturalistic for some contemporary Wittgensteinians, but would Wittgenstein himself have objected to it? (He might have thought that it is science, not philosophy, but that's a different matter.)

contemporary philosophical naturalists. I have argued that the popular view (object naturalism) is in trouble by its own lights, in virtue of its semantic presuppositions. The availability of the subject-naturalist alternative makes clear that the problems of object naturalism are not problems for naturalism per se – not a challenge to the view that in some areas philosophy properly defers to science.

We began with the relevance of science to philosophy. Let's finish with the relevance of science to science itself. Object naturalism gives science not just centre stage but the whole stage, taking scientific knowledge to be the only knowledge there is (at least in some sense). Subject naturalism suggests that science might properly take a more modest view of its own importance. It imagines a scientific discovery that science is not all there is – that science is just one thing among many[10] that we do with 'representational' discourse. If so, then the semantic presuppositions of object naturalism are bad science, a legacy of an insufficiently naturalistic philosophy. The story then has the following satisfying moral. If we do science better in philosophy, we'll be less inclined to think that science is all there is to do.

---

[10] Or more likely, I think, 'several things among many', in the sense that scientific language itself is not monofunctional. I think that causal and modal talk has distinct functions in this sense and, while essential to any interesting science, is not the whole of it. If so, this is enough to show that there is functional plurality within scientific language as well as outside it. More on this in later lectures.

CHAPTER 2

Two expressivist programmes, two bifurcations

Huw Price

The previous lecture focused on naturalism. In that context, my discussion of representation was a means to an end. I argued that it is the role of representationalist presuppositions in much contemporary naturalistic metaphysics that best reveals both the theoretical priority of what I called subject naturalism and the vulnerability of object naturalism. In this lecture, representation itself takes centre stage, though I shall approach it, in part, from the wings: via two views in contemporary philosophy that set themselves up in opposition to mainstream representationalists, at least about certain matters. These two views are the self-avowedly 'expressivist' positions of Simon Blackburn, on the one hand, and Robert Brandom, on the other.

Perhaps surprisingly, the issue of the relationship between these two expressivist programmes has been little discussed. In my view, they complement each other rather well, though there are some apparent points of tension to be negotiated.[1] One tension turns on the fact that Blackburn, like other writers in what I shall call the 'Humean' expressivist tradition, takes for granted a 'bifurcation' between descriptive and non-descriptive uses of declarative utterances. (Blackburn's own version of this view is distinctive in that he lays great stress on the need to explain why some non-descriptive uses of language are nevertheless 'quasi-descriptive', in taking declarative form in the first place.) Brandom, on the other hand, appears to offer us a uniform account of the role of assertoric language, with no place for such a distinction.

This tension is significant but ultimately superficial, in my view. Here, I shall propose that it points to a need for a different distinction – a kind of bifurcation in the notion of representation itself. I shall argue that there are two very different notions, or clusters of notions, both commonly

---

[1] I discuss these issues at greater length in Price (2011a).

associated with 'representation' and various cognate terms, and that there is much to be gained by pulling them apart and recognising that they are distinct.

This bifurcation in the notion of representation requires a considerable reorientation in our intuitive ideas about how language relates to the world – indeed, as we shall see in Lecture 3, it requires that we rethink what we *mean* by 'the world' (recommending a corresponding bifurcation at that point, too). In order to have before us a vivid conception of the view I think we need to reject, I want to begin with a metaphor, intended to capture some of the intuitive representationalist picture and its role in contemporary philosophical thought.

I THE MATCHING GAME

Imagine a child's puzzle book, designed like this. On the left side of the page are some peel-off stickers – perhaps the Opera House, the Harbour Bridge, a koala. The aim of the game is to match each of these stickers to the corresponding object in a picture on the right-hand side of the page. The game is successfully completed when every sticker has been placed in its correct location.

Now think of the right-hand side as the world and the stickers as statements we take to be true of the world. For each statement, it seems natural to ask what *makes* it true – what fact in the world has precisely the 'shape' required to do the job. Matching true statements to the world seems a lot like matching stickers to the picture; and many problems in philosophy seem much like the problems the child faces when some of the stickers are hard to place.

In both cases, the problem stems from restrictions on the options available on the right-hand side of the game. In the first case, the child has to work within the constraints of the picture provided. If she's allowed to draw her own outlines, one for each sticker, the task is easy – engrossing, perhaps, at a certain age, but essentially trivial. But in a preassigned picture the outlines can be concealed or absent altogether, and hence the puzzle can be difficult or impossible to complete.

In the philosophical case, similarly, the game is trivial – not even engrossing, to most temperaments – if for any true statement 'P' at all, we're allowed to say that 'P' is made true by the fact that P. It becomes non-trivial when we impose limitations on the facts on the right – restrictions on the available 'truth-makers' for the statements on the left.

There are various motivations for playing the philosophical game with restrictions of this kind, but by far the most influential, in contemporary philosophy, is the one I discussed in the previous lecture. It rests on two intuitions, or implicit assumptions. The first is a kind of proto-theory about language, in the light of which the game seems to provide a useful informal model of the relation of language to the world. This proto-theory accords a key role to the idea that the function of statements is to 'represent' worldly states of affairs and that true statements succeed in doing so.[2]

I'll call this first assumption (big R) *Representationalism*. Given Representationalism, the second motivation for the popular version of the game is the thought that if this proto-theory is to be incorporated into a mature scientific theory of human language, then the matching model needs to fit within the scope of a broadly scientific investigation of ourselves and of the world we inhabit. After all, as we consider the world as scientists, we see ourselves and our language as one small but rather significant part of it. If the proto-theory is to be incorporated into a scientific perspective, the perspective itself seems to dictate the shape of the available facts and truthmakers. Roughly, the available shapes are the kinds of outlines recognised by natural science.

Notoriously, it turns out that there are many true statements – or *apparently* true statements ('apparently' qualifying either term) – that don't seem to line up neatly with facts of the kind uncovered by natural science.[3] There's a striking mismatch between the rich world of ordinary discourse and the sparse world apparently described by science. Much work in modern philosophy amounts to attempts to deal with some aspect or other of this mismatch. The project is often called simply *naturalism*. In the last lecture I called it *object naturalism*, reserving the generic term for a more basic view – with which, as I argued, object naturalism itself may well turn out to conflict.

The object naturalist's mantra is that there are no facts but the kind of facts recognised by natural science. But it isn't this mantra alone that

---

[2] It may seem inappropriate to call this assumption a proto-theory. The label 'theory' may seem too grand for such an obvious truth, or the label 'proto' too tentative for such a well established canon of philosophy of language. Nothing hangs on the label, however. For the moment, the important thing is the role that this assumption – trivial truth, proto-theory or mature canon – plays in giving rise to the most taxing form of the philosophical version of the matching game.

[3] The problem cases are not just the classic misfits, such as the (apparent) truths of aesthetics, morality and other normative matters, or those of consciousness. Arguably, at least, they include matters much closer to a scientist's heart, such as probability, causation, possibility and necessity, and conditional facts of various kinds. (More on this in the next lecture.)

commits object naturalists to their restrictive version of the matching game. In principle, one could endorse the mantra without thinking that the matching game provides a useful model of the relation of language to the world.[4] The puzzle stems from combining the mantra with Representationalism: with the proto-*theory* for which the matching game offers a metaphor. The proto-theory says that our statements 'represent' aspects of the world. Object naturalists combine this proto-theory with the mantra's restriction on the available truth-makers, and it is the combination that leads to the puzzles.

As we saw, the role of the proto-theory reveals an interesting vulnerability in the object naturalist's own position. By her own lights, the proto-theory counts as a hypothesis about what it is appropriate to say about language itself, from a scientific standpoint. If it turns out to be a bad hypothesis – if good science shows that the proto-theory is a bad theory – then the motivation for the object naturalist's version of the matching game is undermined. But it is undermined from *within* a scientific view of language and its place in the world. In that sense, the undermining wouldn't be an anti-naturalist conclusion. On the contrary, it would depend on convicting some self-styled naturalists of bad science. A good naturalistic account of our own linguistic practice might defeat Representationalism – might reveal it to be a poor theory about the relation between language and the world. The result would be naturalism – subject naturalism, as I put it – without (big R) Representationalism.

In the previous lecture I outlined three reasons for thinking that this threat is a serious one. The first appealed to the attractions of semantic minimalism, which threatens to deprive Representationalism of its theoretical foundations; the second to the kind of challenges Stephen Stich raises to the project of grounding metaphysics on a semantic basis; and the third to concerns about circularity, if the semantically grounded approach[5] is applied to the semantic notions themselves. I argued that these are all reasons for a (small n) naturalist to question Representationalism, to doubt whether the matching game turns out to be a good analogy for the task that confronts a philosophical account of the place of language in the natural world.

But what alternative is there? In this lecture and the next I want to propose a way forward. It depends, of course, on giving up (big R) Representationalism. In one sense, this is a familiar proposal. There are

---

4 Quine provides an example, perhaps, at least under some interpretations.
5 That is, in our present terminology, the matching model.

famous critics of Representationalism in modern philosophy, such as
Dewey, Wittgenstein, Rorty and others in the pragmatist tradition.[6] But
although I'm sympathetic to these criticisms – much more so than most
people in contemporary analytic philosophy – I'm also inclined to try to
cast them in a less iconoclastic form. I agree with these writers about the
location of the pragmatists' Promised Land, at least in outline – that is, I
agree that we need to leave Representationalism behind us – but I'm less
pessimistic than they are that analytic philosophy might reach it, starting
from where it is now.

One ground for optimism, in my view, is that although this non-
Representationalist utopia isn't well marked on the maps in contemporary
analytic philosophy, it is surprisingly close to positions that are now well
marked. The position I want to recommend is now accessible from familiar
places, and even from comparatively popular places. The remaining work
is mainly a matter of marking some trails: of visiting various familiar locations which actually lie close by and of calling attention to the paths that
lead in the right direction. That kind of work – trail-marking, much more
than trail-blazing – is what I'm trying to do in this lecture.

The trickiest part involves some unfamiliar and hazardous territory
around the notion of representation, but I'll approach that, too, from
firmer and familiar ground. Some of the positions I want to use as stepping
stones, or anchors, are associated with various familiar approaches to the
puzzle of the matching game – to the problem that we seem to have a lot
more true statements than naturalistically respectable truth-makers. The
best way to get a sense of where my alternative fits in is to begin there, with
a sketch of the usual suspects.

2 PLACEMENT STRATEGIES

The problem is that of 'placing' various kinds of truths in a natural world.
We seem to have more truths than truth-makers – more stickers than places
to put them. Given the nature of the problem – an apparent mismatch
between the cardinality of two different sets – it comes as no surprise that
there are three basic kinds of solution. One argues that the two sets can
be matched, just as they are; that there's some non-obvious isomorphism
that does the trick. The second maintains that the problem arises because
we've under-counted on the right and that there are more truth-makers

---

[6] As Menand (2001: 361) notes, Dewey was already predicting in 1905 that pragmatism would 'give
the *coup de grace to representationalism*'.

available than we thought. And the third argues that we've over-counted on the left, and that there are fewer statements in need of truth-makers than we thought.

2.1 Isomorphism after all

The first option is *reductionism*, which seeks to convince us of the existence of some non-obvious isomorphism between the crowded tiers of true statements on the left and the sparse natural facts on the right. A noteworthy recent version of this approach is the one due to Frank Jackson (1998), now commonly called the Canberra Plan.[7] And a noteworthy technique for finding sufficient natural facts – not wholly new, but recently popular under the name *response-dependence* – is to appeal to the diversity of human responses to the world and to argue that problem cases may have relational truth-makers, involving such responses.[8]

2.2 Grow the pie on the right

The second option tries to adjust the imbalance by adding facts on the right. It is usually held to comprise two sub-options. One accepts the constraint imposed by naturalism but argues that there are more facts within the scope of natural science than we thought.[9] The second argues that the constraint itself is at fault and that we need to recognise that there are non-natural facts.[10] It is debatable whether the distinction between these two sub-options is more than terminological – an issue as to what we call science – but we needn't discuss that here. What's relevant is what the sub-options have in common, viz., that they attribute the original puzzle to excessive parsimony in our initial assessment of the available truth-makers on the right-hand side of the model.

2.3 Shrink the pie on the left

The third option is to try to reduce the size of the set on the left – i.e. to try to reduce the number of statements we take to require truth-makers. In this case, there are several sub-options:

---

7 I contrast my approach to Jackson's in Price (1997) and Price (2009). In the latter paper, especially, I try to exhibit the way in which Jackson's programme depends on substantial assumptions about language – assumptions closely related to what we are presently calling the Matching Model – and to argue that this is problematic for Jackson's view, in various ways.

8 I discuss this approach in Price (1998).

9 David Chalmers's (1996) view of consciousness is a familiar example.

10 The classic example is Moore's (1903) view of moral facts.

1. *Eliminativism.* Recall that the stickers are supposed to represent true statements. An eliminativist deals with the excess – i.e. with the embarrassing residue, after all the obvious candidates are assigned to their naturalistically respectable places on the right – by saying that we're victims of large-scale error. Large sub-classes of the statements we take to be true are actually systematically false.

2. *Fictionalism.* A similar view offers the same diagnosis of the apparent mismatch between statements and truth-makers, but with an irenic conclusion. The eliminativist compares the false statements in question to the claims of discarded scientific theories and recommends a similar fate. Fictionalists are mellow about falsehood. They embrace the idea of 'useful fictions' – language games in which false claims serve some useful purpose. The practices of making moral or modal claims might be beneficial in some way, for example, despite the fact that the claims concerned aren't literally true. If so, we don't need to find truth-makers, but nor do we need to reject the language games in question.

3. *Expressivism.* The same lesson – that the point of some of the statements on our initial list is not to match worldly facts – is carried a stage further by expressivists.[11] Expressivists maintain that some of the utterances we take to be statements aren't genuine statements at all, but have some other point or function. The hope is that once these pseudo-statements are pruned away, the apparent imbalance between true statements and truth-makers will be eliminated, or at least reduced.

Note an important difference between fictionalism and expressivism – e.g., in the moral case. A fictionalist thinks that moral claims have both an everyday use and a literal use. Taken literally (and interpreted as a moral claim), the statement 'Torture is indefensible' is *false.* Literally speaking, there are no moral facts to make it true. Taken in its everyday sense, however – within the fiction in which we all participate – it may be said to be true. By contrast, an expressivist doesn't have to admit that there is any sense in which such a statement is literally false. On the contrary, says the expressivist, taking it to be literally false is making a mistake about what kind of speech act it is. It isn't the kind of speech act that *has* a literal truth value, in the sense that the fictionalist intends.

---

[11] This is not to suggest that expressivism is a descendant of fictionalism. It might be more accurate to say that fictionalists are proto-expressivists, who haven't yet realised that language needn't wear its logical form on its face.

Thus, an expressivist might hope to agree with everyday moral claims, without having to take anything back, without having to admit (even if only in private, as it were, with her professional colleagues) that all such claims are literally false. She agrees full voice with the everyday folk, and argues that the attempt to raise further issues – Are there *really* any such facts? – rests on a mistake about language. Once we see that moral claims are not genuinely descriptive, the expressivist assures us, we see that such metaphysical issues rest on a category mistake. See things properly and you see that they simply don't arise.

However, it might seem that the advantage of not having to say that our moral claims are *false* comes with a countervailing disadvantage. Doesn't the expressivist have to give up on the idea that there could be some everyday sense in which such a claim is *true*? Indeed, how is the expressivist going to account for the fact that we *call* such claims true and false if they are not really in the business of making claims about how things are?

3 QUASI-REALISM AND THE THREAT OF GLOBALISATION

These issues are best addressed in the version of expressivism called *quasi-realism*, championed over many years by Simon Blackburn. The quasi-realist's project is to begin where expressivism begins, with the thought that the primary function of certain of our (apparent) statements is not that of describing how things are and yet to show how, nevertheless, such expressions might earn a right to all or most of the trappings of descriptive 'statementhood' – in particular the right to be treated as capable of being true and false.

As Blackburn emphasises, the appeal of quasi-realism is to provide a way of dealing with placement problems without resorting either to implausible metaphysics or to the error theory. If successful, quasi-realism explains why the folk practice of making moral claims is in order just as it is *and* explains why any further metaphysical enquiry about whether there are *really* moral facts is inevitably missing the point (in being premised on a mistaken view of what we are doing with moral language).

Quasi-realism is important, in the present context, because the view I'm trying to put on the map can be thought of – in most respects – as a generalised or 'global' version of quasi-realism, a position just further down the same path. To understand how the generalisation proceeds, note first that what expressivism does is to remove some (apparent) commitments from the matching game – to say that the matching model is a bad model of the relation of those commitments to the world. (What quasi-realism in particular adds is an account of why, on the surface, it 'looks as if' the matching model is applicable.) In place of the matching model, presumably, expressivism offers some positive account of the use of the parts of language in question – some account compatible with the basic ('subject naturalist') premise that the creatures employing the language in question are simply natural creatures, in a natural environment.

Typically, of course, expressivists do all of this *locally*. They think that some of our claims are genuinely factual, or descriptive (and, hence, presumably, characterisable in terms of the matching model, in so far as it works at all). And they think that for any of our claims or commitments there's a genuine issue concerning whether it is really factual, or descriptive. In other words, they take for granted what Robert Kraut (1990), following Rorty, calls the *bifurcation thesis* – the doctrine that there is a line to be drawn in language, between descriptive and non-descriptive uses.[12] With this thesis in place, expressivism is taken to be needed when the answer is held to be 'no' – when something that looks superficially like a factual claim is held to fall on the non-descriptive side of the line.

However – this is a crucial point – the bifurcation thesis, and in particular the belief that some claims are genuinely descriptive, play *no role at all* in the positive story, in the case of the commitments the expressivist regards as not genuinely descriptive. In other words, the expressivist's positive alternative to the matching model doesn't depend on the claim that the matching model is *ever* a useful model of the relation between natural language and the natural world. So there's no evident barrier to abandoning the matching model altogether and endorsing *global* expressivism. This is the view that I want to recommend.

A quasi-realist of a more conventional stripe, who does want to hold onto the bifurcation thesis, is committed to a kind of two-tier view of the landscape, with respect to a whole range of notions that we associate with the business of making claims and assertions. In effect, he must think that there are both *loose* and *strict* answers to questions such as: what is it to be a *belief*, an *assertion*, a *statement*, a *judgement*, a *proposition* (even a *fact*)? The loose answer is supposed to tell us what descriptive and quasi-descriptive uses of language have in common, the strict answer what separates the real cases from the merely quasi-cases. The loose answer characterises all the

---

[12] Usually non-indicatives are regarded as non-descriptive by default, and the interesting question is thought to be whether there are non-descriptive indicatives, too.

passengers on the flight, as it were, the strict answer just those who are travelling first class.

I think that a quasi-realist who devotes his energy to arguing that economy-class passengers are entitled to first-class service – that common-ers are entitled to cake, or at least some decent simulation of cake – is in danger of missing some larger questions on either side. What, if anything, entitles the 'real' first-class passengers to this kind of treatment? And what does it take to get on the plane in the first place – what is it that the first- and economy-class passengers have in common? In different ways, both of these questions abstract from the quasi-realist's *local* concerns – that of arguing that a particular vocabulary is entitled to an upgrade, or at least to most of the advantages that would follow from an upgrade – to a more gen-eral question: how do we understand the genuinely descriptive claims (so called)? And what is it that all claims have in common, whether 'genuinely descriptive' or not?

Quasi-realism's commitment to the bifurcation thesis may thus have hampered the enterprise of developing an adequate general theory of judge-ment and assertion (whether strict or loose). If nothing else, I think, it has tended to muddy the waters, by disassociating the issue as to why moral claims (say) take the 'declarative' form that they do from the deeper question as to why *any* speech acts take such a form (strictly or loosely).

For the loose version of these broader questions, the quasi-realist is going to be looking for answers that don't simply presuppose Representational-ism. The whole point is supposed to be that something can properly be an assertion (or a statement, a belief, a proposition, or whatever) in the loose sense, without being in the business of (big R) Representing anything. What the quasi-realist needs, in other words, is an approach to issues such as 'What is an assertion?' that doesn't presuppose the kind of theoreti-cal underpinnings that properly belong, if anywhere, only to the strict cases.

Where are we to find such a thing? It seems to me that there is one pre-eminent candidate in contemporary philosophy, namely, Robert Bran-dom's (1994, 2000) *inferentialism*. Brandom's approach not only offers us an answer to questions such as 'What is an assertion?' – telling us that it is a certain move in a particular game of giving and asking for reasons – but also, crucially, and as Brandom emphasises, gives us an answer that rests on expressivist foundations. So it doesn't presuppose any of those (big R) Rep-resentationalist notions on which a quasi-realist can't afford to be relying at this point.

4 WHAT GIVES STICKERS THEIR PROPOSITIONAL SHAPE?

Thus, I'm attempting to recruit Brandom's inferentialist account of assertion, to answer a question I think Blackburn's quasi-realist should have
been asking a little more loudly: what is it that all declarative claims have
in common (*quasi* and *really* descriptive claims alike, if such a bifurcation
there be)? I'm not sure how either party would feel about being roped to
the other in this way, but in my view the combination has much more
going for it than might appear at first sight. I want to try to convince you
that Blackburn and Brandom are climbing the same mountain, even if they
come to the bottom of it from different directions. (I also want to try to
convince you that the pragmatists' Promised Land is in sight at the top,
but more of that later.)

Reverting for a moment to the metaphor with which we began, the
question of what all declarative claims have in common can be thought
of as the question as to what gives our sentential 'stickers' their distinctive
assertoric or 'propositional' shape. What makes something the kind of thing
that properly figures – or at least, looks as if it properly figures – on the
left side of the game of matching statements to the world? As I say, I think
we find a powerful and plausible answer to this question in Brandom's
inferentialism – in the idea that, most fundamentally, assertions are to be
construed as moves in a linguistic game of 'giving and asking for reasons'.

Brandom doesn't claim that making assertions is the only game we can
play with language, of course, but he does claim that the assertoric game is
both central and indispensable. Contrasting his own view to Wittgenstein's,
he explains that his view requires that language 'has a downtown' – that
assertion is a fundamental linguistic activity, on which others depend:

> By contrast to Wittgenstein, the inferential identification of the conceptual claims
> that language ... has a *center*; it is not a motley. Inferential practices of producing
> and consuming *reasons* are *downtown* in the region of linguistic practice. Suburban
> linguistic practices utilize and depend on the conceptual contents forged in the
> game of giving and asking for reasons, are parasitic on it. (2000: 14)

4.1 A challenge to functional pluralism?

I mention this because at first sight it might seem that Brandom's view thus
challenges Blackburn, too. After all, Blackburn interprets Wittgenstein as
a kind of proto-quasi-realist. When once or twice Blackburn flirts with
global quasi-realism, he offers Wittgenstein as an example of someone who

might be seen as moving in that direction.[13] Where Blackburn's expressivist wants to see a variety of superficially assertoric language games, differently related to various functions and psychological states, doesn't Brandom show us a single practice of making commitments, offering entitlements, giving and asking for reasons? For Brandom, surely, it isn't an option to deflate the notion of assertion, as Blackburn (1998: 167) notes that Wittgenstein himself might do with related notions, such as that of description. On the contrary, assertion is *the* fundamental language game, for Brandom, and the core of his expressivism is an investigation of the nature of this fundamental game.

In my view, however, there's actually no conflict here – quite the contrary, in fact. After all, even Wittgenstein acknowledges the common 'clothing' that makes different language games superficially similar (and thereby misleads us into thinking that they are all doing the same job). It is open to us to say that the key similarity is precisely that various of the different language games all avail themselves of the same inferential machinery. This is thoroughly compatible with underlying pluralism, so long as we also maintain that the various different kinds of commitments answer to different needs and purposes – have different origins in our complex natures and relations to our physical and social environments. It is open to us to say this as long as we reject what is otherwise a competing account of the significance of assertions, viz., that they exhibit a common relation to pre-existing conceptual contents (which puts the basic pluralism at the level of differences of content, rather than differences of function).

Thus I think we can follow Brandom here – agree that language has a downtown – without abandoning the pluralist aspect of Blackburn's expressivism. (It is another question whether the bifurcation thesis survives, but we'll come to that.) To preserve the pluralism, what we need is the idea that although assertion is indeed a fundamental language game, it is a game with multiple functionally distinct applications – a multi-function tool, in effect.[14] So long as the right way to theorise about these applications is in the expressivist's use-based vocabulary, the position is compatible with the kind of functional pluralism of Blackburn's version of Wittgenstein.

---

[13] See Blackburn (1998a: 77–83) and Blackburn (1998b: 166–7), for example.

[14] Brandom warns us against misuse of the idea that language is a tool – that language has a *purpose* – but nothing I say here treads on controversial ground in this respect. (On the contrary, as I'm about to explain, the functional pluralism I have in mind here is of a kind that Brandom himself wants to highlight.)

Indeed, Brandom's project seems not only compatible with this kind of functional pluralism but thoroughly committed to it. Brandom characterises his project as follows:

> Starting with an account of what one is *doing* in making a claim, it seeks to elaborate from it an account of what is said, the content or proposition – something that can be thought of in terms of truth conditions – to which one commits oneself by making a speech act. (2000: 12)

> Pragmatism about the conceptual seeks to understand what it is explicitly to *say* or *think that* something is the case in terms of what one must implicitly know *how* (be able) to *do*. (2000: 18)

Thus, Brandom aims to show how conceptual content arises from pragmatic function, and this could only fail to involve some sort of pragmatic functional pluralism if Brandom were to offer us the *same* functional story for every sort of content. That is obviously not what he intends, however. On the contrary, Brandom's project is to link different kinds of vocabulary to different kinds of practices and pragmatic tasks.[15]

So while Brandom's account may impose a degree of uniformity on language that some Wittgensteinian pluralists might wish to reject – offering us a uniform account of the way in which Wittgenstein's common linguistic 'clothing' is held together, so to speak – it not only allows but actually *requires* that this uniformity coexist with an underlying functional diversity of the kind that expressivists such as Blackburn and Gibbard require. It not only allows but insists that different pieces of linguistic clothing do different things, even though there is an important sense in which they are all put together in the same way and all belong to the same assertoric game.

4.2 What happened to the class system?

But is Blackburn out of the woods, by Brandom's lights? If we follow Brandom in characterising assertions as moves in a game of giving and asking for reasons, what happens to the idea that some *apparent* assertions – e.g., moral claims – are not genuine, first-class assertions? Moral claims certainly seem to count as assertions by these standards, so how can a quasi-realist

---

[15] Indeed, it *couldn't be* what he intends, on pain of falling back into his opponents' camp. If Brandom were to say that we were *doing* the same thing, in the relevant sense, in making any assertion whatsoever, then he would merely have offered us a pragmatic account of assertoric *force* – by coarse-graining to this extreme, his account would simply fail to connect with what *varies* from assertion to assertion and hence would have nothing to say about *content* (or the dimension of variability it represents).

take them to be less than first-class assertions (except by challenging the inferentialist account itself)?[16]

There are actually two issues here, I think. One is the question whether admitting that moral claims (say) are genuine assertions *in the inferentialist sense* would be at all in tension with what expressivists had in mind, when they denied that such claims are assertions. I think the right answer to this question is a resounding 'no'. What expressivists took themselves to be denying was that the primary function of moral claims was that of 'tracking' some distinctive moral feature of reality. This would only be in tension with the thesis that moral claims are assertions in the inferentialist sense, if the inferentialist notion were also a 'world-tracking' notion – and this seems strikingly not the case (more on this in a moment). On the contrary, and as above, the inferentialist notion has the same expressivist bloodlines as Blackburn's quasi-realism, and any conflict at this point is superficial and terminological.[17]

The second issue is trickier. Does Brandom's view of assertion leave any room for a bifurcation thesis, of the kind (and in a place) that Blackburn's local version of quasi-realism requires? Or does it necessarily recommend a more global version of expressivism? Here I want to propose an irenic answer, which offers a qualified 'yes' to both questions (the qualifications saving me from self-contradiction). The proposal depends on something I just mentioned in connection with the first issue, viz., a distinction between the 'world-tracking' kind of representation that expressivists such as Blackburn and Gibbard have traditionally been in the business of denying (to moral claims and to their other target vocabularies), and what I think is a quite distinct notion of representation that emerges from inferentialism. I think that there's a distinction that needs to be clearly drawn here, that has been overlooked, or at least insufficiently remarked, by almost everyone in these debates. I'll call it the *new bifurcation thesis*.

5 THE NEW BIFURCATION THESIS

Let's step back a moment from the issues we have been considering – expressivism, inferentialism, placement problems and so on – and think

---

[16] This objection is like the familiar claim that deflationism about truth and reference defeats non-cognitivism, by making it the case that moral claims come out as truth-apt, by the only standards – rather undemanding standards – that deflationism allows.

[17] However, there's room for argument about where Brandom wants to leave us in this respect, I think. Sometimes he writes as if his project is that of rebuilding Representationalism on pragmatist foundations. On this matter, see Price (2010). Here, I'm taking for granted that whatever his own intentions in the matter, his approach doesn't in fact yield any kind of (big R) Representationalism. More on this below.

about notions of representation as they occur in what (in the nicest sense) we might call more naive, or less 'meta', regions of philosophy and the cognitive sciences. Imagine a survey of notions of representation in play in these fields. Here's a hunch about some neglected structure that I think such a survey would reveal. I think it would reveal that there are (at least) two distinct focii, or conceptual nodes, around which various uses of representational notions tend to cluster.

1. **e-Representation:**[18] On the one hand, we have the *environment-tracking* paradigm of representation, dependent on such notions as covariation and 'indication relations' (Field 1994) – think of examples such as the position of the needle in the fuel gauge and the level of fuel in the tank, the barometer reading and air pressure and so on. In these cases, the crucial idea is that some feature of the representing system either does, or is (in some sense) 'intended to', vary in parallel with some feature of the represented system. (Usually, but perhaps not always, the covariation in question has a causal basis.) In biological cases, for example, this notion gives priority to the idea that the function of a representation is to co-vary with some (typically) *external* environmental condition: it puts the system–world link on the front foot.[19]

2. **i-Representation:**[20] On the other hand, we have a notion that gives priority to the *internal* functional role of the representation: something counts as a representation in virtue of its position or role in some cognitive or inferential architecture. Here it is an *internal* role of some kind – perhaps causal–functional, perhaps logico-inferential, perhaps computational – that takes the lead.

Of course, it is usually taken for granted that these two notions will fit together in some intimate way. Typically a view that gives initial priority to the latter will then want to read it as a sophisticated version of the former – such is the grip of Representationalism. But my point is that this assumption isn't compulsory. It is open to us to maintain – and to offer as a remedy for some of our present difficulties – that these two notions of representation should properly be kept apart, not pushed together.

It takes some effort to see that the two notions of representation might float free of one another, but I think it is an effort worth making – all the

---

[18] 'e' for *environmental* or *externalist*.

[19] Even if the relevant piece of the world is sometimes something within the skin, as it were, as in the case of pain or thirst.

[20] 'i' for *internalist* or *inferential*.

more so when the systemic-functional notion in question is a rich, normative, linguistic notion of Brandom's kind, rather than some sparer causal–functional notion of mental representation. The vista that opens up is the possibility that representation in the systemic sense is a much richer, more flexible and more multi-purpose tool than the naive view assumes.[21]

Once the distinction between these two notions of representation is on the table, it is open to us to regard the two notions as having different applications, for various theoretical purposes. In particular, it is open to us to take the view that at least by the time we get to language there isn't any useful external notion, *of a semantic kind* – in other words, no useful, general, notion of relations that words and sentences bear to the external world, that we might identify with truth and reference.[22]

5.1 Two notions of external constraint

True, we need to explain how the two notions are so easily run together, but for an expressivist, used to the idea that language plays tricks on us, this seems no huge challenge. The key, in my view, is to recognise a systematic confusion between *two notions of external constraint*. The first of these is the kind of 'in-game externality' provided by the norms of the game of giving and asking for reasons – the fact that, *within the game*, players bind themselves, in principle, to standards beyond themselves. This is a theme I've explored elsewhere. (See Price [1988] and Price [2003], for example.) In my view, the most illuminating route to a pragmatic theory of truth is to see it as associated with this kind of in-game externality – as a normative constraint, external to any individual speaker, to which speakers necessarily take themselves to be subject, in playing the game of giving and asking for reasons. It is an 'in-game' notion in precisely the sense that winning itself is an in-game notion, in a game such as chess: you don't understand the notion of winning unless you understand what it is to play the game.

The second notion of external constraint goes with that of covariance – and hence 'normal', 'intended' or 'proper function' covariance – between a tokening of a representation and an element of an external environment. In this sense, a token fails the constraint if it is a counter-example to the general or intended pattern – a 'false positive' or a 'false negative'. As these terms

---

[21] Once again, quasi-realism provides a useful stepping stone. The quasi-realist is already committed to the idea that something can behave for all intents and purposes like a 'genuine' belief, even though it has its origins at some 'non-cognitive' level.

[22] Note that this is a conclusion that semantic minimalists have already come to (directly, as it were).

themselves indicate, it is easy to run this notion together with the in-game norms of truth and falsity (thus confusing *in-game* answerability for *environmental* answerability), but this is a mistake.[23] The two notions have their origins in two distinct notions of representation. The former belongs in a particular (normative, inferentialist) version of the systemic-functional notion, which characterises representations in terms of their roles in networks of various kinds. The latter belongs with notions of representation as environmental covariance. My new bifurcation thesis claims that these are not two competing accounts of a single species of representation but two quite different beasts; and that it is this fact, not the old bifurcation thesis, that is the key distinction that expressivists need to make their project run smoothly.

6 WHITHER THE OLD BIFURCATION THESIS?

With the new bifurcation thesis in hand, let's return to the old bifurcation thesis. Does anything survive of the distinction that that thesis was trying to draw, if we view matters as I have recommended? My irenic proposal wants to offer a qualified 'yes' at this point. The qualification depends on a distinction between two versions of the question, corresponding to our two notions of representation.

The first question is whether, *if we restrict ourselves to discussing the matter in i-representational terms*, there is room for the idea of what I called the first-class/economy-class distinction – for the idea that some assertions are *genuinely* descriptive, or *genuinely* representational? So far as I can see, the answer to this question must be 'no'. This is not to say that there will not be distinctions between vocabularies to be drawn in i-representational terms. It might be, for example, that we find significant differences in the ways in which different assertoric vocabularies participate in the game of giving and asking for reasons – 'no-fault' disagreements might be treated as possible in some cases but not in others, for example.[24] And that fact in turn might have an explanation in terms of other features of vocabularies – e.g., in terms of differences in their 'functions', in some sense (including, perhaps, their e-representational functions). But these *explananda* will not themselves lie at the i-representational level. So long as we restrict ourselves to

---

[23] As I'll explain in the next lecture, one source of the confusion seems to be that the in-game notion has the character of faithfulness to an external realm of facts, which can make it seem like the second notion, if we fail to notice that the realm of facts in question is itself a product of the game.

[24] I explore this idea in Price (1988).

the vocabulary associated with the i-representational level, in other words, we should not expect to be able to formulate any remnant of the old bifurcation thesis.

The second question is whether there is room in this picture for the idea that some *subset* of representations in the i-representational sense are also representations in the e-representational, 'environment-tracking' sense. That is, is it open to the quasi-realist to say something like this: 'I accept that moral claims and scientific claims are on a par in the i-representational, inferentialist sense – both are full-blown, first-class assertions, in that sense. But scientific claims nevertheless have a world-tracking, e-representational character that moral claims lack'? I think it is open to a quasi-realist to say this, and this is the core of my irenic proposal. But I think it is important to be clear what this does and doesn't involve. The point is not that being an i-representation and being an e-representation somehow 'come to the same thing' in the case of scientific assertions – these are still different notions, answerable to different masters – but that the two distinct characterisations may both be appropriate, in some cases.

By way of analogy, observe that tomatoes and aubergines are fruit in one sense, vegetables in another. (Rhubarb goes the other way, perhaps.) Obviously, there are two notions of fruit in play and not a lot of mileage in insisting that one notion is primary – that the class of fruit in one sense divides up into *real* fruit and *quasi*-fruit, according to the other sense. We could say this, of course, in either direction, but it's not going to add anything to what we knew already. If we met someone who was troubled by the question whether rhubarb was *really* a fruit, the kindest thing would be the kind of gentle terminological therapy that we philosophers are so good at: 'It all depends on what you mean by "fruit"!' Similarly, I want to suggest that there isn't much mileage in the question whether some representations in one sense are also representations in the other sense. The important thing is what we learn by noticing that there are two notions in play. [25]

I shall return to the issue of the status of scientific language in the next lecture, and consider again the question of what sense, if any, my view can make of the claim that scientific language is 'primary' – that scientific ontology is privileged, and uniquely deserving of realist commitment. (By

---

[25] Note also that the concession that some representations in the systemic sense may also be representations in the covariance sense does nothing to re-inflate the metaphysics-grounding uses of the notion of representation. On the contrary, if we want to regard a particular class of i-representations as also counting as e-representations, it will be because we think we already know what lies at the 'world' end of the relevant covariance relation.

that stage, we shall have on the table a proposal to distinguish two notions of 'world', paralleling the distinction I have drawn here between two notions of 'representation'.) To close this lecture I want to return to the analogy I offered at the beginning, to try to clarify the senses in which the view I am recommending differs from an orthodox representationalism.

7 SEPARATING *CONTENT* FROM *CORRESPONDENCE*

The view I'm challenging can be thought of as a loosely articulated combination of two fundamental assumptions about language and thought. The first assumption (call it the *content assumption*) is that language is a medium for encoding and passing around sentence-sized packets of factual information – the *contents* of beliefs and assertions. The second assumption (the *correspondence assumption*) is that these packets of information are all 'about' some aspect of the external world, in much the same way. For each sentence, and each associated packet of information, there's an appropriately 'shaped' aspect of the way the world is, or could be – viz., the state of affairs, or fact, that needs to obtain for the sentence to be true. The orthodox view bundles these two assumptions together (not recognising that they are distinct). Once both are in place, it is natural to regard language and thought as a medium for mirroring, or representing, these sentence-sized aspects of the external environment and passing around the corresponding packets of information from head to head. My proposal rests on pulling the two assumptions apart, on regarding them as having quite different theoretical allegiances, the content assumption with *i-representation* and the correspondence assumption with *e-representation.*

Foregrounding the content assumption for the moment, my default model for a conception of its natural home is provided by inferentialism.[26] According to an inferentialist, contents and content differences are 'instituted', as Brandom puts it, by the complex inferential relationships among and between linguistic items.[27] Roughly speaking, we might say that contents correspond to 'nodes' in an inferential network. But these nodes may themselves be associated with many different kinds of functional relationships, in the complex interaction between language users and their physical environment – there is no requirement whatsoever that each node have an *e-representational* role, where the correspondence

---

[26] Though, as I noted, I think that an analogous point could be made in the context of other i-representational models, computational or causal–functional.

[27] More on Brandom's views about this in the next lecture.

assumption would gain some traction. This is not to say that they *cannot* have such a role – on the contrary, my irenic proposal rests on the thought that some of them will do so, to some extent. The point is simply to insist that these are different issues – content and correspondence answer to different masters.

The proposal is that from the inside – as ordinary language users – we don't notice these underlying functional differences between one sort of content and another. We talk about 'facts' of many different kinds – e.g., about tastes and colours, or right and wrong – as easily as about shape and position. The differences are only visible from a theoretical perspective, by asking about the different roles that commitments about these various matters play, in the lives of creatures like us. Facts thus become a kind of projection of informational structures made possible by language, echoing Strawson's famous remarks: 'Of course, statements and facts fit. They were made for each other. If you prise the statements off the world you prise the facts off it too' (1950: 137). And there is plurality in the resulting realm of facts, reflecting the underlying plurality of functions of kinds of assertoric commitments. (More on these themes in the next lecture.)

The most interesting part of the project is then to explain *how there come to be* statements with particular contents, by thinking about the practical role of the particular instantiation of the assertion game that produces tokens with such content. There is a new dimension of variability at this point, corresponding to the plurality of available functional roles – again, more on this in the next lecture. The general advantage of this pragmatic direction of explanation is that it is easier to account for the distinctive practical role of the concepts in question – e.g., moral or probabilistic concepts – if we *begin* with that role, than if we begin elsewhere and try to work our way to the use.[28] Once again, traditional expressivists saw this advantage locally. My project seeks to institute it globally. My aim is thus to have all the advantages of traditional expressivism, without the big disadvantage: the need to make good the bifurcation thesis – to find a radical divide in language, where usage marks none.

To get a sense of the big picture, let's go back to the sticker analogy. Think of the systemic, inferential notion of representation as offering an account of what gives a sticker its 'propositional' form in the first place. The placement problems arose from the fact that there are a lot

---

[28] In the moral case, the problem in question is what Michael Smith (1994) calls the moral problem; for probability, it is the problem of justifying something like Lewis's Principal Principle (1980); and so on.

more stickers given form by their systemic inferential roles than truth-makers on the right-hand side of the game, in the world as seen by natural science.

My recommendation is that we deal with this problem by *playing a different game*. In place of the old project of matching stickers to shapes in the natural world, I recommend the project of explaining (in naturalistic terms) how stickers *obtain* their characteristic shapes. Freed of the requirement that they must bear semantic relations to the natural world, stickers – or representations in the systemic, in-game sense – can now occupy a new dimension of their own in the model, orthogonal to the natural world. Like the figures in a pop-up book, they stand up from their bases in the natural world, without being constrained to match or resemble anything found there.

Of course, a pop-up book does all the work for us, as we open the page. For a more illuminating metaphor, let's make the construction into a puzzle – a kind of three-dimensional jigsaw puzzle. We begin with a large collection of shapes or pieces, each of them a statement we take to be true, and a large board or playing surface, depicting the natural world (in such a way as to give prominence to our own situation, as creatures with certain attributes and situation, within that world). In effect, our task is then to solve two kinds of puzzle simultaneously. We need to arrange subsets of the pieces into clusters, fitting them together so that (as in an ordinary jigsaw puzzle) the shape of each is defined by its conceptual relations to its neighbours (and eventually, perhaps, to the super-cluster of all the pieces). And we need to position each of the resulting clusters in the correct place on the board as a whole so that its edges bear the right relations to particular features of the situation of the speakers (ourselves, in this case) who are depicted on the board.

For example, the pieces representing probabilistic statements need to bear certain internal relations to one another, corresponding to the inferential or functional links that define internal representations and their conceptual components. But they also need to bear the right functional relations to the decision behaviour depicted on the underlying board, to count as *probabilistic* statements at all. Thus, at least roughly, the first stage of the puzzle is concerned with what makes a piece of the puzzle a *statement* at all; the second stage with pragmatic factors about its use that may play a crucial role in determining *what* statement it is. (Missing altogether is the idea that the latter fact is determined by some matching to a shape already discernible in the natural world.)

Thus we have a model in which there is a substantial *internal* notion of representation – a substantial theory as to what gives a piece or a pop-up figure its content, or propositional shape – but no substantial *external* notion of representation, at least at this point.[29] As the model illustrates, moreover, internal notions of representation are not constrained by the cardinality of the natural world. So long as we find roles for pieces which are not that of matching outlines in the natural world, we can happily allow that there are many more pieces than available outlines. In effect, this is the original pluralist insight of expressivism and quasi-realism, here given a more attractive home, in a version of the picture in which external representation disappears altogether, for content-determining purposes.

As we've seen, the view thus combines plurality at one level with unity at another, resolving the tension that plagues other forms of expressivism and pragmatism. But it shares with conventional forms of expressivism an important philosophical moral: it warns us that what looks like a problem about the nature of some part of reality – e.g., about colours, or moral properties, or numbers – may be better addressed as a question about the role of certain kinds of vocabulary in the lives of creatures like us. The moral is that philosophy's debt to science is properly repaid not by looking for these things within the scientific world but by explaining in scientific terms how natural creatures like us come to think and speak in these ways.

8 CONCLUSIONS

I have proposed that expressivists such as Brandom, on one side, and Blackburn, on the other, can be seen as working two sides of the same street. Thus, Brandom, on the more abstract side of the street, offers us an expressivist – i.e. crucially a non-Representationalist – account of the general assertoric game. Whereas Blackburn – engaged, like other Humean expressivists, with the particular philosophical debates in which expressivism emerges as an option – begins with the attractions of expressivism in contrast to other approaches in those cases. I've tried to show that these two starting points are entirely complementary, and mutually supportive. And I've offered a framework for thinking about where the street leads. I've suggested that the crucial step – missed, I think, on both sides of the street – is a distinction between two notions of representation.

---

[29] As I have emphasised, the model still allows for an external or e-representational notion to play a role *at a different point.*

To end this lecture with my tongue in my cheek, let me say that I'm amused to find myself recommending these two notions of representation. Until recently I had thought of myself as a straight up and down anti-representationalist, in the tradition of Dewey, Wittgenstein and Rorty. But now – even if I'm still opposed to big-R Representationalism – I find that far from being an eliminativist about representation, I'm heading in the other direction: I'm a *dualist*, not a *nihilist*!

CHAPTER 3

Pluralism, 'world' and the primacy of science
Huw Price

In the previous lecture, I distinguished two nodes, or 'attractors', for the notion of representation, as it figures in contemporary philosophy. One node ('i-representation') emphasises position in an inferential or functional network, the other ('e-representation') stresses correlation with an aspect of an external environment. I recommended that rather than trying to encompass both nodes in a single account of representation, or to privilege one at the expense of the other, we should simply recognise that they are distinct. There's a legitimate theoretical role for both notions, in other words, but not as the two ends of the same philosophical stage-horse. Better, I urged, to let each notion stand on its own two feet, and to allow them to live their separate lives.

I talked loosely about the idea that i-representations 'do many jobs', and I claimed that there is thus a new degree of freedom in a proper theory of language and thought – an extra dimension of variability – which is necessarily invisible in traditional representationalism, when i-representations and e-representations are not distinguished. In this lecture, I want to begin by saying something more about this potential plurality of i-representations – about what it consists in, *how* the different cases differ from one another. I'll do this by appealing once again to the genetic affinities between the programme I'm recommending and the traditional 'Humean' expressivism of writers such as Blackburn. From that point, the rest of the lecture goes like this.

I'll begin by stressing the way in which the picture I'm recommending reverses the order of explanation between *use* and *factual content*. (I'll note an affinity at this point with the way in which Brandom characterises the project of pragmatism, as he sees it.) I'll then discuss the implications of this picture for the notion of the *world*, as it figures in contemporary philosophy. Here, I think we need to recognise a deep conflation between two distinct notions, each respectable in its own terms, but deeply misleading when confused. Not surprisingly, perhaps, I want to suggest that this conflation is a kind of metaphysical image, or complement, of the conflation I've identified between two notions of representation. As with representation, then, my strategy is to make the notion of the world tractable by splitting it in two. One notion, linked to the traditional conception of the world as the totality of the facts, cleaves to the notion of i-representation. The other notion, that of the world as the natural environment, cleaves to e-representation and to the standpoint of subject naturalism.[1]

Next, returning to some issues I mentioned at the end of the previous lecture, I'll discuss the objection that this view amounts to a concession that the scientific perspective is 'primary' – that the facts of science are the real facts, and the rest, at best, some sort of quasi-fact. If successful, this objection would lead us back in the direction of the old bifurcation thesis and the view that while science is description, all else is mere projection. But I'll argue that it isn't successful. I'll argue that it mistakes a kind of merely perspectival primacy for the view that science alone is *really* 'in the referring business'. It misses the point that every assertoric vocabulary is equally in this business *by its own lights*, and that the apparent primacy of science, within the subject naturalism here proposed, reflects the fact that the lights of the enquiry *are* those of science. (To mistake this for an absolute primacy is to mistake science for metaphysics.) And I'll back this up with reasons for thinking that we find the relevant kind of functional pluralism *within science* – so that it can't be true, as this line of argument wants to claim, that *description* itself is one of the relevant functions, uniquely associated with scientific language. Once we know what to look for, on the 'expressive' side, we find it within science, too.[2]

I'll finish with some brief remarks about pluralism, distinguishing the functional plurality of i-representations from the more familiar pluralism often discussed with respect to particular 'levels' in the conversational game: in science, morality and elsewhere. These are horizontal pluralisms, mine a vertical pluralism, to use a distinction I introduced elsewhere (Price 1992).

---

[1] Which way, if either, goes the notion of the world as everything that *exists*? Initially a faithful Quinean, I want to answer that question in terms of the scope of existential quantification, but to rebel against the master in claiming that it needn't be just in science that existential quantification finds a role. The world of existents thus goes the same way as the world of the totality of the facts, under my interpretation. See Price (2007) for more on this.

[2] Here the argument will appeal in particular to the *modal* aspects of science, where the case for an interesting functional explanation seems to me to be very strong. This means that science could only be 'genuinely descriptive', in these terms, if the modal is in principle eliminable from science.

I THE DIVERSE UNITY OF I-REPRESENTATIONS

I've referred to a new dimension of variability within the class of i-representations – a dimension I've claimed is systematically obscured by the orthodox picture, which runs together the two notions of representation. But what does this variability consist in, and what is the plurality to which it is supposed to give rise? My first-pass answer, as I suggested in the previous lecture, is that the variability is just what traditional expressivists in the Humean tradition were getting at when they suggested that evaluative or modal claims (say) had a distinctive linguistic role – that of 'expressing' a particular sort of practical stance, or a psychological state with particular practical consequences.

For traditional expressivists, of course, these distinctive functional roles were supposed to contrast with the 'descriptive' function of 'genuine' factual claims. Thus there was thought to be a *prescriptive–descriptive* distinction on the evaluative side and what we might term a *predictive–descriptive* distinction on the modal side. The picture I have recommended wants to reject, or at least severely qualify, these traditional dichotomies. But this needn't involve any major revision to the *positive* account of the functions of what these expressivists took to lie on the non-descriptive side.

Some examples. The evaluative and normative cases are familiar, so I'll concentrate instead on examples of 'predictive' expressivism. Best known, perhaps, is the view known as probabilistic *subjectivism*, although this view needs to be interpreted with some care to fit the present mould. Subjectivism about probability is often characterised as the view that probabilities *are* degrees of belief, so that statements about probabilities are statements *about* degrees of belief. This needs to be distinguished from the view that ascriptions of probability should be understood as *expressions of* degrees of belief, and it is the latter view I have in mind here.[3] Crudely put, the view is that creatures who are decision-makers under uncertainty find it useful to tie their credences to a topic suitable for debate and consensus, and that's what the notion of probability provides. *By* discussing propositions about probability – by coordinating beliefs about *that* – speakers can coordinate their credences. That's what talk of probability is 'good for', on this view. The distinctive 'objects' of such talk – the probabilities themselves – inherit their properties from the functional task, from the credences, or dispositions to betting behaviour, to which *talk* of probability gives voice. (More in a moment on the order of explanation here exemplified.)

3 This distinction illustrates something very general about the viewpoint – more on this in a moment.

There's an analogous view of causation, which takes it to differ from probability mainly in that it reflects the distinctive perspective of a creature who takes herself to have the ability to *intervene* in her environment – in other words, an agent. In other work (see, e.g., Price [1991], [2012]) I've argued that the causal viewpoint can be treated as a kind of special case of the probabilistic viewpoint, where the probabilities concerned are probabilities of outcomes conditional on *actions*, assessed from the distinctive epistemic standpoint of the agent herself. (Creatures who were gamblers, but not agents within the realm on which they gambled, would not be in a position to occupy the latter standpoint, and hence would have no use for causal talk.)

As a final example, consider the tradition associated with writers such as Ryle (1950) and Ramsey (1990), that treats conditionals and law-like generalisations as something like rules, or inference-tickets: conditional commitments, to make one move in the language game, *in the event that one makes another* – to believe that *q* if one should come to believe that *p*, or to treat something as a B, if one should come to treat it as an A.

These examples all illustrate the basic idea. Particular, contingent features of a creature's practical circumstances – e.g., that she is a *decision-maker under uncertainty*, or an *agent*, or a bearer of *epistemic dispositions* – provide the source of the variability in this 'missing dimension'. Each of these features constitutes what we might call a *practical stance* – a practical situation or characteristic that a creature must instantiate, if the language game in question is to play its defining role in her life.[4] The variation in these practical stances is the source of the functional variation of i-representations, which I want to treat as entirely of a piece with the variability highlighted in traditional expressivist views of these same matters.

As for a traditional expressivist, this variability lies at the level of use conditions rather than truth conditions. The stance is something like a practical precondition of the language games in question; and, at a more detailed level – the level of possession of a particular credence, say – it provides an appropriateness condition for a particular utterance within the game. In particular, it isn't a truth condition. For traditional expressivists, the way to say this was to say that the utterances in question *don't have* truth conditions. For me it is a little more complicated. The utterances do have

---

4 This needs qualification in the following respect. Just as blind people can learn to apply 'visual' concepts, so, in all or most of these cases, speakers who do not occupy the relevant stance could presumably pick up the vocabulary in question by exploiting at second hand the abilities of those speakers who do.

truth conditions, from the point of view of their users – the speakers playing the game. Indeed, 'It is probable that P' is true iff it is probable that P. But, as I stressed above, these truth conditions are not to be identified with the use conditions, or stance.[5]

What's most distinctive about my proposal, compared to those traditional expressivist accounts, is that in place of their *bifurcation* between expressivist language – where this kind of functional story was taken to be appropriate – and what they thought of as genuinely *descriptive* discourse, I want to offer an overarching unification. I want to propose a single, *unitary* account of the assertoric form, an account compatible with the idea that it can be put to work in these various distinct ways.

On my view, then, all these functionally distinct moves in the language game *are* genuine assertions, in the only sense now available. But what is this sense? How can we *characterise* the notion of assertion so that, despite their functional differences, utterances of these various kinds can all count as genuine assertions?

In the previous lecture I gave you the low-carbon answer to this question: we should just coast in Brandom's wake at this point, helping ourselves to his account of assertion. (One of the main points of the previous lecture was that Brandom's notion is thoroughly compatible with the pluralism of my Humean expressivism.) I now want to add to this energy-saving answer a more labour-intensive proposal for reaching what I think turns out to be the same point (with a better view of the surrounding landscape, along the way).

At its simplest, my proposal is that the assertoric language game is simply a coordination device for social creatures, whose welfare depends on collaborative action. It helps to reduce differences among the behavioural dispositions, or other variable aspects of speakers' situations, on which such action depends. Of course, it is hardly news that assertion can be thought of in this way. But whereas tradition would have said that *what gets coordinated* are beliefs about the world, my view says that while this isn't exactly *wrong* it puts the explanatory emphasis in the wrong place.

The first step to getting things right is to recognise that the coordination task has another dimension – a dimension corresponding to the functional

---

5 I disagree with someone (e.g., the probabilistic subjectivist, or Jackson and Pettit 1998) who claims that the use conditions are actually truth conditions not so much in thinking that they make the *wrong* choice of truth conditions but in thinking that they are wrong to assume that there is a theoretical issue to be settled at all, in these terms. As a deflationist, I simply deny that. Within the vocabulary in question, of course, claims have their disquotational truth conditions, but I recognise no semantic notion that would give us a fact of the matter from any other standpoint.

variability. *What gets coordinated* thus varies from case to case, depending on the practice or functional task – i.e. the *stance* – that underlies the class of utterances in question. For probabilistic claims it is credences or dispositions to betting behaviour, for conditionals it is inference-tickets, and so on. Each case brings with it a new *practical* respect in which the members of a speech community may differ and hence a new sense in which it may make a difference to their collective lives whether they take steps to coordinate. For better or worse, that's the crucial difference that flows from bringing the case within the scope of the assertoric game.[6]

This is a story that needs a lot more telling, of course. I've told it in a little more detail elsewhere (e.g., in Price [1988] and Price [2003]), but much remains to be done. For the present, however, I'll simply offer two reasons for optimism about this aspect of the programme. The first is that it doesn't seem controversial that assertion functions as a coordination mechanism, in something like this way. That looks just *obvious*, from the traditional standpoint. My move is simply to take that obvious truth and give a new twist to our understanding of what gets coordinated – to reverse the order of explanation between practice and semantic content, in a way I'll explain in a moment. But since that reversal takes place beneath the surface, as it were, it doesn't affect the plausibility of our 'obvious' observation. (It gives the subject matter of the observation a new and more important role, but the tradition can hardly deny that the material is there to be put to use.)

The second ground for optimism is that this project seems to align so well with what, as I've said, I take to be the leading current proposal for saying something substantial about the assertion game, that of Brandom. Certainly, more needs to be said about how Brandom's wheels fit on my axles – how the resulting vehicle can be steered in the direction I want to take it – but that's a much less daunting task than inventing the wheels from scratch.

2 THE PRAGMATIC CONSTRUCTION OF CONTENT

There is another respect in which my proposal aligns well with Brandom's. In the previous lecture, I characterised my view in terms of two assumptions about language and thought: the content assumption, that language is a medium for encoding sentence-sized packets of factual information, and the correspondence assumption, that these contents are all 'about' some aspect

---

[6] One of the advantages of this proposal, I think, is that it helps to explain our varying inclinations to play the assertion game, with respect to different topics – in Price (1988) I explored this idea in terms of the variability in the possibilities for no-fault disagreements, from case to case.

of the external world, in much the same way. As I said, my proposal rests on pulling the two assumptions apart, retaining the content assumption but sidelining the correspondence assumption, replacing it with a more pluralistic understanding of the role of content in our complex interaction with our environment.

The project is thus to explain *how there come to be* statements with particular contents, by thinking about the practical role of the particular instantiation of the assertion game that produces tokens with such contents. This amounts to a reversal of the orthodox view of the relative priority of content and usage, or semantics and pragmatics. Here's Brandom's description of what I take to be a closely related contrast between these two orders of explanation:

> An account of the conceptual might explain the use of concepts in terms of a priori understanding of conceptual *content*. Or it might pursue a complementary explanatory strategy, beginning with a story about the practice or activity of applying concepts, and elaborating on that basis an understanding of conceptual content. The first can be called a *platonist* strategy, and the second a *pragmatist* (in this usage, a species of functionalist) strategy. One variety of semantic or conceptual platonism in this sense would identify the content typically expressed by declarative sentences and possessed by beliefs with sets of possible worlds, or with truth conditions otherwise specified. At some point it must then explain how associating such a content with sentences and beliefs contributes to our understanding of how it is proper to use sentences in making claims, and to deploy beliefs in reasoning and guiding action. The pragmatist direction of explanation, by contrast, seeks to explain how the use of linguistic expressions, or the functional role of intentional states, confers conceptual content on them. (2000: 4)

Brandom goes on to say that his own view is 'a kind of conceptual pragmatism':

> It offers an account of knowing (or believing, or saying) *that* such and such is the case in terms of knowing *how* (being able) to do something … The sort of pragmatism adopted here seeks to explain what is assert*ed* by appeal to features of assert*ings*, what is claimed in terms of claim*ings*, what is judg*ed* by judg*ings*, and what is believed by the role of believ*ings* … – in general, the content by the act, rather than the other way around. (2000: 4)

Later, Brandom distinguishes between views that understand the conceptual 'in representational terms' (2000: 7) and his own view, which seeks 'to develop an expressivist alternative' to this 'representational paradigm' (2000: 10).

In these respects, then, my project seems well aligned with Brandom's. In other recent work (Price 2008, 2010), I have explored some possible divergences at later stages – these depend on some issues of interpretation of Brandom's project – but it seems clear that he and I begin in very much the same place.[7]

2.1 The mirror and the key

My project turns on a contrast between the view of informational content as a passive, 'reflective' sampling of something 'external' and that of it as an active product of an inferential and conversational game – a game whose distinct applications are distinguished by variation at two ends: in the *users*, as well as in the *world*. I'm thus proposing that we abandon the passive conception of representational content in favour of a more active, relational metaphor: that of the *key*, which is adapted at one end to the shape of the user, at the other end to the shape of some part of the environment.

The important question then becomes something like this: in virtue of what features of the environment, and what features of the circumstances of the language users, does the particular variation of the assertion game that generates *these* contents prove itself to be useful? It is the second part of the question that corresponds to the new dimension of variability which is obscured by traditional representationalism (and uncovered but misunderstood by traditional expressivism).

The difference between my position and traditional expressivism requires that I say something very different about the the issue of word–world relations. Traditional expressivists held onto the old representationalist story for discourses they regarded as genuinely descriptive and told a different, functional story elsewhere. My story is in one sense more complicated and in another sense much simpler. It depends on a bifurcation in the notion of the *world*, but not in that of *assertion*.

3 THE DUALITY OF WORLDS

[W]here there are no sentences, there is no truth ... the world is out there, but *descriptions of the world* are not. (Rorty 1989: 4–5, my emphasis)

---

7 A possible difference concerns the notion of practice. There is room for a range of views on the question as to what extent the relevant practices are constrained by our natures and physical circumstances. At one extreme would be the view that we are universal practitioners, capable of turning our hands to any practice at all, given the right instructions. At the other extreme would be the view that, as Louis Armstrong puts it with respect to jazz, 'If you gotta ask, you ain't never gonna know.' – i.e. you have the relevant practices innately (or otherwise naturally), or not at all. Both extremes are implausible, but there are a lot of possibilities in between. Brandom may be closer to the former extreme than me.

At the end of the previous lecture I offered my bifurcation in the notion of representation as an alternative – in some ways, a very sympathetic alternative – to Rorty's rejection of big-R Representationalism. To make the transition a happy one, however, we need to face up to a corresponding bifurcation in the notion of the *world.* This notion, too, I want to suggest, has two nodes, or conceptual attractors, that need to be clearly distinguished – and, once distinguished, kept apart, rather than uncomfortably bundled into the same skin. I began this section with the above quotation from Rorty – a much-quoted fragment from the introduction to his *Contingency, Irony and Solidarity* – to illustrate that he, of all people, here seems unconscious of the need for the distinction. After all, what is Rorty, of all people, doing in combining the idea that the world is 'out there' with that of *descriptions of the world.* Isn't this plain old representationalism? (As we'll see, there are ways to read Rorty to avoid that consequence, but they need the distinction I'm about to draw.)

3.1 Worlds of states of affairs

It is often noted that notions such as *belief, statement, state of affairs* and *fact* seem to go hand in hand with those of *assertion*, and *truth* itself.[8] And in arguing that we should think of the use of i-representations as genuinely assertoric, in what turns out to be the most interesting theoretical sense available, I've recommended, in effect, that we should respect this intuition: i-representations should be regarded as genuinely *factual*, too, in the best sense of the term we now have.

But a venerable tradition in metaphysics thinks of the *world* as the totality of facts, or states of affairs. Thus the world is held to *be* 'a world of states of affairs', in David Armstrong's phrase;[9] or simply 'everything that is the case', in the opening words of the *Tractatus* (Wittgenstein 1922). How is this conception of the world to be reconciled, if at all, with the relaxed, multifunctional notion of fact and state of affairs I've just recommended? On the one hand, the idea that the world is everything that is the case seems so uncontroversial that they could hardly fail to get along; on the other, the result seems likely to collide head-on with any *metaphysical* use of this notion.

8 This sort of remark is especially common in the context of approving discussions of deflationary theories of truth, but its plausibility doesn't seem to depend on deflationism.

9 'My hypothesis is that the world is a world of states of affairs. I think that I am saying the same thing as those who have held that the world is a world of facts' (Armstrong 1993: 429).

Why do they collide? Because all sides will agree, presumably, that what facts *we take there to be* depends on what kinds of assertoric claims our language equips us to make (as well as on what particular claims, of each kind, we take to be true). But functional pluralism about kinds of assertion seems to stand squarely in the path of any sort of metaphysical closure, or totality. If there is in principle no totality of possible kinds – no set of all possible functionally distinct assertoric language games – then nor can there be any totality of all the facts, apparently.

There seems to be a totality from where we stand, as it were – as players of a particular assemblage of assertoric language games – but we might have stood somewhere else (it depends on a host of contingencies about our circumstances and natures). This doesn't commit us to saying, implausibly, that if we had gone in for different language games the facts would have been different, only that if we'd gone in for different language games we would have made factual claims different, from (i.e. not translatable as) any that we actually make. Here, proper attention to use–mention distinctions saves us from implausible idealism.[10]

Thus we get something like not a plurality of *worlds*, but a plurality of *ways of world-making*. Or, rather, what we get is one way of world-making, the only way – viz., the adoption of a practice of making factual claims – but now recognised to have a plurality of potential applications, associated with the plurality of possible assertoric language games.

Before we turn to the second notion of the world, it is important to see that there's nothing spooky going on with respect to the first. In particular, there's no sense in which our adoption of a new language game 'gives concrete being' to a world or realm of facts that didn't exist before we started to play the game. The story is much more banal than that. Adoption of a new language game gives concrete being to … a new language game! That is, it puts us in a position to endorse a new collection of factual claims. But there's no perspective, external or internal, from which it is appropriate to say that the adoption of the game has 'brought the facts into being', or anything of that kind. We can't speak about the facts in question until we

[10] I think it also saves us from conflict with the argument of Davidson (1974). A standpoint that merely *mentions* the language games of foreigners does not incur the obligation to interpret them in the home language and hence to render the 'alien' conceptual scheme in terms of our own. This doesn't mean, *contra* Davidson, that we recognise an irreducibly *different* conceptual scheme. So long as we merely mention the foreigners' utterances, we do not attribute them a conceptual scheme at all – that's not the enterprise in which we're engaged. Davidson will say that we therefore don't treat them as language users, but I think this is terminological – if Davidson wants to keep the term 'language', we can use another.

play the relevant game, and within the game, very special cases aside, it certainly won't be appropriate to say that we *created* the facts. (There's no soapbox here for the village idealist.)

3.2 The world as the natural environment

The first notion of world (call it the *i-world*) went with that of i-representations. The world in the first sense is simply what our i-representations are *about*, in the proper deflationary sense of 'about' – among other things, as I've stressed, it is a world only visible from *within* (i.e. to *users of*) the vocabularies in question.

The second notion of world goes with that of e-representation. In this sense, the world is simply the natural environment – what we have in view in the scientific project. This project includes, as a small fragment, the kind of enquiry that might have a use for the notion of an e-representation, when the focus of the investigation is a particular aspect of human behaviour (our own *linguistic* behaviour) and its context. Here, the notion of an e-representation provides one among many conceivable relations between the relevant aspects of us, on the one hand, and our environment – the *e-world* – on the other. (The relations that figure in the expressivist's functional explanations provide other examples.)

I want to be neutral, for present issues, on some controversial issues about the constitution of the e-world, in this sense – neutral, in particular, on issues of reductionism and pluralism within science. (I'll say something briefly about the latter at the end of this lecture, but only to contrast scientific pluralism with the kind of pluralism associated with i-representations.) However, I want to stress that there's nothing metaphysical about the notion. It doesn't presuppose an Archimedean viewpoint, outside thought and language altogether, but simply an ordinary, first-order scientific viewpoint. Roughly, the e-world is visible only from within science in precisely the same sense as the i-world is visible only from within the viewpoint of users of assertoric vocabularies in general. Indeed, the e-world simply *is* the i-world of the scientific vocabulary. (Our own scientific vocabulary, too, not some transcendental scientific vocabulary.)[11]

---

[11] Note that the fact that the e-world can be properly contained in the i-world, despite the fact that our own vocabularies are all proper objects of scientific study and thus items themselves in the e-world, depends on the fact that not all investigations of a vocabulary need be committed to the ontology to which the vocabulary itself is committed. The crucial points here are the use–mention distinction and rejection of substantial semantic properties.

Once again, the view I'm recommending is that the i-world and the e-world are both useful notions to have in our philosophical vocabulary, so long as we don't make the mistake of confusing them. Traditional positions, naturalist and non-naturalist, might be seen as arguing that one or other is primary – one or other is *the* world. I want to say that that argument, like the analogous argument about representation on which it feeds, rests on an equivocation.

In the next section I want to turn to an argument that tries to resuscitate one side in this debate, claiming that the kind of account I have offered itself reveals the primacy of the e-world. Before I turn to that, let's return to my quotation from Rorty, to illustrate the way in which the distinction between two notions of world makes things go smoothly: '[W]here there are no sentences, there is no truth ... the world is out there, but descriptions of the world are not' Rorty (1989: 4–5). If it is the e-world that is 'out there', then the contrast is misleading (by my lights, and surely by Rorty's), because not all descriptive sentences are descriptions *of the e-world*. But the remark stands if we read both occurrences of 'world' as 'i-world'. For in this case it amounts to an affirmation – *from the inside*, as it were – that the existence of the i-world doesn't depend on our linguistic practices.

Similar points apply to this famous remark from P. F. Strawson, the earlier part of which I quoted approvingly in the previous lecture: 'If you prise the statements off the world you prise the facts off it too; but the world would be none the poorer. (You don't also prise off the world *what the statements are about* – for this you would need a different kind of lever)' (1950: 137, my emphasis). Once again, I want to say that this is fine if we read it 'from inside our language games', with our i-worlds in view. From this vantage point, the italicised phrase can be given a deflationary reading, and the remark as a whole can be read as emphasising that although our language games are 'mind-dependent' (or better, 'situation-dependent'), the objects they commit us to are not. We cannot speak of those objects except within the game concerned, but, from that standpoint, the right thing to say – neglecting the obvious reflexive cases – is that the objects *don't* depend on our practices. (As I put it before, no standpoint for simple-minded idealism.)

If we try to read Strawson's remark in terms of the e-world, however – as a remark from the anthropological perspective, in which we stand outside the language games in question – then again the italicised phrase is problematic, by my lights. In fact, it is problematic in two (albeit closely related) ways: first, in assuming that there is a notion of 'aboutness' in play, from this standpoint, and second in assuming that what statements are about must lie in the e-world.

4 ISN'T SCIENCE 'PURELY DESCRIPTIVE'?

At this point, some of my opponents – especially traditional expressivists – are likely to ask how my view really differs from theirs. Why shouldn't we say that the e-world – the natural environment – just *is* the *real* world, as these expressivists do, and regard my view as a victory for the view that combines realism about the natural world with irrealism about other matters or *real* realism about science with *quasi*-realism about other vocabularies?

As the latter way of putting the question makes clear, this is related to a broader issue, raised in the previous lecture. Does my view leave any room for Blackburn's distinction between (as I put it there), loose and strict notions of assertion? Or does it necessarily recommend a kind of global version of quasi-realism – a budget-travel global expressivism, that allows the economy-class passengers to take over the whole plane?

In the previous lecture I recommended the latter view, the economical alternative, though with an important concession. I suggested that the distinction between i-representation and e-representation offers scope for a compromise: it allows us to say that although all the relevant declaratives are genuine assertions in (the inferentialist's version of) an *i-representational* sense, nevertheless some are more in the *e-representational* business than others. In this way, I suggested, we can make sense of the intuition underlying the old bifurcation thesis, that not all declarative utterances are equally in the business of 'tracking the world'. (We can say this so long as we are clear that it is an *e-representational* notion of tracking that we have in mind.)

Can a traditional quasi-realist do better than this, by defending the (old) bifurcation thesis in some stronger form? It seems to me that there are at least three ways in which such an attempt might be made – three ways in which a class of genuine assertions, or factual statements, might be argued to be distinguished from the broader field, in the way that quasi-realism and its non-cognitivist ancestors traditionally assumed (thereby leaving the language of science in a privileged position).

1. *Logical form*: It might be argued that there are logical or grammatical marks of 'genuine' as opposed to 'quasi' statementhood.
2. *Ontology*: It might be held that my own view gives an ontological primacy to science (or perhaps to some subset of science).
3. *The fate of the expressive component*: It might be argued that for some vocabularies – again, perhaps, those of science – the expressive component of the account simply falls away, leaving us nothing else to say, except that the claims in question are 'purely descriptive'.

Concerning the first of these proposals, however, it seems to me that it is simply inconsistent with the idea that we should look to Brandom's inferentialism for our account of assertion. For, if inferentialism supplies our account of the distinctive grammar and logic of assertion – and if I am right in claiming that what it captures is the loose rather than the strict notion – then it follows that the grammar and logic go with the loose version, not with anything else. But there is more to be said about the second and third proposals.

4.1 Ontology and the perspectival fallacy

The second option – roughly, realist about the-world-as-described-by-science but at best quasi-realist about other topics – is a version of what is sometimes called *Eleatic* realism (or Eleatic naturalism). One appealing version of the Eleatic criterion for realism holds that we should be realists about a class of entities (about Xs, say) when Xs figure in causal explanations of our talk and beliefs 'about' Xs (i.e. of talk which has the superficial form of talk about Xs). Blackburn canvasses such a criterion as the basis of a distinction between quasi-realism and genuine realism, for example: 'A quasi-realist [e.g., about value] can mimic our formal practice with the concept of truth or fact. But surely he cannot give the facts any role in explaining our practice. To do so is to embrace their real distinct existence, or so it might seem.'[12]

Of course, the task of seeking the causes of our beliefs and utterances – 'explaining our practice', as Blackburn puts it – is just a small part of the scientific enterprise as a whole. The Eleatic criterion is likely to appeal to the general case, saying that the mark of the real is to be needed in causal explanations in general not merely in causal explanations of our own practices. But the restricted project will serve to illustrate my general point: as we engage in this explanatory project, there is an inevitable but potentially misleading difference between the scientific vocabulary and others. We are engaged in a scientific practice, seeking explanations for various other practices (or, indeed, for scientific practice itself). In other words, we are *employing* scientific vocabulary, to *theorise about* the function and genealogy of vocabularies in general.

In general, presumably, the explanations we offer from this scientific perspective will appeal to extra-linguistic states of affairs of various

---

[12] Blackburn (1980: 31); cf. Blackburn (1984: 257). Blackburn goes on to call attention to some difficulties for this suggestion; here, as elsewhere, he is by no means an unqualified Eleatic naturalist.

kinds – to the various features of ourselves and our environments that explain our linguistic practices (scientific and otherwise). Thus, roughly, it is characteristic of the project that it appeals to non-linguistic ontology in the service of explanations of various kinds of linguistic behaviour. In the case in which the latter behaviour involves quantification over a distinct ontology of its own – an ontology of moral values, in the moral case, for example – the explanatory project embodies the starkest possible asymmetry between this ontology and that of science. It *invokes* scientific ontology while *ignoring* moral ontology. And how could it be otherwise? We *use* scientific vocabulary but *mention* the various object vocabularies with which we are concerned. (Our *explanandum* is *the use of moral language*, not *moral states of affairs*.)

No wonder, then, that the natural facts that play a role in explaining our practices *look* privileged from this perspective. They are privileged, *from this perspective*, for it simply *is* the scientific explanatory perspective. One mark of this privilege – perhaps the most misleading – is that the perspective entitles us to formulate the disquotational platitudes for terms and sentences in the scientific vocabulary but not for others. To say something of the form:

$$\text{'P' is true iff P}$$

we have to *use* the sentence we substitute for P. The same goes for something of the form:

$$\text{'X' refers to X.}$$

Since our imagined explanatory perspective merely *mentions* the target vocabulary, expressions of this form are admissible only in the case in which the target vocabulary and the explanatory vocabulary are one and the same – in other words, only in the case in which the meta-vocabulary provides the use of the term in question. Hence it can easily seem that the meta-vocabulary is *uniquely* representational, or referential.

In both a semantic and an ontological sense, then, scientific discourse can easily seem to be privileged. The error, I've urged, is to mistake a genuine but merely perspectival privilege for something stronger – for an *absolute* ontological criterion, or for the conclusion that only scientific discourse is genuinely truth-conditional. The best defence against this error lies within the explanatory project itself. If reflection on the genealogy and functions of quantification, and semantic vocabulary, leads to the kind of conclusion I've recommended – in other words, to a view that is essentially unitary about these aspects of language, across vocabularies with different functional origins – then we have what we need to meet this challenge: an explanation of the *appearance* that scientific discourse is privileged in these ways, without the need for any substantial, non-perspectival distinction to account for this appearance.[13]

Thus, functional pluralism offers a natural way to deflate the Eleatic intuition – to explain it as a product of a kind of perspectival fallacy. We functional pluralists should certainly embrace the project of explaining our linguistic practices – for that way, if all goes well, lies a scientific foundation for the suggestion that different parts of language serve different functional ends, in some sense overlooked by object naturalists. As I suggested at the end of the first lecture, the upshot would be that science might properly take a more modest view of its own importance. Object naturalism would be defeated from within, as it were, by a scientific discovery that science is just one thing among many that we do with the linguistic tools of assertion and ontological commitment. And this project itself does not accord any special status to scientific ontology, in anything other than the perspectival sense. (No basis here, in other words, for metaphysical privilege.)

4.2 Expressivism all the way down?

The last suggestion is that the material for a distinction between genuine and quasi-description might lie within expressivism itself – that the expressivist project will simply run out of steam at some point and find nothing to say other than that the remaining statements are genuine statements, devoid of any expressive component. I want to offer two reasons for thinking that this outcome is unlikely, the first pitched at the idea that the purely descriptive residue would equate with the language of science, and the second more general.

4.2.1 Science and the status of modality
A popular philosophical conception of science combines two thoughts. On the one hand, science is supposed to aim for the perspective-free standpoint, the view from nowhere. On the other, its fundamental concern, at least *inter alia*, is supposed to be with the modal character of the world: with laws

---

[13] If this seems doubtful, note that we can consider our linguistic practices from other perspectives. We can evaluate them, in various senses, for example. (Arguably, in fact, they cannot count as full-blown linguistic practices – as 'sayings', or 'assertings', say – unless they are taken to be subject to normative assessments of various kinds. But the present point doesn't depend on this claim.) If we invoke evaluative or normative properties in this context, the resulting ontological commitment is once again a product of the perspective – a product of the framework in play, as a Carnapian might put it.

of nature, causal powers and objective probabilities and dispositions. My kind of expressivism raises the possibility that science itself might provide us with good reason to challenge this philosophical conception of science – with good reason to think that these two characteristics, combined in the popular conception of science, are actually incompatible.

How could this happen? Well, suppose, as I suggested earlier, that we came to accept an expressivist genealogy for causation and other modal notions. In essence, this would be a scientific account of a particular aspect of human linguistic and cognitive practice, explaining its origins in terms of certain characteristics of ourselves, as epistemically limited creatures, embedded in time in a particular way. A corollary would be that uses of these very concepts in science – including, indeed, in this very explanation – would themselves be held to reflect the same embedded perspective. Thus, some aspects of current scientific practice would be revealed *by science* to be practices that only 'make sense' from this embedded perspective – so that if, *per impossibile*, we could step outside this perspective, these aspects of science would cease to be relevant to us.

Would this be a *reductio* of the expressivist account of causation? Or a fundamental challenge to science? Neither, in my view. On the contrary, it would be continuous with a venerable scientific tradition, a tradition in which science deflates the metaphysical pretensions of its practitioners, by revealing new ways in which they are unlike gods. Science has not only survived, but thrived, on this diet of self-deprecation. Why should the present case be any different, if some of science's own core categories and activities turn out to be perspectival in a newly recognised way, a way that depends on the peculiar standpoint that science's own practitioners occupy in time?[14]

In general, the status of modal discourse provides a particularly fascinating focus and potential application for the kind of pragmatism I want to recommend. For the moment, the crucial point is that it provides a major

---

[14] Would the relevant aspects of current science then stand revealed as bad science? No, I think, for the perspectivity of (some aspects of) current scientific practice would have turned out to be entirely appropriate, given its role in the lives of creatures in our situation. In that sense, it is not 'bad science' and doesn't need to be reformed or eliminated. As Blackburn has long stressed, unmasking the expressive character of a concept need not lead to simple-minded 'rejectionist' anti-realism – we may continue to use the concept, and even to affirm, in a variety of ways, the objectivity of the subject matter concerned, despite our new understanding of what is involved (of where we 'stand') in doing so. In appreciating this perspectivity, however, we get a new insight into the nature of the non-perspectival world, which 'looks like this', from our particular point of view. So there's some good news, too, for 'detached' science.

potential challenge to the view that science is uniquely 'in the describing business', a challenge from within science itself (i.e. from within the scientific investigation of human modal vocabulary). But in philosophy more generally the cement of the universe has become the concrete from which many metaphysical edifices are constructed. With representationalism, modality is one of the twin foundations of much of contemporary metaphysics; so a great deal rests on these issues.

4.2.2 The pragmatic foundations of generality

The suggestion we're considering is that we might find genuinely descriptive language where the expressivist programme simply runs out of steam: where there is nothing to say about the role, function or genealogy of a concept, other than that it serves to represent some feature of the speaker's environment. In a recent paper (ancestor of his contribution to present volume) Blackburn himself characterises this suggestion rather nicely (without wholly endorsing it):

A similar fate awaits us, in many peoples' view, if we pose [an expressivists'] external-sounding question about at least the coastal waters of science. How come we go in for descriptions of the world in terms of energies and currents? Because we have learned to become sensitive to, measure, predict and control, and describe and refer to, energies and currents. That is science's own view of how we have got where we are, and there is none better. (2007: 7–8)

But, as I've noted elsewhere (Price 1988, 1998), there is a powerful objection to this kind of suggestion in the lessons of Wittgenstein's rule-following considerations, especially as elaborated by Kripke. One of the lessons of these considerations is that our use of general terms inevitably depends on shared but contingent dispositions to generalise in the same way from a small number of exemplars. Actually, the point applies equally well to names and other singular terms, for these, too, depend on shared dispositions concerning reapplication. Language use is a dynamic, diachronic activity, and even singular terms need to be reapplied when reused. The lesson of the rule-following considerations is that all of these cases depend on contingencies in us – contingent, shared dispositions to 'go on in the same way' in the *same* way.

The point I want to emphasise is that these contingent dispositions are themselves *practical stances*, in the sense I've been using that term. In other words, they are contingent features of speakers, on which the use of particular vocabularies depends – and which can't in general be construed as aspects of the *content* of claims made in these vocabularies. (They are background pre-conditions of language, in other words.) As long as these stances are on a par with all the others, they reveal a respect in which all of language has the kind of dependence on contingent characteristics that was the mark of the expressive.[15] In this positive sense, then, the expressivist project casts its distinctive illumination over everything, though to different degrees in different places. The old bifurcation thesis thus gets replaced by a kind of gradation, with no extreme case at the right-hand end. (In terms of the irenic proposal of the previous lecture, we could put this last point by saying that although some vocabularies are more in the e-representational, e-world-tracking business than others, there are no pure cases – no cases in which the contingencies on the speakers' side go to zero, as it were.)

5 TWO KINDS OF PLURALISM

Finally, a note about pluralism. In an early paper (Price 1992), I distinguished two kinds of philosophical pluralism. One kind – I called it 'horizontal pluralism' – I took to be exemplified by Quine's ontological relativity and other forms of scientific relativism. Here the plurality consists in the possible existence of a range of alternative scientific world views, each empirically adequate to more or less the same degree, and none, even in principle, having privileged claim to provide a 'truer' description of the world. I pointed out that horizontal pluralism is not confined to science. In ethics, for example, it is the familiar thesis that there is a range of equally coherent moral viewpoints, none objectively superior to any other. Why is this a case of horizontal pluralism? Again, because different moral systems are all nevertheless moral systems. They have something in common in virtue of which they may be counted to be different ways of performing the same linguistic task. It is a nice question how this 'something in common' is to be characterised, but there must be an answer if relativism is not to degenerate into the trivial point that the same words may mean different things for different people.

I contrasted this kind of pluralism with 'vertical pluralism', the view that philosophy should recognise an irreducible plurality of *kinds* of discourse – ethical as well as scientific, for example – and mentioned Wittgenstein, as well as Goodman and Rorty, as examples of pluralists of this vertical sort.

---

[15] With similar possibilities for no-fault disagreements, etc. See Price (1988 Chapter 8).

I've mentioned this distinction now because scientific pluralism has enjoyed a resurgence in recent years, notably in the work of Nancy Cartwright (1999) and John Dupré (1993). Hence it seems important to distinguish the kind of pluralism I've been defending from such forms of scientific pluralism. It is an interesting issue whether the distinction is a sharp one. On the one hand, after all, I've noted that it might be a consequence of my view that we find functional plurality within science, for example in the distinction between modal and non-modal vocabulary (or between different kinds of modal vocabulary). While on the other hand, we might well want to distinguish Cartwright's and Dupré's version of scientific pluralism from anything that Quine signed up for – and to explain the difference, perhaps, by appeal to a vertical dimension. I suspect, actually, that there's a further distinction we'll need, between two kinds of verticality: one corresponding to something like differences in levels of description in a world in which we find patterns at many levels, the other corresponding to my functional pluralism.

These distinctions need a lot more work. For the moment, I conclude with a distinction between two sources of pluralism. One explains it in terms of a pre-existing plurality of structure in the natural world (external to us), the other in terms of plurality in our natures and circumstances, and hence in the uses we find for assertoric language games. The distinction may not always be sharp, but it is deep and important, in my view – and naturalism leads us astray, unless we keep it in mind.

PART II

Commentaries

CHAPTER 4

Pragmatism: all or some?

Simon Blackburn

I EVERYDAY REPRESENTATION

The conference at which an ancestor of this paper was first delivered was unusual for me.[1] If we think of philosophers who emphasise reference, representation, fact, truth, truth-makers and ontology as conservatives, on the right, and we think of those who talk instead of expression, discourse, norms and social practices as radicals on the left, then I am usually attacked from the right. My quasi-realist, right-wingers say, pretends to give us what we want by way of facts and truth but is really only offering us a sham: fools' truth, or fools' facts. He is insufficiently enchanted by truth-makers and ontology and the paradises of metaphysics. But on this occasion I was much more likely to be ambushed by the left. The quasi-realist, it might be said, plays along with too much of the stock-in-trade of the right, retaining notions of reference and representation and even attacking iconic figures of the left for their more wholehearted expulsion of any such notion anywhere and everywhere. The quasi-realist is not a card-carrying revolutionary, they say, but an arrant trimmer. In Huw Price's more sympathetic eyes, I have been a valiant but sad Moses figure, who helped to show the way to the Promised Land but who could never manage to enter it himself. And, as any student of politics knows, the temperature when agitators of different shades of pink air their differences rises just as high as it does when they rail against those on the right.

I do not like high temperatures, so I did not want to justify standing in one place or another, or staring at the promised land of pragmatism only

[1] Expressivism, Pragmatism and Representationalism, at the Centre for Time, University of Sydney, August 2007. The paper is intended to be self-standing, but it owes its existence to the generous, yet critical, work of Huw Price and others – see Macarthur and Price (2007), Price (2010) and Price (2006). Another ancestor of the paper was previously given to the philosophy faculty at Murcia, and I owe thanks to Angel Garcia Rodriguez for the invitation and opportunity.

from a distance, but to offer a kind of apologia for not knowing where to stand. I find that knowing where to stand requires me knowing where to stand on a lot of other issues, such as Quine versus Carnap on the difference between external and internal questions, minimalism in the theory of truth, the best way to tell the kinds of genealogical or anthropological stories that are the stock-in-trade of the left or even what to think about things such as functionalism, or the external world. So all I could try to do was to sensitise the audience to some of my difficulties and then, in a cooperative and conversational spirit, to ask for guidance.

I can best introduce the issues by referring to a discussion Huw Price gives of a passage from my book, *Truth*. I had written about Rorty's substitution of a norm of solidarity for a norm of truth:

> To many of us, however, the solution looks worse than the problem: language is not there to represent how things stand—how ridiculous! It is as if Rorty has inferred from there being no innocent eye that there is no eye at all. For after all, a wiring diagram represents how things stand inside our electric bell, our fuel gauge represents the amount of petrol left in the tank, and our physics or history tells how things stand physically or historically. (Blackburn 2005: 153)

Price (2006) quotes this, alongside a similar passage from Frank Jackson (1997), who had expressed astonishment at conferences where people attack representational views of language 'who have in their pockets pieces of paper with writing on them that tell them where the conference dinner is and when the taxis leave for the airport'. Price takes us as examples illustrating how something called 'anti-representationalism' often meets with something close to incomprehension, and he goes on to quote as an ally Robert Brandom who also talked of the way in which a representationalist paradigm is 'taken for granted' even in fields outside analytical philosophy.

But Brandom probably had other disreputable branches of philosophy and theory in mind, whereas the opinion voiced in my passage, and I think in Frank Jackson's, was not intended as a philosophical defence of a philosophical position called representationalism. It was intended only as a Wittgensteinian reminder that the term 'representation' and its cousins have perfectly good *everyday* uses. A historian may represent the court life of James I in a somewhat lurid light. Captain Cook's charts represented the coastline of New South Wales with astonishing accuracy. The petrol gauge and the wiring diagram and the menus and timetables can do what they are supposed to do, or fail. These are not philosophers' sayings but simply parts of the everyday. We mention them not as things that demand a particular philosophical approach all by themselves, but as 'an assemblage of reminders': the data that any such approach must end up respecting. In Moorean vein, I would suppose that any philosophy that ends up denying them is far less likely to be right than they are. My problem with Rorty was that he was not, in my judgement, respecting them, but at any rate in his persona as cultural agitator and prophet, gleefully bent on trampling on them. Of course, this is going to leave a problem of distinguishing the legitimate everyday use of such notions, from anything more philosophical and more suspect. It might even turn out that there is nothing there, no articulate philosophical theory to reject or oppose, but that is for later.

Huw Price and David Macarthur did not present themselves as cultural storm troopers, bent on excising reference and representation from the everyday. Rather, they say that for the pragmatist the crucial thing is not to answer questions about the function of language in ways that encourage *metaphysics* (Macarthur and Price 2007: 95). On this I would like to be at one with them but want to insist that neither petrol gauges nor timetables, nor in general the Wittgensteinian reminder of the everyday that I offered should encourage metaphysics. Again, however, there may be some difficulty about identifying the enemy. One radical pragmatist, Robert Kraut, has raised the pertinent question whether the reflections that prompt metaphysics are themselves legitimate social and intellectual parts of the culture so that Rorty's campaign against them is inconsistent with his own tolerant cultural holism. Kraut writes:

The point is not that entrenched practices are unsusceptible to criticism; some concepts and distinctions – despite their prevalence – are surely dangerous (at least, by our lights) and ought to be jettisoned. But Rorty's revisionary desire to drop various distinctions (for example, that between *scientific knowledge* and *cultural bias*) strains at his own culture-holism: he should do more philosophical/interpretive work to understand the role played by such distinctions. Just as we are inclined to ask 'What are we DOING when we moralize?' (the refrain commonly prompting noncognitivisms of various sorts), we should be equally prepared to ask 'What are we DOING when we offer metaphysical hypotheses?' A thoroughgoing pragmatism should earn us the right to moralize, modalize, and – here's the rub – metaphysicalize. That's something we like to do; a good anthropological story should say why, and not portray us as dysfunctional imbeciles for scratching ongoing metaphysical itches. (Kraut, personal communication)

The point is surely correct. Rather than an overarching confidence that there is something bad out there called metaphysics, the right attitude must be much more piecemeal. When we come across a piece of philosophical (reflective) theorising, we ask whether it helps, whether it rings true, takes us somewhere it is valuable to go or offers a 'perspicuous representation' of one of our practices.[2] And the answers may vary, as may people's standards for perspicuity. For some ('realists'), the question of what we are doing when we talk of numbers or duties or possible worlds is sufficiently answered by insisting that we are talking of numbers or duties or possible worlds. To others, of a more ambitious cast, this is hopelessly flat-footed, and we have to dig deeper. If a Carnapian external question about a piece of discourse is worth asking, some of us think, it is not worth answering with the flat-footed response.

It is easy to stray from the everyday into philosophical theory, or attempts at it. If the ten commandments represent our duties, in the same way as the menu represents the available food, then what is there to oppose in the 'philosophical' theory that talks of us as responsive to, reflecting on, referring to, duties? Doesn't the 'theory' follow seamlessly from the talk? The cross-border traffic works both ways, because it is also easy to move from philosophical theory into the everyday with what to my eye is often an alarming nonchalance. An example is this sentence from Davidson, although it is no worse than many others: 'There is, then, very good reason to conclude that there is no clear meaning to the idea of comparing our beliefs with reality *or confronting our hypotheses with observations*' (Davidson 1986: 324, my italics). Here what starts life supposedly as a deep philosophical objection to correspondence theories of truth, instantly metamorphoses into the rejection of a perfectly everyday activity, and one absolutely essential to our lives as rational beings. Davidson here falls over a precipice, but he has only himself to blame, since he often skips carelessly along its edge, as here, talking about the confrontation of beliefs with reality: 'No such confrontation makes sense, for of course we can't get outside our skins to find out what is causing the internal happening of which we are aware' (Davidson 1983: 144). Personally I find I can perfectly well confront my complacent belief that there are plenty of eggs in the fridge with the stark reality of there being few or none, certainly without getting outside my skin and almost always without being aware of any internal happenings, except when gastric rumbles and gurgles are propelling me to the kitchen in the first place.[3]

Perhaps this casual attitude is explained by a Quinean refusal to distinguish Carnap's 'external' questions, about some kind of thing we say, from 'internal' questions that arise within the form of saying itself. The external

---

[2] The usual translation of Wittgenstein's goal of an 'Übersichtliche Darstellung' of a piece of language.

[3] I am not denying that Davidson's essays on the foundations of epistemology are deeply important, nor is it right to take these two sentences as typical. But they illustrate a problem.

question is posed, about a piece of language or discourse of some identified kind, when we ask how to explain the fact that we have come to think and talk like that: why do we go in for possible world talk, arithmetical talk, ethical or normative talk, and so on? Carnap himself was fighting 'metaphysical' attempts to answer external questions, although the precise interpretation of his own attitude to them is not entirely clear: a plausible view sees him as embracing a pragmatic, and perhaps expressivist, line according to which one external view or another manifests what is fundamentally a policy decision.[4] I suspect that Rorty and perhaps other neo-pragmatists were influenced by Quine's rejection of an external/internal boundary, supposing that if representation has no proper use in answering the external-sounding question, since it introduces metaphysics, then it must have no proper use in the internal workings of the discourse itself. But that must surely be a mistake: indeed, relying on the Moorean priority of the everyday, we might just as well reverse it and say that since 'representation' and its cousins have a respectable place inside discourses, they can freely be used in theorising about them as well. If this is the upshot, then the problem with what I called flat-footed realism is not that it is false but that it is flat-footed.

It is perhaps worth noticing that any such dissolution of the internal/external distinction would have nothing to do with rejection of the analytic–synthetic distinction, which at best bears on Carnap's own construction of such a question. There is no trace of the analytic–synthetic distinction, for instance, in Hume's distinction between the anatomist and the painter, in connection with ethics. Nor is there any metaphysics in his own way of tackling the question; as he himself indignantly insists, if you find metaphysics in his account of ethical thinking, 'you need only conclude that your turn of mind is not suited to the moral sciences' (Hume 1902: Appendix 1 p. 289).

The evident reason Carnapians can maintain the distinction is that simply insisting on the everyday is compatible with offering different *interpretations* of it, such as those offered by expressivists in their various domains. The propriety of everyday talk offers a datum, but it does not offer a self-extracting philosophical 'ism': representationalism, which the propriety of the sayings therefore establishes. It just means that if we set such an 'ism' up either as a good thing or as a target,

---

4 I am indebted to Robert Kraut for alerting me to some of the ambiguities in Carnap's own view. Kraut raises the possibility of what to me would be a very congenial interpretation according to which Carnap himself allows an expressive function to 'metaphysical' sayings.

then we ought to be sure what it is. And if the propriety of the every-day talk is a datum, then pragmatists would do well to ensure that what they attack as 'representationalism' does not encompass the everyday so that the ordinary human baby gets thrown out with any undesirable bathwater.

2 PRACTICES

One could, indeed, see Rorty himself as simply offering an interpretation of the everyday use of 'truth', 'description' or 'representation', in spite of his frequently derogatory remarks about them. The interpretation I went on to discuss in the work to which Price and Macarthur refer was that in offering everyday remarks that allow sayings to be true or to say how things stand, or to represent the way things are, we deploy nothing more than a norm of solidarity with others (Blackburn 2005: 160ff.). I argued that this was inadequate for familiar reasons that boil down to this: that justifying ourselves to our peers is often quite different from getting things right, and it only offers even a pale surrogate for truth provided our peers are fully paid-up practitioners of the discipline that matters: fellow historians, if we are doing history; fellow lawyers, if we are interpreting law; fellow scientists, if a scientific question is on the table. But to achieve *that* status, these peers must have mastered techniques and norms of practice that go beyond what is properly comprehended as 'discursive' or belonging to discourse. For their opinions to be worth listening to they need to be more than good inference-makers, for example. They need to be masters of the sextant or the archive or the laboratory, or at least to be well attuned to the results of those who are masters of these things. They need to be plugged into techniques or practices, and they need to follow the norms that belong to them. It is those that entitle them to a hearing in the *après*-truth coffee lounge where we try to become of one mind about something. We must not gaze at this coffee lounge where the scientists and historians congregate to chat and try to become like-minded about things, without remembering that it is a small oasis surrounded by the laboratories and instruments and libraries with which they work. One could indeed try saying that the laboratories and instruments and libraries are in turn simply parts of a normative discursive practice: their use is the way to find yourself successful where it matters, in the coffee lounge. But that would be like saying that training as a batsman is not done with the purpose of enabling you to cope with the bowling but in order to garner applause and solidarity from the team afterwards in the dressing room. It's an odd opposition to mount and, in fact, a false way of looking at the run of sportsmen once it is mounted.[5]

I could put this in Sellarsian terms by saying that Captain Cook, for instance, might literally have had an entry rule for an element of his chart. You do not write a figure indicating a depth unless you have dropped a piece of lead to the bottom and measured the number of marks on the line. Had he not followed many such rules meticulously, his charts would not be revered, as they are, for their representational accuracy. There are also ways to use his chart to navigate the waters around the coast, and rules determining when this is done properly. The chart is useful because there is a harmony between the entry rule, getting the chart to say that there are two fathoms of water in a strait, say, and the exit rule or practice, which gives you success in sailing a boat drawing anything less than two fathoms, but no more, through the strait. But there is no useful contrast here between coping and copying: the chart enables you to cope because it represents correctly the amount of water in the strait. *There is no other explanation of the successes that attend sailors who use it.*

Price (2006: 613) has wondered how, if I stand as close to Wittgenstein as I have claimed, I yet cast aspersions on Rorty, who represents himself – if we may now be permitted the term – as standing at least equally close. The difference is that my Wittgenstein, trained as an engineer, was far more prone to emphasise norms of *technique* or *practice*, than purely conversational norms. In fact, to my eye there is something rather comical about imagining the aristocratic and misanthropic Wittgenstein paying much attention to conversation at all, unless he was conducting it.

A pragmatist, or anyone else, would be perfectly right to insist at this point that the norms governing investigation are *our* norms. It is we who determine what we want to know and how to set about finding it out. In one sense this is obviously true but in another it may be misleading. For it is not simply down to us and our conventions whether any particular investigation is well adapted to give us results about what we want to know. Finding which do and which do not can be a long, sticky and fallible process. We cannot solve it by decision or convention. It is a matter of making ourselves into good instruments for detecting how things stand, and that is no easier than making a good petrol gauge or a good sextant.

---

5 False because vulnerable to the same kinds of argument that Bishop Butler advanced against the similar relocation of human motives in psychological egoism.

I think that the practices of everyday assertion are sufficient as well to help with one problem Huw Price (2006: 607) raises for me. Here he contrasts a *heterological* practice with an *autological* one, introducing the contrast with two kinds of exam. Of the question whether Aristotle was Belgian, one asks the same question in order to test the pupil's knowledge of where Aristotle was born, and the other asks in order to find out what the pupil thinks. A sincere answer is all that is required in the second practice; the first deploys another more exacting norm or standard. Price points out, rightly, that for all deflationism tells us about the truth predicate, we could be in either practice. The autological pupil can say 'it is true that Aristotle was Belgian' as easily as saying 'Aristotle was Belgian' and still get the tick. Hence, Price concludes, more remains to be said about norms of assertion than anything deflationism gives us. For, in general, we are in heterological practices. Sincerity is not enough.[6] I have been concerned to defend the heterological parts of ethics, which does not stop with the swapping of responses but includes a healthy practice of disagreement and doubt and persuasion, at least partly because it is more important for us to be of one mind and to have a tale about why we are minded as we are, when the topic is whether early term abortion is to be banned than when the topic is whether Jackson Pollock was a disaster. In the empirical sciences, heterologicality is more visibly a part of the practice since our responsibility to verification procedures is a firm norm for assertion, and falling short in implementing them is a firm reason for criticism and dissent. In Bernard Williams's terms, we do not merely want the person producing the timetable to be sincere, but to be accurate. The term 'accurate', however, introduces nothing beyond minimalism: we want our informant to say that the plane leaves at 1.00 p.m. if and only if the plane does leave at 1.00 p.m., and so on in general. An autological practice would look different: we would want our informant to say that the plane leaves at 1.00 p.m. if and only *he believes* that the plane leaves then, and so on, and this is at best a desire that might be appropriate in a psychotherapist rather than someone bent on catching a plane.

3 A DEFINITION OF PRAGMATISM

So much for the everyday. With it firmly in place – although, as I have already said, potentially ripe for further interpretation – what remains of

---

[6] I say 'in general' because there are, I think, conversational practices which pretty much approach it. Much vocalisation in art galleries, for instance, and especially modern art galleries, is little more than autological. We effuse and compare effusions rather than trying to get something right. The same may be true of religious sayings in general.

an 'ism' for pragmatism to oppose? Price gives us a great deal of help here, in the kind things he says about my quasi-realist programme as a kind of Trojan horse for introducing pragmatism into the representationalist citadel, or as a shining example for the rest of the movement to follow. He has also said some very useful things about the relation between the kind of expressivism that quasi-realism tries to help and minimalism in semantics. Putting the two sides together, I think we can identify pragmatism in something like the following terms.

You will be a pragmatist about an area of discourse if you pose a Carnapian external question: how does it come about that we go in for this kind of discourse and thought? What is the explanation of this bit of our language game? And then you offer an account of what we are up to in going in for this discourse, and the account eschews any use of the referring expressions of the discourse; any appeal to anything that a Quinean would identify as the values of the bound variables if the discourse is regimented; or any semantic or ontological attempt to 'interpret' the discourse in a domain, to find referents for its terms, or truth-makers for its sentences (Macarthur and Price 2007: 96). Instead, the explanation proceeds by talking in different terms of what is *done* by so talking. It offers a revelatory genealogy or anthropology or even a just-so story about how this mode of talking and thinking and practising might come about, given in terms of the functions it serves. Notice that it does not offer a classical reduction, finding truth-makers in other terms. It finds whatever plurality of functions it can lay its hands upon.

I do not offer this as a prescriptive, defining description of neo-pragmatism. Some thinkers who like the label may reject the whole enterprise of answering a Carnapian external question rather than giving an answer of a certain shape to it. But it will serve for the moment, and with it in front of us we can now put in place Price's compelling use of minimalism about truth and other semantic notions, as a useful, or indeed vital, prop for pragmatism. Minimalism simply assures us that a pragmatist who has completed his explanation need not worry at finding truth, or other semantic notions, woven into the target discourse. By minimalism, they will be serving the same logical purposes, such as enabling generalisation to take place, there, as they do anywhere else.

All this is entirely in accord with the approach expressivists such as Gibbard and myself have taken to the ethical, which can encompass the more general area of the 'normative'; it shows us standing on the same podium as pragmatists, and possibly with a few campaign decorations showing as well.

What then of the fear, voiced by Wright (1992), Boghossian (1990) and others, that minimalism is inconsistent with expressivism, or at least deeply in tension with it? That fear arises only if it is worries about whether ethical terms represent, or ethical sentences can be true, or about what truth-makers they have, that motivate us to set out on the explanatory story. For then there is a threat that the minimalism would itself dismiss and dissolve the worries that set the whole enterprise going. Our discourses would wear their own 'perspicuous representation' on their own faces, and this would give encouragement to the flat-footed realist or representationalist.

But we can now see that there are two answers to this charge, which eventually coincide. One would be that it is not *those* worries, or *just* those worries, that motivate the enterprise. But the more interesting reply is that it *is* those worries but that they can be expressed without the explicitly semantic vocabulary. After all, *minimalism itself forces this possibility upon us.* If there is a legitimate worry somewhere, put by employing a notion of truth, then by minimalism it ought to be capable of expression without it. If we can skip up or down Ramsey's ladder without cost or concern, then equally we must be able to frame genuine problems that arise when we do use the vocabulary, without so doing.

In the moral case, for example, we might start by saying that we are worried by the idea of a moral *fact*, but freely move to saying that it wasn't *facts* that were the problem, ready to be dissolved by minimalism, but morality. Thus, suppose we express a discontent with our understanding of ethics, by saying with John Mackie that we do not see how we can credit ourselves with knowledge of moral facts, when we are conscious that a faultless difference, such as being born in another, equally admirable culture, would have led us to an opposite opinion on what those facts are. And suppose someone tries to soothe us with minimalist thoughts about facts. There is no worry, they say, of this kind, since we no longer theorise in terms of facts: minimalism shows us how to dispense with them as thick or robust elements in any theory. Well and good, we should reply, I now express my worry without mentioning facts: I do not see how to claim that I know that p when I am conscious that a faultless difference, such as being born in another, equally admirable culture, would have led me to think that $\sim p$. In general, I continue, I adhere to norms that suggest that I should not maintain knowledge when I also accept that an equally defensible view suggests the negation of what I claim to know. And I can't see how to exempt myself from the accusation that this is what I am doing in the present case.

I do not say that this 'argument from relativism' is particularly compelling – in particular, the admission that the other culture is equally admirable is usually one we do not make, and without it the worry solves itself – but it is just as compelling put without mention of truth or fact as with it.

Or again, suppose Mackie comes out with an argument from queerness, framed in terms of the mysterious magnetic properties of supposed moral facts. Thanks to minimalism we can rephrase this: Mackie fails to see how being convinced that p can by itself involve being motivated to do some related thing, without there being an additional, independent and contingent component of desire in the agent. Again, we may or may not be impressed, but the new phrasing is on all fours with the old.

In other areas we find the same kind of transformation. If a worry about numbers were put in terms of the difficulty of referring to abstract, non-located, causally inefficacious objects, and deflationism about reference gallops in to help, the worry will relocate itself in the question of how we know about abstract, non-located, causally inefficacious objects. Or, it might tellingly ask why we should be concerned about them. And the philosophy of mathematics again gets a motivation and a foothold. A similar transformation could be offered for puzzles about reference to possible worlds. In each case, the substantive puzzle can be relocated away from the insubstantial notions of representation and reference.

4 LOCAL OR GLOBAL?

Returning to the characterisation of pragmatism given above, we should now see not a binary opposition, between pragmatism and some competitor called representationalism, but at least a fourfold division of alternatives. We could hold out for pragmatic stories *everywhere*. The opposition would be flat-footed representationalism *somewhere*. Or, we could hold out for pragmatic stories *somewhere*, and the opposition would be flat-footed representationalism *everywhere*. The last of these is, I suppose, the position manifested by those conservative philosophers with whom I started, who automatically react to any pragmatic story by reaching for notions of truth, truth-condition, truth-makers, and their kin, and proclaiming that these lie beyond the pragmatist's grasp. I stand shoulder to shoulder with Price and others in finding that attitude reprehensible. Still, all that is needed to oppose it are *local* pragmatisms, for which, of course, I am more than happy to sign up.

On the other hand, I am much less certain about *global* pragmatism, the overall rout of the representationalists apparently promised by Rorty and perhaps by Robert Brandom. The reason is obvious enough. It is what Robert Kraut, investigating similar themes, calls the no-exit problem. It points out, blandly enough, that even genealogical and anthropological stories have to start somewhere. There are things that even pragmatists need to rely upon, as they produce what they regard as their better understandings of the functions of pieces of discourse. This is obvious when we think of the most successful strategies of the pragmatist's kind. A Humean genealogy of justice, for example, talks of human beings with limited capacities, very definite needs, situated in a relatively niggardly environment where it is hard to satisfy those needs and therefore having to evolve cooperative mechanisms regulating mutually beneficial conduct, restraint and coordination. A wider Humean genealogy of values in general talks of natural propensities to pain and pleasure, love and hate, and an ability to take up a common point of view with others. It postulates a human nature in which some particle of the dove is kneaded together with the wolf and the serpent and provides a story of our evaluative practices on that basis. A broadly Fregean genealogical story of arithmetic and then mathematics more generally would start by placing us in a world of kinds of objects with distinct identity conditions, such as tigers and eggs and warriors, and then a capacity to tally them, with there being an advantage to us in being able to rank pluralities of them by their magnitude: three tigers are more of a problem than one, five eggs are better than three; eighteen warriors coming our way make for a disaster, although we could probably fight off ten. And so on.

Such genealogical stories start with a common-sense background of us, and a world of physical objects, with distinct locations, changing only according to distinct regularities with a distinct speed limit. In the books in which he provides a genealogy of morals, Hume simply takes all that for granted, just as a Fregean account of arithmetic takes the tigers and eggs and warriors for granted. If we ask the Carnapian external question about all *that*, then we face a choice point. It may be that we take an Aristotelian, or perhaps Wittgensteinian, line on the priority of the everyday. There is simply no place for 'first philosophy' to stand behind the *endoxa*, the given in our common-sense situation. This attitude would be that of *quietism*, or the rejection altogether of at least some external questions. If we insisted instead on posing the Carnapian external-sounding question, how come that we go in for descriptions of the world in terms of surrounding middle-sized dry goods?, then the answer is only going to be the flat-footed stutter or self-pat on the back: it is because we are indeed surrounded by middle-sized dry goods. That answer, obviously, draws on the referential resources of the object language and, according to the account in front of us, amounts to a victory for representationalism over pragmatism. It is because it is no better than a stutter that I call it flat-footed representationalism. A similar fate awaits us, in many people's view, if we pose a Carnapian external-sounding question about at least the coastal waters of science. How come we go in for descriptions of the world in terms of energies and currents? Because we have learned to become sensitive to, measure, predict and control, and to describe and refer to, energies and currents. That is science's own view of how we have got where we are, and there is none better. In these areas we might want to echo another sentiment of Davidson's: 'The causal relations between our beliefs and speech and the world also supply the interpretation of our language and our beliefs' (1986: 331). Here there is no further enterprise of going behind the world to 'interpret' our sayings and beliefs in yet more perspicuous terms.

5 ROLLING PRAGMATISM?

We may think our spade is not turned so quickly and that we can dig below our everyday landscape. Hume thought so when he tackled the external world in *Treatise*, I.iv.2, but he never revisited the dig, perhaps because the trench could not be shored up with the materials he had left himself and collapsed upon him. Berkeley thought our spade was not turned so quickly, and others influenced by Descartes, such as Hobbes, did so too. The aim will be to see reference to everyday objects as an instrument for coping with something else, and the only plausible candidate will be the order-liness of experience, the only 'given' that looks capable of distinguishing experience of a real independent world from a mere 'rhapsody of sensation'. As Peter Strawson so marvellously indicated in *Individuals* (1992), the possibility of spatial organisation of the world requires orderliness, stability and repetition, giving rise to the idea of a revisit to the same place, and the reidentification of the same kind of thing, rather than the substitution of a qualitatively identical but different thing. But whether this is a genuinely distinct and satisfying 'genealogy' for the concepts of a public world is, obviously, extremely doubtful, and to many contemporary philosophers it would be complete heresy, facing a battery of objections, from those centred on the impossibility of recognising orderliness, or effecting reiden-tifications, in a purely private world (Wittgenstein) to those querying the possibility of even something so basic as awareness of time in such a world (Kant).

It would be very odd if either classical pragmatism in its early American dress, or neo-pragmatism as we have it now, depended on the old Cartesian priority of the inner against the outer. And it would be even more odd to see Wittgenstein as any kind of champion of a global pragmatism which is trying to take over the common-sense homeland of representationalism by using materials fashioned from the inner life of consciousness. It would be nearly as odd to take Davidson as a similar champion of the inner. Instead, neo-pragmatism attempts a genealogy by taking certain *social* facts for granted, including conversation, inference, scorekeeping, and other discursive activities, and constructing its genealogy of reference and everyday ontology on that basis. I see this as an interesting exercise, but I find myself very unclear about the motivation: epistemologically or cognitively I should have thought that what people say is a special case of what things do, and the child's reidentification of its rattle and bricks and its ability to locate itself comes at around the same time and requires the same cognitive resources (it may require different neural resources) as its similar reidentification of its mummy and daddy and its discernment of structure, pattern and repetition in what they are saying to it. Similarly, as someone who thinks that genealogical stories about norms and values are our best examples of neo-pragmatism in action, I am sceptical about reversals that give the learner's sensitivity to norms priority over its sensitivity to the recurring elements of its environment. Generally speaking, you learn that you must stop at red lights only after you have learned to recognise red lights.

It has been well said that every explanation must start somewhere, but there is no particular place that every explanation has to start. So one could imagine a kind of rolling global pragmatism. Whenever an area of discourse becomes a target for philosophical theory and we find ourselves worrying about its ontology or the kind of epistemology or the kind of saying about the world that constitute it, step aside to a place that, at least for the moment, seems not so worrisome and essay a pragmatic story about the utility of the target way of thought and talk, given an environment composed in the other, less demanding way. A rolling pragmatism would differ from a foundational pragmatism in that there would be no objection to patching it together from piecemeal, and together potentially circular, explanatory projects. You might explain our penchant for ethics and normativity taking middle-sized dry goods, and some facts about human nature and human needs for granted. You might explain the way we think about the ongoing identity of human beings in terms of our concern with psychological connectedness, and you might explain our talk of psychology in turn in terms of sensitivity to behaviour. You may talk about our sensitivity to powers and dispositions and talk of that kind of talk as a way of organising patterns in the Humean mosaic and reactions to them, as Hume's own theory of causation did. But then thought in terms of a Humean mosaic might in turn be explained as a kind of abstraction out of things presented to us in our everyday lives in the external world. And if the external world is the problem, then rolling pragmatism might equally step aside to construct a genealogy from our exposure to the Humean mosaic. Global pragmatism would be a patchwork of local pragmatisms, living by taking in each other's washing. There never comes a point at which our spade is turned and explanation can go no further, although, as the case of the external world suggested, it may often be open to doubt whether the explanations on offer always deserve the title, or always avoid drafts covertly drawn on the very kind of thing about which we are talking, and therefore failing to explain that kind of talk in the pragmatist way. I am not sure that rolling pragmatism would appeal to pragmatism's founding fathers – James, for instance, at least in his later empiricist and neutral monist phase, seems much closer to being a closet foundationalist – but it is the best I can do to sympathise with anything like a global programme.

In terms of rolling pragmatism, the flat-footed 'explanation' of a mode of discourse simply by citing our having cottoned on to an ontology, or the facts, or the truth-makers, would be abandoning the only kind of worthwhile philosophical explanation there could be. It would be announcing that our spade had been turned, and then, amazingly, patting ourselves on the back for this fact.

Although, I think we ought to ask why Rorty, of all people, with his desire to sink philosophy and its explanatory pretensions, should have minded about that. Common sense's answer to the Carnapian-sounding question, from within common sense, and science's answer from within science, should surely be a model for freedom from philosophy, not a target of contempt. What they model is the vanity of any philosophical ambition to step outside and to do better. It is the rolling global pragmatist who is an addict of new, philosophical, explanatory perspectives. The representationalist, on this account, is the true minimalist, and true quietist, modestly and sometimes admirably shying away from theory. 'Representationalism' on this story is what is left when philosophy becomes very, very boring. But some, such as Wittgenstein, Davidson and especially Rorty might say, in at least some areas, none the worse for that.

6 SO WHERE ARE WE LEFT?

In its classical form, pragmatism knew that its relationship to realism was fraught:

Realism manifestly is a theory of very great pragmatic value. In ordinary life we all assume that we live in an 'external' world, which is 'independent' of us, and peopled by other persons as real and as good, or better, than ourselves. And it would be a great calamity if any philosophy should feel it its duty to upset this assumption. For it works splendidly, and the philosophy which attacked it would only hurt itself. (Schiller 1907: 459)

Contrary to Dewey, perhaps far from burying it pragmatism should be seen as vindicating realism. This view has other supporters: it is found in James and, perhaps most famously, in Quine. In effect, what is happening here is that Carnap's external question is allowed, even in the case of the external world. The request for a 'perspicuous representation' is not dismissed out of hand as 'metaphysical', but instead it is given a (rather sketchy) pragmatic answer. The 'language' or mode of thought that embraces external, independent, public objects earns its living. It works, and nothing else of which we have the faintest conception does so. So we are to embrace it.

Theorists who like their pragmatism, or their realism, global rather than local may scent an opening here. If in this way pragmatism vindicates realism about chairs and tables, why not about possible worlds, numbers, rights and duties, selves, the passage of time and all the other posits of our everyday speech? These parts of thought or language also earn their keep, so should we not accept the inevitable and announce ourselves as representationalists and realists about them too?

My answer is that we should not because if we look back at the description of pragmatism that I gave we find there is a huge asymmetry between the case of common sense and what I called the coastal waters of science, on the one hand, and cases like possible worlds, numbers and rights and duties or the passage of time on the other. For in embracing the common-sense scheme we embrace not only the tables and chairs it posits but a *distinct view about our relation to them*. We must think of ourselves as causally influenced by them and sensitive to their multitude of properties: their positions, their creation, their destruction, their appearances and changes. To say that we mirror their doings now becomes a way of summarising a whole host of facts about our sensitivities that come along with first positing them: that if my chair collapses I will notice it, that if the table dances around or bursts into flames I will register that, that were it to grow in size it would have all kinds of other consequences that I could also register, and so on and so on. A mirror is quick to reflect the surrounding scene; I am not quite so quick but I do such a good job that comparing myself to a mirror becomes almost irresistible.

Furthermore, nature itself has imprinted its demands upon us. Our visual systems, for example, are hard-wired and modular in the sense that their output lies outside our control and outside the influence of other cognitive functions. We might know that the conjurer is not producing an egg out of thin air, but we cannot stop seeing the act as if that is exactly what he is doing. Other areas lack this fixity: ethics, for instance, attracts attention partly because while its demands seem so absolute to those of us who were well brought up, we also know that they are interpreted differently, or are even invisible to those who were not.

Finally, the doings of the items of common sense are directly witnessed, reflected in experience or what Kant called intuition. Their whole life, as it were, consists in their role as systematisers and explainers of experience. There is therefore no option of embracing the scheme while holding back on its own explanations of why we do so. Whereas in the other cases there is every prospect of bracketing the existence of possible worlds and the rest and coming to understand why we go in for the mode of thought in question in other terms. In other words, there is every prospect of giving an anthropology or genealogy which is itself free of the commitments in question.

As already touched upon, there is the traditional empiricist option of wrestling the common-sense example into the same shape as the others by going fundamentally private: indeed, one might argue that this option is already foreshadowed by Quine with the very idea of a 'posit', since the model is one of a theoretical entity posited in order to help with some independently known phenomenon. But, as I have said, this seems not to be the neo-pragmatist intention, taking us back, as it does, to the dark days before Wittgenstein and Sellars. From this point of view, Quine's cheerful assimilation of common sense to basic science was a throwback to the bad old days in Vienna.

A more promising, or at any rate a more up-to-date, strategy for a global theory would be to urge that more is involved with the common-sense scheme than meets the eye. It is only to a superficial glance, it might be said, that chairs and tables form part of a scheme that can be separated from modality, arithmetic or normativity. It is here that various arguments against the possibility of 'disentangling' the one part of discourse from the other come into play. I believe that they all fail and that the natural presumption of difference remains. Even in cases where disentangling is genuinely impossible, the different strands making up our thought can be separately identified. There is no understanding that we are confronted by a chair that does not embrace understanding that it has various causal powers or that various counterfactuals are true. Yet causation and counterfactual thought are ripe for the kind of attempt at perspicuous representation that expressivists have always offered. The good things Hume said about causation do not disappear because causation is so firmly entrenched in our most basic modes of thought. All that follows is that we can discern a plurality of functions more often than we might have expected. But then it was never more than a pious hope that perspicuity would require simplicity.

CHAPTER 5

Global anti-representationalism?

Robert Brandom

I REPRESENTATIONAL SEMANTICS AND EXPRESSIVIST PRAGMATICS

Huw Price is one of the boldest and most original voices of pragmatism in
the generation after Richard Rorty and Hilary Putnam. Two particularly
interesting ideas he has been developing recently are subject naturalism and
global expressivism.[1]

The term by contrast to which 'subject naturalism' is defined is 'object
naturalism', which is the kind usually associated with the term 'naturalism'.
It aspires to a particular kind of semantic account of some vocabulary or
discursive practice. More particularly, it offers a representational account.
That is, it says what objects and properties that vocabulary talks about,
what range of facts it states or expresses. That representational semantic
strategy accounts for the 'object' side of object naturalism. The 'naturalism'
side is a matter of the semantic metavocabulary that is employed, in part
to specify the ontology: what kinds of things the vocabulary in question
represents. It is to be a naturalistic vocabulary. That is a genus that comprises
a variety of species, including at least the vocabulary of fundamental physics,
vocabularies of the special natural sciences, or, least demandingly, ground-
level empirical descriptive vocabulary, including both observational and
theoretical vocabulary.[2]

By contrast, subject naturalism is the project of using a vocabulary that
is naturalistic in one of these senses, not as a *semantic* metavocabulary but
as what in *Between Saying and Doing* (Brandom 2008) I call a '*pragmatic
metavocabulary*'. That is, it is to be used to describe what the discursive

---

[1] I am thinking especially of Price (2004) and Macarthur and Price (2007). The other essays in
Price (2011b) can also be consulted with profit in this connection.
[2] Note that one ought not just to assume that only vocabulary that is descriptive in a sense that contrasts
with prescriptive, or, more broadly, normative (not the only way of thinking about description) can
have observational uses.

85

practitioners who deploy the vocabulary in question *do*, the practices they engage in, or the abilities they exercise, in virtue of which they count as using that vocabulary. The idea is to formulate in the favoured vocabulary necessary and sufficient conditions for doing what one needs to be doing in order thereby to be saying what can be said using the vocabulary, rather than (as with a semantic metavocabulary) for saying in different terms what they can say in that vocabulary. This is telling the sort of story familiar to us from the many instances of the genre we find in Wittgenstein's *Investigations* (1953). Instead of worrying about what the vocabulary says about how things are with whatever it is it talks about, how it is describing or representing the world as being – a model that might or might not fit with the use of the vocabulary in question – we describe how the use of the vocabulary is taught and learned. If there is nothing mysterious about that, and if we can say in our favoured terms just what one needs to do in order to use the vocabulary correctly, Price argues, then the vocabulary should count as naturalistically acceptable, regardless of whether we have anything to say about what it represents.

As a somewhat fanciful example, consider someone who is puzzled about what is represented by indexical and demonstrative vocabulary. Are there indexical and demonstrative *facts*, over and above those expressible in non-indexical terms? If not, why aren't indexical terms freely interchangeable with nonindexical ones (as the phenomenon of the essential indexical, pointed out by Perry [1979] and Lewis [1979] shows they are not)? If so, what are these peculiar items? (One might imagine here some naturalistic analogue of the theologians who worry that a deity who is not spatio-temporally located could not think the sort of indexical and demonstrative thoughts we express using 'here', 'now' and 'this'.) The fact that we can formulate rules sufficient to specify the correct use of indexicals (at least for ordinary, spatio-temporally located speakers) – including the uses that are demonstrably not interchangeable with the use of any non-indexical terms – entirely in non-indexical terms[3] should be enough to dispel any concern that there is something spooky or mysterious going on. Some thought like this seems to be behind Wittgenstein's stories about the use of terms such as 'pain' and 'rule'. If the practices themselves are all in order from a naturalistic point of view, any difficulties we might have in specifying the kind of things those engaged in the practices are talking about, how they are representing the world as being, ought to be laid at the

---

3 As I argue in the Appendix to Chapter 2 of Brandom (2008).

feet of a Procrustean semantic paradigm that insists that the only model for understanding meaningfulness is a representational one.

The term by contrast to which 'global expressivism' is defined is 'local expressivism' about some particular vocabulary. One of the central examples here is the expressivism about terms of moral evaluation that has been developed by Allan Gibbard and Simon Blackburn. The thought is that the best way to understand this sort of vocabulary is to think about what one is doing in using it, what subjective attitudes one is expressing, rather than how one is supposedly representing or describing the objective world as being. On this line, the essential thing about normative vocabulary is its use to express an attitude of commendation, approval or practical commitment. For understanding this particular kind of vocabulary, that expressive role is central, rather than any descriptive or representational role that it might also be thought to play. An essential part of what recommends an expressivist approach to some vocabulary consists in the *contrast* it emphasises between the functioning of that vocabulary and the functioning of ordinary empirical descriptive vocabulary. But Price wants us to consider radicalising the expressivist approach so as to adopt it in understanding the use of *all* vocabularies. A *global* expressivism would be a way of implementing the move from object naturalism to subject naturalism.

What global expressivism and subject naturalism have in common is the rejection of *representationalism*, by which I understand a commitment to having the concept of representation play a fundamental explanatory or expressive role in semantic theory. That is the aspect of these views I want to focus on here. Let me begin by making some further distinctions. One thing at issue between object naturalism and subject naturalism is whether one is concerned with what one is *saying* or thinking, or with what one is *doing* in saying or thinking it. As I want to use the terms, this is the distinction between *semantics* and *pragmatics*: the study of the *contents* of utterances and other episodes and the study of the *acts* being performed in producing or exhibiting them. In addition to engaging in a semantic project, what Price calls 'object naturalism' is committed to a particular form of semantics: *representational* semantics. It aspires to an account of content in terms of what is being represented, talked or thought *about*. The semantic project need not take that form. One might, for instance, take inference or information rather than reference or representation as the central concept in one's semantic theory. Finally, object naturalism is committed to formulating its representational semantic theory in a vocabulary restricted to *naturalistic* terms, in one of the various senses in which a vocabulary might qualify as 'naturalistic'. So, as I understand it, 'object naturalism' is a project characterised by three, in principle independent, commitments: to a naturalistic representational semantics.

In understanding subject naturalism to be concerned in the first instance with pragmatics rather than semantics, I do mean to emphasise that subject naturalism and object naturalism are not necessarily incompatible enterprises. One might pursue both projects: using a naturalistic vocabulary to specify what the users of a certain vocabulary are doing when they deploy that vocabulary, and using a naturalistic vocabulary (perhaps the same one) to say what it is they are talking *about*, how they are representing or describing the world as being, when they deploy that vocabulary. Of course, these need not be construed as simply independent enterprises. What I have called 'methodological pragmatism' is the view that the point of introducing a notion of semantic content or meaning (and hence the source of the criteria of adequacy of the resulting theory) is to explain or at least codify central proprieties of their pragmatic *use*. What motivates Price to make his first distinction is the observation that naturalistic scruples will have been respected – the commitments that motivate restricting ourselves to naturalistic vocabularies when explaining intentional phenomena will not have been violated – if we offer naturalistic accounts of the pragmatics of some discourse, even in the absence of a representational semantics couched in the same vocabulary. That is exactly what local expressivist accounts of the significance of moral normative vocabulary aspire to offer.

I want to put the issue of naturalism to one side and just consider some of the relations between representational semantics and broadly expressivist pragmatics. As a matter of fact, I am sceptical about the prospects for a naturalistic pragmatic metavocabulary, sufficient to say what one needs to do in order to be able to say even all the things we can say by deploying naturalistic vocabularies themselves. For the principle object of the study of pragmatics is *proprieties* of use: how it would be *correct* to use various kinds of vocabulary. Understanding pragmatics that way does not by itself rule out the possibility of a naturalistic pragmatic metavocabulary. For one might be able to offer a pragmatic metavocabulary for the deontic normative metavocabulary in which those proprieties of use are specified. The most promising approach I know of for specifying such proprieties in a naturalistic metavocabulary is Ruth Millikan's selectional teleosemantics.[4] But this is not the line of thought I want to pursue here.

4 The issues in the vicinity of naturalistic pragmatic and semantic metavocabularies are intimately related to the distinction between the aspirations for *reductions from below* and *reductions from above*

One thing that Price sees as promising about the possibility of being a local expressivist about some kinds of vocabulary is that it shows that we need not accept global semantic representationalism: the view that for any legitimate vocabulary it must be possible to offer a representationalist semantics for it – on pain of its not turning out to be legitimate after all. A successful local expressivism about some vocabulary would show that while it might be *possible* to offer a representational semantics for that vocabulary it is not *necessary* to do so in order to show it to be legitimate. For there are other legitimate things one can do with language, other expressive functions besides representing or describing that it can perform. This is a theme that was near and dear to Wilfrid Sellars' heart. In a 1957 essay, 'Counterfactuals, Dispositions, and the caused Modalities', he takes as his principal target what he calls the 'tendency to assimilate all discourse to describing', which he takes to be primarily 'responsible for the prevalence in the empiricist tradition of "nothing-but-ism" in its various forms (emotivism, philosophical behaviorism, phenomenalism)' (Sellars 1957: Section 103):

[O]nce the tautology 'The world is described by descriptive concepts' is freed from the idea that the business of all non-logical concepts is to describe, the way is clear to an *ungrudging* recognition that many expressions which empiricists have relegated to second-class citizenship in discourse are not *inferior*, just *different*. (Sellars 1957: Section 79)

Sellars is here rejecting a *global descriptivism*. Now, not all discursive representations are descriptions: demonstratives and indexicals are not, for instance. But Sellars' discussion makes it clear that this sort of difference is irrelevant to his point. He would have been just as happy to say that not all declarative sentences should be understood as representing states of affairs. In particular, he takes modal claims to have the expressive function of making explicit rules of inference, which he takes to entail that they are not to be put in a box with descriptive claims that purport to say how things are. Sellars should be understood here as rejecting a *global semantic representationalism*, on the basis of a local expressivism about alethic modal

(in Dennett's useful phrase). In Chapter 1 of *Making It Explicit* (Brandom 1994), I aspire to, if not a *reduction* from above of normative vocabulary in terms of *socially* articulated attitudes and practices, at least an *explication* of it from above. For I want to understand the normative statuses that *confer* conceptual content as themselves *instituted* by socially articulated practical normative attitudes. McDowell and others have complained that this is a kind of residual naturalism. I would reply that it is precisely a naturalism of second nature and that I am just talking about the fine structure or mechanism that implements what McDowell wants to be entitled to say.

vocabulary. I will have more to say about this sort of local expressivism further along.

Without going into details of the case of modal vocabulary at this point, I want to make two observations about the conclusions Price and Sellars draw from the different local expressivisms they consider. First, it is at any rate not obvious that playing some expressive role that is not itself descriptive or representational rules out *also* being susceptible to a representational semantic treatment. (After all, it is having something to say about how expressivist analyses need not rule out discerning also a descriptive content – and so being able to respond to the Frege-Geach embedding objection – that is what distinguishes contemporary moral expressivism from its earlier incarnations.) Further collateral premises of some sort will be required to secure that inference. Second, supposing such auxiliary methodological hypotheses to have been supplied, the result of any particular local expressivism will be at best an argument against global semantic representationalism, not an argument for global semantic anti-representationalism: the conclusion Price seems to be aiming at, that the content of *no* vocabularies, not even ground-level empirical descriptive vocabulary, should be understood semantically in representational terms. Anti global-representationalism is weaker than global anti-representationalism. The latter will require, as Price is fully aware, *global* expressivism, together with whatever collateral commitments are needed to secure the inference from the applicability of a non-representational expressivist pragmatics to the unavailability of a representational semantics.

2 RORTY AGAINST REPRESENTATIONALISM

In at least taking seriously global semantic anti-representationalism, Price joins that other great neopragmatist, Richard Rorty. Thirty years ago, in his *magnum opus*, *Philosophy and the Mirror of Nature* (1980), Rorty offered a stunning diagnosis of the ills of contemporary philosophy as the culmination of working through ideas around which the whole of modern philosophy since Descartes had been built. The therapy he proposed is even more radical: reject those ideas root and branch and figure out how to do what we need to do with the sparer, more naturalised, more historicised neo-pragmatist vocabulary generated by a picture of vocabulary use as a part of the natural history of a certain kind of creature, as at once a coping strategy and an instrument of self-formation and transformation. The two master ideas of Enlightenment philosophy that Rorty blamed for setting us on an ineluctable path to the bottomless abyss we now confront are representation and experience. He saw these concepts as by now so thoroughly contaminated and infected with disastrous collateral commitments as to be forever entangled with them. He despaired of the project of producing sanitised, hygienic successors. The only safe way to treat these leper's rags, he thought, is to burn them.

I have by and large followed my teacher in rejecting the notion of experience as too burdened by noxious baggage – in particular, by the myth of the given – to be worth trying to recruit for serious explanatory and expressive work in philosophy. 'Experience' is not one of my words – literally: it does not occur in *Making It Explicit* (Brandom 1994), which contains many words. However, I broke with Rorty in trying to show why it is necessary and how it is possible to recover a notion of representation that is freed of the burdens and consequences he saw as inevitably encumbering it. In effect, where he thought that prudence requires building a fence that keeps the public out of sight of the edge of the abyss, I claimed that one much nearer would suffice to avoid catastrophe. John McDowell, in his magisterial *Mind and World* (1994), while acknowledging the dangers Rorty pointed to, endorses the rehabilitation of *both* of Rorty's suspect Enlightenment master concepts. His principle explicit concern is precisely with the notion of experience that I join Rorty in eschewing. In general, he thinks no barrier need be erected, no radical pragmatist measures taken. He shows us how to hop sure-footedly along the very edge of the precipice, with the confidence and insouciance of a mountain goat. And, indeed, I do not think he succumbs to the siren-like temptations of the deep. He does not, in fact, fall into the myth of the given. But I still want to say, 'Kids, don't try this at home. This man is a professional. If you try it, it will end in tears.'

Now, in this sketch I have also followed Rorty's rhetorical example and used rather melodramatic terms: 'abyss', 'leper', 'catastrophe', and so on. But what, exactly, is the problem that leads Rorty not only to reject global semantic representationalism but to recommend global anti-representationalism? It is perhaps less easy than it ought to be to glean a crisp answer to this question from the text of *Philosophy and the Mirror of Nature*. The somewhat equivocal response to this powerful book is, I think, partly to be explained by the fact that its readers could generally tell quite well what Rorty was claiming and recommending but had a harder time discerning exactly why he did so. And if you are urging that we must burn down the old town and strike out for the frontier, you'd better be able to be very clear about the danger or threat that calls for such a drastic response.

I think Rorty's diagnosis of the ills of semantic representationalism falls under two general headings: (1) a characterisation of life-threatening symptoms and (2) an etiology of them. He is much more explicit about the first part than he is about the second. The proximal difficulty is that thinking of our broadly cognitive and intentional relations with our environment principally in terms of our *representing* things as being thus and so (thinking of the mind as a 'mirror of nature') requires, he thinks, commitment to various kinds of epistemically *privileged* representations. Prime among these, in their twentieth-century analytic form, are what is *given* in sensory experience and cognitively transparent *meanings*. What is wrong with the genus of which these are both species is that the privilege in question is essentially magical in nature. Representations of these sorts are understood as having a *natural* or *intrinsic* epistemic privilege so that their mere occurrence entails that we know or understand something. They are self-intimating representings: having them counts as knowing something. But there is no way to cash out this sort of intrinsic authority in terms of the practices of using expressions or interacting with each other or our world. Rorty sees the middle years of the century as having unleashed a rising tide of *social pragmatism* about *normativity*: the view that *all* matters of authority and responsibility, entitlement and commitment, are ultimately matters of social practice. The later Wittgenstein adopts this standpoint to make fun of the idea of us as having automatic, intrinsic, infallible access to what we experience and what we mean. More pointedly, in 'Empiricism and the Philosophy of Mind' (1956), Sellars mounts a broadly pragmatist critique of the idea of things known simply by being in some sensory state, and in 'Two Dogmas of Empiricism' (Quine 1951), Quine does the same for the idea of things known simply by our grasp of our own meanings. (Rorty took it as persuasive evidence of how hard it is fully to disentangle ourselves from this particular tar baby that Sellars seemed to hold on to a version of the analyticity Quine had discredited, and Quine remained committed to the sensory given.[5] Carnap, of course, embraced both forms of givenness.)

So Rorty's first claim is that we should realise we have been driven to a philosophical impasse when we find ourselves committed to representations characterised by a sort of intrinsic epistemic privilege that is magical in virtue of its supposed intelligibility independently of the role the representings in question play in our actual reason-giving practices. His therapeutic

---

5 I think this picture is unfair to Sellars – though not to Quine. This story has been told with particular force and clarity by Michael Williams, in his *Groundless Belief* (1977).

recommendation is that the pragmatist critique that revealed the idea of this kind of epistemic privilege as incoherent be radicalised and extended. But we can ask, why should the recommended surgery extend to the excision of the whole notion of representation? That is, why should our theoretical response take the form of global anti-representationalism? Why not just give up the idea of representations characterised by this objectionable sort of epistemic privilege? Rorty's answer is that representational semantics has epistemological consequences. Unless some representations are intrinsically intelligible – grasped just by being there – understanding our cognitive and intentional relations to the world in representational terms puts an epistemological intermediary (a set of representations) between thinkers and what they think about. In this way, it excavates a gulf between mind and world. Semantic representationalism accordingly makes us patsies for epistemological scepticism, which then calls out for foundations in privileged representations. The sensory given and cognitively transparent meanings are foundationalist regress-stoppers on the side of premises, and of inferences, respectively. That is why Sellars and Quine between them should be understood as mounting a comprehensive pragmatist refutation of epistemological foundationalism. Rorty concludes that if we begin, as Descartes and Kant, for instance, taught us to do, with a semantic understanding of knowledge and meaning in terms of representation, we will end with the unpalatable alternatives of epistemological scepticism or an untenable epistemological foundationalism. That is why he sees a form of pragmatist global anti-representationalism as the preferred way out of the impasse.

My impression is that many philosophers who are principally concerned with semantic notions of meaning and content are unmoved by this line of thought because they are inclined to some such response as this: 'I am not at all worried by the supposed "threat" of epistemological scepticism. I am perfectly prepared to take for granted the common-sense and scientific picture of us as natural organisms adapting to and in constant causal commerce with a natural environment, which renders moot the extravagant suspicions of demon-deceiver or brain-in-a-vat scepticism. Concern with how one might in principle respond to such traditional, ultimately Cartesian epistemological worries does not and should not exert any constraint on my choice of semantic explanatory primitives.' There is certainly something to this response. But it is not clear that broadly epistemological issues can be neatly severed from more narrowly semantic ones. I suspect, for instance, that the return of (objectionable) sensory givenness in two-dimensional semantics is not a contingent feature of some ways of working out that idea but essential to the programme itself. And McDowell argues persuasively in *Mind and World* (1994) that subscribing to the myth of the given is an intelligible, though ultimately unsustainable, response to the entirely legitimate demand (not just in the context of epistemology but even in the context of semantics) that the world we are talking and thinking about be intelligible as exercising not only *causal*, but also *rational* constraint on our talking and thinking. Apart from that, he thinks, the very idea of empirically contentful judgements is bound to go missing.

I think the deep reason for the inextricable intertwining of broadly epistemological with narrowly semantic concerns is an animating insight about which in *Philosophy and the Mirror of Nature* Rorty is not as explicit as he is about the bearing of the options of scepticism or foundationalism on semantic representationalism, but which I think is present nonetheless. The forces that push representationalists towards semantic and epistemological foundationalism in the form of commitment to sensory, logical or semantic givenness (i.e. analyticity) ultimately stem from concern with the question of what it is to *understand* representations as such, what it is to grasp representational content, what one must *do* to count thereby as taking or treating something in practice *as* a representation, as pointing beyond itself in this distinctive intentional way. Only the possibility of a suitable answer to that question can keep representations from having the significance of a veil interposed between representers and a represented world. (Rebecca West asked rhetorically why one would want a *copy* of the world: 'Isn't one of the damn things enough?') The idea of epistemically privileged representations ('givens') represents one, flawed, answer to that question. Semantic representationalism will only be as viable as the alternative answers it can make available.[6]

It seems to me that one of the cardinal advantages of semantic inferentialism over representationalism is precisely the availability of such an answer. Grasping a conceptual content is a kind of practical know-how: mastery of an inferential role. That is being able to discriminate good from bad material (i.e. content-dependent) inferences in which it plays an essential role either in the premises or in the conclusions. Typically, such mastery will be both partial and fallible. But one counts as grasping a concept in so far as one knows what else one would be committed or

---

[6] I think this is essentially the argument of the first half of the Introduction to Hegel's *Phenomenology* (1931), but that is a story for another occasion. I have discussed what I take to be Kant's and Hegel's answers to this question in Chapters 1 and 3 of *Reason in Philosophy: Animating Ideas* (Brandom 2009).

entitled to by applying it and what would commit or entitle one to do so.[7] There appears to be no equally straightforward and natural answer to the question of what grasp of representational purport consists in – of what one must in practice be able to do in order to count as taking and treating something *as* a representing, as answering for its correctness (in a distinctive sense) *to* how it is with what, in virtue of playing that distinctive normative role as authoritative, is intelligible as being represented by that representing. I am not claiming that no such answer can be constructed,[8] only that the representational model does not come with one similarly ready to hand.

The basic thought behind raising the question is that meaning and under-standing are coordinate concepts, in the sense that neither can be properly understood or explicated except as part of a story that includes the other. Meanings are what one in the first instance understands, and talk of mean-ing in isolation from talk of what it is to grasp or to understand that meaning is idle. Michael Dummett, Donald Davidson and Crispin Wright are philosophers of language who have made this principle the centrepiece of their thought about meaning. If it is accepted, then semantics is inextri-cably bound up with broadly epistemic issues – where the broad sense of 'epistemic' refers not just to knowledge (a matter of knowing that) but also to understanding (a matter of knowing how). Of course, this view is not universally accepted. Jerry Fodor, in particular, considers the commingling of issues that are epistemic in this sense with properly semantic concerns to be the great bad of contemporary philosophy of mind and language. I don't want to argue the point here, just to register the dispute and to claim that Rorty's rejection of representationalism (indeed, his endorsement of global anti-representationalism) is rooted in his endorsement of what we

---

7 It is only in the presence of substantial optional collateral methodological commitments that such an approach is obliged to go on to pick out, among material inferences, a distinguished proper subset that plays some privileged role in the individuation of contents, or in assessments of grasp of them – for instance, inferences whose material goodness is underwritten by conceptual content *rather than* contingent facts about how the world is. Assessments of agreement and disagreement (hence of communication), whether within the practice or by a theorist looking on, are underwritten by assessments of whether two interlocutors have bound themselves by the same norms (so applied the same concept), even though they have different partial, fallible takes on what those norms require and permit.

8 So, for instance, for the simplest grades of representation, mapping and tracking (relations I under-stand in terms of the possibility of *us*, the theorists, being able to make inferences from map facts to terrain facts), being able to navigate among representeds by consulting representing is certainly a responsive, and probably a correct, answer to the question. For practical intentional systems (those intelligible as having goals) goal satisfaction with respect to represented achieved by consulting rep-resentings plays a similar role. Millikan (1984) offers a sophisticated response relying on her central notion of proper function within a reproductive family.

might call the 'entanglement thesis'. My own view is that it is a thesis about the relation between semantics and pragmatics – between theories about meaning or content and theories about what one needs to *do* in order to count as applying concepts with that meaning or deploying vocabulary that expresses that content. In so far as that is the right way to understand it, it is entailed by methodological pragmatism: the view that meaning should be thought of as a theoretical concept and meanings as postulated to explain proprieties of use, that is, of the activities of those who express them.

3 SEMANTIC ATOMISM AND SEMANTIC NOMINALISM

Does endorsing methodological pragmatism or its consequence, the entanglement thesis relating the concepts of meaning and understanding,[9] require one also to endorse global anti-representationalism – that is, the denial that representation can play a fundamental explanatory, or even expressive, role in an acceptable semantic metavocabulary?[10] This is a complicated question. In the closing portions of this paper I describe one perhaps unexpected dimension along which the issue ramifies. But first I want to point to two views in the vicinity, two forms that semantic representationalism often takes, that on this basis I think we *should* reject.

The first is *semantic atomism*, the idea that the semantic contents of at least some episodes, states and expressions can be made sense of one by one, each independently of all the others. The master idea animating Sellars' rejection of the sensory given is a *semantic* one, which then turns out to have (anti-foundationalist) *epistemological* consequences. The idea of sensory givenness is the idea of there being episodes that qualify as knowings (in a sense that includes their being available as suitable premises in inferences whose conclusions also count as knowings, in part in virtue of those inferences) that are *non-inferential*, not only in the (unobjectionable) sense that the process that results in the occurrence of those episodes is

---

9 I think of the entanglement thesis as a reciprocal sense-dependence claim, in the sense I define in Chapter 6 of *Tales of the Mighty Dead* (Brandom 2002b). As such, it stands in apparent tension with the claim that it is entailed by methodological pragmatism, which asserts an *a*symmetric relation between pragmatics and semantics. The bridge principle or auxiliary hypothesis I have in mind as relating them is the claim that once a set of theoretical concepts have been incorporated into a vocabulary, by being related inferentially to each other and to some observational vocabulary conceived of as antecedently available, the concepts expressed even by observational terms (those that have non-inferential, reporting uses) can be articulated in part by their inferential relations to the newly introduced theoretical vocabulary.

10 Later I will distinguish between explanatory and expressive versions of representationalism and so of anti-representationalism.

not an inferential process (but a matter of exercising, *inter alia*, a reliable differential responsive disposition), but also in the (objectionable) sense that its possession of the content it has is independent of any inferential relations to *other* contentful episodes. When Sellars talks about the ideology of givenness requiring that the occurrence of some contentful episodes does not depend on any prior 'learning', the learning he means is mastery of *other* concepts. (After all, it would be no problem for anyone on either side of the debate about givenness to allow that one might need some sort of training regimen to master the reliable differential responsive dispositions involved.) That is, the point is grounded in a denial of semantic atomism. My discussions of this point usually involve parrots[11] – I won't trample again on that well-worn ground. Suffice it to say here that semantic atomism is hard to maintain for anyone committed to the entanglement thesis. Meaning is holistic because understanding is.

If that line of thought is right, then *atomistic* representationalism should be rejected. But there is no necessity for semantic representationalism to take an atomistic form (though its more empiricist versions have tended to do so). When Descartes, impressed by Galileo's geometrical treatment of time by lines and acceleration by areas, wanted to replace traditional resemblance theories of the relation between appearance and reality by an account in terms of a more abstract notion of representation, his model was the relations he had discovered between discursive algebraic equations and geometric figures. '$x^2 + y^2 = 1$' and '$x + y = 1$' do not *resemble* the circle and line that they represent. They represent those figures in virtue of the facts relating the whole *system* of equations to the whole *system* of extended figures, in virtue of which, for instance, one can compute the number of points of intersection between the figures by simultaneously solving the corresponding equations. This original understanding of representation in terms of global isomorphism is an essentially holistic one.

The second, related, pernicious form of semantic representationalism is semantic *nominalism*. This is the view that takes as its semantic paradigm the designation relation between a name and its bearer (what it is a name *of*), or between sign (signifier) and signified, and assimilates *all* varieties of the representing/represented relation to that model. (Contemporary semiotics takes this shape, as does much structuralist and post-structuralist thought, downstream from Saussure. Derrida was at various points sufficiently

---

[11] Taken as an organising trope to particularly good effect by Jeremy Wanderer, in the opening chapter of his recent book *Robert Brandom* (Wanderer 2008).

within its grip that his alternative to Saussure's signifier/signified model was to take it that signifiers designate ... other signifiers.) What this approach misses is the Kant-Frege lesson that *sentences* are special. They are prior in the order of *pragmatic* explanation because it is using some expressions as declarative sentences, making *judgements* or *claims*, that is what makes something a discursive practice or ability in the first place. It is items in this category that a knower can take responsibility for (Kant), attach pragmatic, paradigmatically assertoric, force to (Frege) or use to make a move in a language game (Wittgenstein). As Frege taught us, our understanding of predicates should derive from our understanding not only of singular terms but also of sentences. So using the designational model for predicates and using it for sentences are intimately related moves. Methodological pragmatists are obliged to take the category of sentences as *semantically* fundamental, precisely because of their *pragmatic* priority.

A popular idea is that what sentences represent in the sense of designate is a special kind of thing: states of affairs. The thought is that what *true* sentences designate is *facts*, and some states of affairs are merely *possible* facts, designated by false sentences. This model inevitably leads to metaphysical extravagance. For there are lots of different kinds of sentences because there are many different ways of using sentences (things one can do with them). Pretty soon one must worry about logical facts and states of affairs (including negative and conditional ones), modal facts and states of affairs, probabilistic ones, normative ones, semantic and intentional ones, and so on, and corresponding kinds of properties to articulate each of them. One of the motivations for various local expressivisms is precisely to avoid such extravagance. Indeed, Wittgenstein in the *Tractatus* (1922) adopts what can be thought of as a local anti-representationalism about logical vocabulary, precisely to avoid having to postulate the kind of logical properties and relations (such as negation and conditionality) that his picture theory of representation forbids. But his tinker-toy approach, treating states of affairs as arrangements of objects, offers no account of modal or normative facts, only a token, unworkable approach to probabilistic ones, and treats semantic and intentional facts as in principle inexpressible. In doing so he opens the gate to a path he did not himself take: to treating these other kinds of vocabulary also in a non-representational, locally expressivist fashion. For he showed that even if one's semantics is at base representationalist, it need not take the form of semantic nominalism. (Jerry Fodor's 'divide and conquer' semantic methodology acknowledges the same lesson.)

Representationalism invites, but does not entail, semantic nominalism. But one of the basic criteria of adequacy for any representationalist account must be its treatment of *sentences* and what they express. This demand sometimes surfaces in the form of the issue of characterising the distinctive 'unity of the proposition'. This is another criterion of adequacy (along with offering an account of understanding coordinate with that of meaning, and rejecting semantic atomism) that inferentialist approaches automatically satisfy. For to be propositionally contentful, according to this approach, just is to be suitable to play the role both of premise and of conclusion in inferences, which articulate the content of the proposition.

In sum, these arguments do not rule out making essential use of representational vocabulary in semantics, so long as the account meets at least three conditions. First, an account must be offered of the uptake or grasp of representations as such – what one has to *do* to count thereby as taking or treating them *as* representings of some represented things. That is a normative status: according to things a distinctive kind of *authority* over the correctness of one's claims, thereby making oneself *responsible* to them. For that is what it is to take it that one is talking or thinking *about* them. Second, the account must be consistent with the pragmatic priority of sentential contents. Third, it must acknowledge the way the semantic content of some expressions, states or episodes is essentially related to that of others, to which one might or might not be committed. Semantic representationalism invites and encourages the denial of these insights, but it does not *entail* them. In fact, I do not think Rorty would have claimed an entailment. He was happy enough with a sort of guilt by association. He thought that representational semantics had been so intertwined with bad epistemological projects that it was irretrievably tainted. Indeed, he recommended jettisoning not only *representational* semantics but semantics in general, as a handmaiden to bad epistemology.

4 MEANING–USE ANALYSIS AND THE EXPRESSIVE ROLE OF REPRESENTATIONAL VOCABULARY

There is another direction from which it is possible to address the nature and therefore the viability of the project of semantic representationalism. Price has pointed out the possible bearing of expressivist pragmatic theories of what one is *doing* in applying the concepts expressed by some vocabularies on the feasibility and utility of representationalist accounts of their semantic contents. I endorse a sophisticated expressivism with regard to logical, modal and normative vocabulary. This is quite a different line of thought than that motivating contemporary expressivist treatments of moral normative vocabulary, for instance in Gibbard and Blackburn. I call my version a 'sophisticated' expressivism to mark the fact that the expressive role taken to be shared by both classical and modal logical vocabulary and normative vocabulary is one possible role picked out from a structured space of possibilities. That space is structured by the basic meaning-use relations I identify in *Between Saying and Doing*. The most important of these are one set of practices or abilities being sufficient to *deploy* a particular vocabulary (PV sufficiency), a vocabulary being sufficient to *specify* a particular set of practices or abilities (VP sufficiency), and one set of practices or abilities being sufficient (for instance by either algorithmic or pedagogical elaboration) for *implementing* another set of practices or abilities (PP sufficiency) (Brandom 2008, Chapter 1). Various expressive roles are then determined by the specific pragmatically mediated semantic relations they stand in to practices and other vocabularies. The simplest such complex meaning-use relation is being a *pragmatic metavocabulary*: the relation a vocabulary V' stands in to another vocabulary V when V' is VP sufficient to specify practices or abilities that are PV sufficient to deploy the vocabulary V.

That is not the expressive role that I take logical vocabulary to play – the genus the logical species shares with the modal and normative species of vocabulary. Complex meaning-use relations can be botanised by their meaning-use diagrams. The diagram for being a pragmatic metavocabulary is a simple composition (Fig. 5.1).[12]

The meaning-use relation of which I take logical vocabulary to be paradigmatic is that of being elaborated from and explicitating of some feature of practices or abilities that are PV necessary to deploy any autonomous discursive practice – for short, being LX for every ADP. This means that there is some set of practices or abilities necessarily exhibited by any autonomous discursive practice – any language game one can play though

---

[12] The conventions of this diagram are:

- Vocabularies are shown as ovals, practices or abilities as (rounded) rectangles.
- Basic meaning-use relations are indicated by solid arrows, numbered and labelled as to kind of relation.
- Resultant meaning-use relations are indicated by dotted arrows, numbered and labelled as to kind and the basic MURs from which they result.

The idea is that a resultant MUR is the relation that obtains when all of the basic MURs listed on its label obtain.

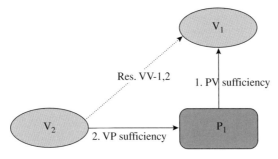

Figure 5.1. Meaning-use diagram: pragmatic metavocabulary.

one plays no other[13] – that can be elaborated into a set of practices sufficient to introduce vocabulary that is expressively powerful enough to specify the original practices. So, in having mastered a natural language, one already knows how to do everything one needs to know how to do, in principle, to deploy a vocabulary that is expressively powerful enough to specify the basic set of abilities on the basis of which the new vocabulary was introduced.[14]

The meaning-use diagram for that complex meaning-use relation is the more intricate one shown in Figure 5.2.

I cannot say enough here to make these diagrams, and the relations they present, graphically, truly intelligible, never mind to say what reasons there are to think that modal and normative vocabulary play structurally identical expressive roles. I offer these arcane images only to give some flavour of the structure that permits the botanisation of an infinite, recursively generated class of expressive roles, with a hitherto undreamt-of precision.

---

[13] As I use the term, to be a *language* game, a *Sprach*spiel, to be a verbal, and not just a vocal practice, some performances must be accorded the pragmatic significance of *claimings*, utterances with *assertional* significance, which accordingly count as the use of declarative sentences expressing propositional content. Wittgenstein's Sprachspiele are not autonomous discursive practices in this sense.

[14] It may be worth mentioning in passing that I am not offering an account of logical vocabulary (*inter alia*) that is *metalinguistic* in any ordinary sense. For, first, it does not involve *mentioning* the non-logical expressions it is applied to, but *using* them in a distinctive way. Of course, as McDowell points out in 'Quotation and Saying That' (1980), mentioning an expression *is* a way of using it. That the sort of use involved in my account is quite different from the use that amounts to mention is clear from how indexicals, demonstratives and foreign-language expressions behave in, say, conditionals. Again (and closely related), the logical vocabulary is not restricted to a metalanguage distinct from the object language but is *added to* the object language. One would get closer by looking at indirect discourse, which shares these features. The closest thought in the vicinity would be that 'If *p* then *q*' means something like 'That-q follows from that-p.' But any such model would require a *lot* of commentary.

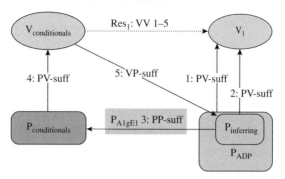

Figure 5.2. Elaborating-explicating (LX) conditionals.

That is the structure within which my local expressivism about a variety of vocabularies is located.[15]

The sort of expressivism about logical, modal and normative vocabulary that consists in understanding them as LX for every ADP is essentially, and not just accidentally, a *local* expressivism. Not all vocabularies can play *this* particular expressive role. Autonomous discursive practices *must* contain vocabularies playing *other* expressive roles – for instance, observational vocabulary that reports features of the non-linguistic bits of the world (ones that are not themselves the deployment of vocabularies). So *this* sort of expressivism is not a candidate for extension to a *global* expressivism.

However, one of the vocabularies I am a local expressivist about is representational vocabulary itself. By this I do *not* mean deflationism about traditional technical semantic vocabulary: 'true', 'refers', 'denotes' and like cognates. I do in fact endorse a distinctive kind of deflationism about such locutions, understanding them as anaphoric proform-forming operators.[16] In spite of specific differences, generically, this view belongs in a box with Paul Horwich's (1998). I mean something possibly more fundamental. For I am also a certain kind of deflationist about the representational dimension of intentionality itself. In the last chapter of *Between Saying and Doing*, I offer an account of intentionality as a 'pragmatically mediated

---

[15] I construe this view about the expressive role characteristic of logical, modal and normative vocabulary as developing, extending and generalising the approach Wittgenstein takes to narrowly logical vocabulary in the *Tractatus* (1922). For there he saw that one need not follow Russell's logical atomism in acknowledging a distinct realm of *logical* facts, over and above the non-logical ones. One can instead construe logical vocabulary as playing an expressive role that is quite distinct from the representational one played by logically atomic vocabulary.

[16] See *MIE* (Brandom 1994), Chapter 5, and Brandom (2002b).

semantic relation'. I do not discuss representational vocabulary there. But the account of its expressive role that I offer elsewhere[17] is an expressive, deflationary one. (Sebastian Knell is very good on this point in his book [2004].) In fact, though the case would have to be made out – as I do not do in *Between Saying and Doing* and will not do here – the expressive role assigned to paradigmatic representational locutions (the 'of' of 'what I am thinking of'. . . etc.) is *also* to be LX of some features essential to ADPs.

The vocabulary I am interested in is the ordinary, non-technical natural language vocabulary that expresses the idea that besides what we say or think there is also what we are talking or thinking *about*. I take this distinction to be the phenomenon that motivates various semantic theorists to introduce technical notions of representation, and initially picks out their topic. They want to elaborate, in a controlled way, the representational dimension of discourse that shows up pre-theoretically in our talk about what we are talking *about*. What distinguishes the 'of' and 'about' that express intentional directedness (the representational dimension of thought and talk) from the 'of' of 'the pen of my aunt' and the 'about' of 'the book weighs about five pounds'? I think it is their use in *de re* ascriptions of propositional attitudes. That is, the home language game of this vocabulary is ascriptions such as 'John believes *of* the green tie that it is blue', and 'When Mark says "ordinary language" he is talking [thinking] *about* the language of classical mechanics.' So, for instance, if we want to know whether some alien language has locutions for making explicit the representational directedness of their thought and talk, and which locutions those are, the place to start is by looking for expressions that have the pragmatic significance and conceptual content of *de re* ascriptions of propositional attitudes. The expressions that mark off the *de re* from the *de dicto* portions of such ascriptions (in lightly regimented English, what goes inside the scope of the 'of' from what goes inside the scope of the 'that') is then the explicitly representational vocabulary.

To understand the representational dimension of discourse, then, we need to understand what is made explicit by *de re* ascriptions of propositional attitude.[18] The way to do that, I have argued, is to look at what

[17] In Chapter 8 of *MIE* (Brandom 1994), Chapter 5 of *AR* (Brandom 2000), Chapter 3 of Brandom (2002), and in Brandom (2004).

[18] Although it is not obvious, the anaphoric account of the expressive (substitution-inferential) role distinctive of the classical semantic vocabulary of 'true' and 'refers' takes its place within the framework provided by *de re* ascriptions of propositional attitudes, via the insight that what I have called

one is *doing* in asserting a *de re* ascription. And here I have argued that from the pragmatic, deontic scorekeeping point of view one is doing *two* things in making any ascription of a propositional attitude. One is in the central case *attributing* a commitment, typically to someone else. That one is doing that by explicitly *saying that* the individual has that attitude is what distinguishes *ascription* of the attitude from the simple attribution of the attitude, which may otherwise be practically implicit in what one does. But because in ascribing one is *saying* something, in the sense of asserting it, one is also *undertaking* or *acknowledging* a commitment. Each bit of vocabulary deployed in the ascription must accordingly do double duty pragmatically. It contributes to the specification both of the claim responsibility for which is being attributed and of the claim responsibility for which is being undertaken. The question can then arise whether the choice of some way of expressing the claim being attributed is itself something for which responsibility is being attributed, along with the ascribed claim, or undertaken, along with the ascribing claim. Segregating some expressions within the scope of a *de re* operator, such as 'of' or 'about', is a way of making explicit that responsibility for using *those* expressions to specify the content of the claim ascribed is being undertaken, along with the ascribing claim, rather than attributed, along with the ascribed claim. Thus, if I say, 'Kant came to believe of his loyal and long-suffering servant Lampl that he was conspiring against Kant', I make it clear that the specification of Lampl as 'loyal and long-suffering' is one that *I* am taking responsibility for, *not* one I am attributing to Kant as part of the attitude I am ascribing to him. The semantic device that performs the pragmatic function that is the converse of that performed by the representational vocabulary that segregates the scope of the *de re* portion of an ascription is scare quotes. So, picking up the remark of another, I might say something like 'That ˢinspiring national leaderˢ is nothing but a self-interested kleptocrat.' Here I *attribute* responsibility for using that expression, while undertaking responsibility for the claim being made.

The pragmatic expressive function that determines the semantic content of representational vocabulary is marking the crucial distinction of social perspective between commitments (assertional and identificational

---

(in *Making It Explicit*) 'ascription-structural anaphora' – paradigmatically, the 'it' in 'John believes *of* the green tie that it is blue' – is the *intra*sentential correlate and codification of *inter*personal anaphoric inheritance of (substitution-inferential) content. That is why we can say 'Senator McCarthy believed of the first sentence of the Communist Manifesto that *it was true.*' I discuss this issue in greater detail in Chapter 8 of *Making It Explicit.*

= substitution-inferential) that are *attributed* and those that are *acknowledged* or undertaken. That is a very different job from describing how the world is. This vocabulary helps us keep our social books straight on who is committed to what – something we must be able to do in order to be able to deploy empirical descriptive vocabulary, but nonetheless something quite distinct from what we do with such vocabulary. A central observation of Kant's is that what we might call the framework of empirical description – the commitments, practices, abilities and procedures that form the necessary practical background within the horizon of which alone it is possible to engage in the cognitive theoretical activity of describing how things empirically are – essentially involves elements expressible in words that are *not* descriptions, that do *not* perform the function of describing (in the *narrow* sense) how things are. These include, on the objective side, what is made explicit as statements of *laws*, using alethic modal concepts to relate the concepts applied in descriptions. On my account, the representational vocabulary we use in natural language to make explicit the intentional directedness of our speech and thought performs a similar framework-explicitating function, but on the subjective side of the ones undertaking and attributing commitments concerning how things are.

So my form of local expressivism is peculiar (though not unique) in that it includes the vocabulary we use to make explicit the representational semantic dimension of discourse – exactly the semantic vocabulary by contrast to which the pragmatic expressivist vocabulary is usually introduced. The account has the consequence, however, that that representational dimension turns out to be ubiquitous. *Every* vocabulary can be used in expressing commitments that can be both attributed and acknowledged. Every vocabulary can figure in *de re* ascriptions and so be talked about in representational vocabulary. (In fact, the vocabulary of *de re* ascriptions can itself be used to ascribe such ascriptions *de re*.) So representational vocabulary makes explicit an essential and ubiquitous dimension of conceptual content. This is a kind of global semantic representationalism, underwritten by a *local* expressivism about representational vocabulary itself.

What I am doing, I think, is just filling in Price's notion of i-representation. At least, I want to offer this account of what is expressed by *de re* ascriptions of propositional attitudes for that purpose. But I also want to emphasise how serious the need for such a filling-in is. For, as things stand at the end of his Descartes lectures, I think the notion of i-representation is a mere placeholder – the mark of an aspiration rather than the specification of a serviceable concept. My reasons for saying that will emerge if we ask what makes the notion of i-representation a notion of a kind or sense of 'representation'. If, as Price recommends, we look for it horizontally, at the relations states and locutions stand in to other states and locutions, to the functional role they play in a system of others, rather than vertically, to their mapping or tracking relations to something outside the system, what is it about such roles that justifies us in treating them as *representations* in *any* sense? Price likes the idea – at the core of my own thought – that a decisive line is crossed when we become entitled to think of the relations they stand in to one another as *inferential* relations. Indeed, I think we then become entitled to think of them (for the first time) as expressing *propositional* contents. For me, such contents are just what can play the role of premises and conclusions of inferences – what can both serve as and stand in need of *reasons*. But what results from that view is at least to begin with a notion of i-*expression*, not i-*representation*. For what does expressing propositional contents in *this* sense have to do with *representation*? Here it looks as though Price is seeking to procure by terminological fiat what can legitimately be secured only by honest toil.

To be sure, once propositional contents in this functional, inferential sense are on board, we will be able to appeal to a deflationary account of truth – either Horwich's sophisticated development of Quine's disquotational approach, or, what I take to be much more expressively and technically flexible and powerful, the anaphoric account of 'is true' as a pro-sentence-forming operator and 'refers' as a pronoun-forming operator – to underwrite the Tarskian T-sentences. But again, what does this notion of truth have to do with *representation*? The way it swings free of the traditional connection between truth and representation is precisely what makes the theory deflationary.

Price does have a substantive and important *pragmatic* account of truth – as coming into play with the possibility of social *disagreement* and procedures for resolving such disagreements. (I'm thinking here of his 2003 essay 'Truth as Convenient Friction'.) This is a rich and promising line of thought. But here, too, a lot more work needs to be done to elaborate from it a sense of 'representing' *things* and their relations to each other and to us. I offer the story I am gesturing at here (and have told elsewhere), about why what is expressed by *de re* ascriptions of propositional attitudes is present wherever propositional contents in the inferential-functional sense are in play as a way of redeeming the promissory note that Price has issued under the rubric of 'i-representation'.

What I am advocating is a *soft* global semantic representationalism. It is an account of the *expressive* role of representational vocabulary that shows the same expressive function that makes it ubiquitously available to express a crucial dimension of conceptual contentfulness also *dis*qualifies it from playing a fundamental *explanatory* role in an account of the semantics of at least some discursive practices. For the expressive role characteristic of representational vocabulary (like that of logical, modal and normative vocabulary) can itself be fully specified in a social, normative, inferential pragmatic metavocabulary that does *not* itself employ representational vocabulary. In the context of a commitment to methodological pragmatism – the claim that the point of theoretically postulating semantic properties associated with discursive expressions, episodes and states is to explain or at least explicate features of their use – this means that the invocation of semantic primitives (unexplained explainers) such as representation, in *this* case, the case of representational vocabulary itself, is unnecessary. That is why the view is *explanatorily* deflationary about representational vocabulary, though not at all *expressively* deflationary about it. (Paul Horwich agrees with me about the first part of this claim, but I am not sure that he agrees about the second. Davidson, in 'Reality without Reference' [in 2001a] can also be considered as enrolled in this cause, in giving [I would claim] a basically inferential account of truth conditions and then denying that they can be *generated* by referential/representational primitives – which, on the other hand, are computed from the truth conditions and, accordingly, do not function as primitive or explanatory-foundational.)

The question remains: just how deflationary is it to provide this sort of non-representational pragmatic metavocabulary? It opens up a space for a view that *is* deflationary, according to which this sort of account in terms of pragmatic metavocabulary is all there is to say about the vocabulary in question. No further semantic questions should be asked or could be answered. Price might be tempted by such a view. But it also seems compatible with acknowledging that at least in some cases an orthodox representational semantic metavocabulary might *also* be available.[19] That is, we can ask, does this sort of deflationary *explanatory* anti-representationalism about what representational vocabulary expresses entail a global explanatory anti-representationalism? I do not see that it does. For it might well be that although representational vocabulary need not be used in specifying the

---

[19] Compare: it is one thing to understand what it is to introduce a range of singular terms and the objects they refer to by *abstraction* – that is, by means of an equivalence relation on some antecedent vocabulary, picking out objects that count as (more) *concrete* relative to this procedure. It is something else (it requires more argument to be entitled) to understand the objects to which one thereby gains semantic access as *abstract objects*. For presumably the latter are objects to which we can *only* gain semantic access by a process of abstraction. It is at least not obvious that Frege, for instance, believed in abstract objects in this sense.

use of representational vocabulary itself (because its expressive role can
be fully specified in a non-representational, social-normative-inferential
pragmatic metavocabulary)[20] nonetheless in order to specify the proprieties governing the use of ordinary empirical descriptive vocabulary, its
distinctive expressive role requires specification with the help of a representational semantic metavocabulary. I have talked so far only about
discursive representational vocabulary. But this is not the only candidate for
a representational semantic metavocabulary. In addition there are at least
three others: those that express *mapping* relations (static), those that express
tracking processes (dynamic) and those that express the *practical* intentional
directedness of goal-seeking systems.[21] I think the expressive role characteristic of each of these kinds of representational vocabulary can also be
made fully explicit in an *inferential*, itself non-representational pragmatic
metavocabulary. Understanding (practically taking or treating) something
as a representation in the mapping sense is exercising the ability to make
inferences from map facts to mapped facts. Tracking is updating a map
in that sense so as to keep the map inferences good as the mapped facts
change. Taking or treating something as a practical intentional system is
understanding its behavior in terms of sample pieces of practical reasoning.
Here, too, the possibility of an adequate non-representational pragmatic
metavocabulary for these varieties of representational vocabulary would
not seem to rule out their playing fundamental roles in a semantic metavocabulary for some other vocabulary – quite possibly, empirical descriptive
vocabulary. Though I cannot pursue the point here, the semantic-epistemic

---

[20] The relation being asserted cannot straightforwardly be put by saying that discursive representational
vocabulary and the social-inferential vocabulary that serves as a pragmatic metavocabulary for it
turns out to be reciprocally reference-dependent, but *not* reciprocally sense-dependent. I think that
latter claim is also true (and the expository strategy of Part II of *Making It Explicit* depends on it).
But the pragmatic metavocabulary relation involves special features that are not part of the generic
reference-dependence-without-sense-dependence story. I discuss these concepts in Chapter 6 of
Brandom (2002).

[21] As I explain in Chapter 6 of *Between Saying and Doing* (Brandom 2008), the fundamental pragmatist
commitment is to explaining *discursive* intentionality in terms of *practical* intentionality. Thus in
Making It Explicit (Brandom 1994), the claim is that discursive scorekeeping can be understood as a
particular structure of practical intentionality, the sort exhibited already by non-linguistic creatures
– a structure that then in turn can be used to understand discursive intentionality. So there is
an interaction between fundamental pragmatism and the entanglement thesis. For the notion of
understanding that the latter appeals to as coordinate with the notion of meaning is a *practical* one:
a kind of knowing *how*, an ability to *do* something. The denial of semantic atomism then follows
from an appreciation of the systematicity of the answers to the question about the kind of practical
understanding that grasp of representing as a representing consists in.

entanglement thesis will give us important clues about relations between semantic metavocabularies and their pragmatic metavocabularies.

5 CONCLUSION

What are we to conclude? Rorty and Price agree that the evils representationalism is prey to require, or at least make advisable, global anti-representationalism. The sort of expressivist, deflationary, pragmatic account of what one is *doing* in *using* representational vocabulary that I am advocating suggests that this response is an overreaction. I have tried in this essay to assemble some analytic materials that might help us towards a more nuanced conclusion. Once one has freed oneself from the idea (and the auxiliary hypotheses that enforce the association) that semantic representationalism need take a nominalist or atomist form, must fail to appreciate what is special about sentences or has to enforce a disconnection between semantic issues of meaning and epistemic ones pertaining to understanding, representational vocabulary can be understood as peforming an important, indeed essential, expressive role in making explicit a discursive representational dimension of semantic content that necessarily helps articulate every autonomous discursive practice.

Further, we can rigorously distinguish the quite different expressive roles played by different kinds of vocabulary. (Brandom 2008 shows how.) So no argument that depends on the impossibility of offering one kind of semantics or pragmatics for some vocabularies, and others for others, is going to be plausible or sustainable. When we do that, we discover that it is possible to specify the expressive roles characteristic of various important kinds of vocabulary – among them logical, modal, normative and representational vocabularies – entirely in a social, normative, inferential, *non*-representational pragmatic metavocabulary. In the context of a commitment to methodological pragmatism, then, there is no *need* to postulate, as part of semantic theory, representational explanatory primitives in order to explain the use of such vocabulary (since methodological pragmatism says that that is why we postulate semantic theoretical features such as meanings). And the vocabularies of which that is true include, I claim, discursive representational vocabulary. So we do *not* need to *use* the concept of representation (or i-representation, or e-representation) in order to understand what we are *doing* when we use the concept of (discursive) representation.

I have also claimed that it does *not* follow (even in the context of collateral commitments to methodological pragmatism and to semantic-epistemic entanglement)[22] that the use of ordinary empirical descriptive vocabulary, which plays quite a *different* expressive role from that of logical, modal, normative or representational vocabularies, is not best explained by appeal to a semantics that is couched in (i- or e-) representational terms. Price makes much of the fact that any *local* expressivism is committed to drawing a *line* between the discourses or vocabularies that should be treated *representationally* and those that should be treated *expressively*, in their semantics. He is, I think, inclined to scepticism about the possibility of drawing such a line in a principled way. I do not think that *this* argument will work. On my account, logical, modal and normative vocabulary plays the distinctive expressive role of being LX for every ADP. That is not true of ground-level empirical descriptive terms. Perhaps they are best understood to be representing features of the objective world, by responsive mapping and tracking, indeed, even in the practical acting sense.

Even if that is so, we still have to worry about what it means that the use of the representational vocabulary appealed to in our semantics can itself be rendered *non*-representationally. For I think we do not know how the possibility of offering a certain kind of pragmatic metavocabulary for a vocabulary relates to the kind of semantic metavocabulary it is amenable to. In this case, the question is what does the possibility of offering a social-normative-inferential pragmatic metavocabulary specifying the expressive role of representational vocabulary say about the possibility of *also* offering an explanatorily representationalist semantics for it, or for other vocabularies? (The question mark in my title is meant to indicate that I do not claim to know the answer to this question.)

I conclude that we have just not yet sufficiently explored (and so do not now know enough about) the relations between pragmatic metavocabularies and semantic metavocabularies, for vocabularies playing very different expressive roles to be able to answer to this question. In the

---

[22] I have tried to be clear about the collateral methodological commitments within which I am assessing consequences. They include methodological pragmatism and semantic-epistemic entanglement (with the holism about meanings that results, in the context of relatively weak auxiliary hypotheses). One response might be: 'No doubt one can derive all sorts of extravagant consequences, if one is allowed to make use of substantially *false* collateral premises. But why should we care?' But I think this would be too quick. Meaning (like representation) is a *theoretical* notion. And that means that what we *mean* by 'meaning' is determined in no small part by the collateral commitments available to conjoin with it as auxiliary hypotheses in reasoning about it. They help determine what sense of 'meaning' we are exploring.

wake of the Frege-Geach embedding argument against classical meta-ethical expressivism, Blackburn, Gibbard and Railton pioneered a new level of sophistication in thinking about the relations between non-descriptive expressive roles and descriptive content. Price has placed their enterprise in a much larger, more global theoretical setting, raising issues about the relations between the pragmatic metavocabularies in which we specify what we are *doing* when we use any kind of vocabulary and the semantic meta-vocabularies in which we specify what we are *saying* or *meaning* when we use them. My principle aim here has been to clarify the state of play that I understand as resulting from that recontextualisation, to indicate how some of my own work on expressive roles and pragmatic metavocabularies might contribute to greater analytic clarity on these issues and finally to say something about the challenges for further research that confront us as we try to discern and navigate the next level of fine structure in the relations between expression and representation, and between pragmatics and semantics generally.

CHAPTER 6

Naturalism, deflationism and the relative priority of language and metaphysics

Paul Horwich

I INTRODUCTION

As its title suggests, the topic of this paper lies at the intersection of three central debates within philosophy.

One of them is the clash between *truth*-based approaches to empirical semantics (which form the mainstream) and a less popular *use*-theoretic point of view, variously known as 'inferentialism', 'expressivism' and 'semantic deflationism'. The issue here, in a nutshell, is whether the word–world relation of *reference* and the derived property of *truth* are to be given central roles in characterising the nature of meaning and hence in explaining the import of understanding for verbal behaviour. Perhaps it should be acknowledged, rather, that the concepts of truth and reference are exhausted by trivial equivalence schemata that imply their unsuitability for causal-explanatory work (but enable them nonetheless to serve as useful expressive devices). And if so then, in so far as word meanings exert a causal influence on linguistic activity, their grasp will have to be constituted in some non-referential way – e.g., by basic propensities of word usage.[1]

Second, we have the issue of naturalism. There is undeniably a vast, unified network of objects, properties and facts that bear spatial, temporal, causal and explanatory relations to one another – a network incorporating observable phenomena, the elementary particles, fields, strings, etc., of physics for which those phenomena provide evidence, and all the macroscopic objects and events built out of such elements. But is *everything* located within this network, as naturalism dictates? Or do certain perfectly

---

[1] The truth-based approaches are developments of projects initiated by Frege, Davidson and Montague, aimed, in the first instance, at showing (respectively) how each sentence's truth value, or truth condition, or truth value in a possible world, depends on the referents of its words and its structure. The use-based approaches evolved from verificationism. Contemporary variants include Brandom's explanation of meaning in terms of *normative attitudes* to word use, Gibbard's in terms of *normative facts* governing word use, and the present author's in terms of *natural laws* of word use.

real features of the world lie outside it – perhaps numbers, or possibilities, or values, or meanings?[2]

And, third, there's the debate over whether questions of metaphysics – most of which appear superficially to be about the non-linguistic, non-cognitive world – can be answered only, and merely, by attention to our linguistic and conceptual practices. It is tempting to think that in order to settle whether or not bachelors are invariably unmarried one must examine not bachelors themselves but rather our use of the word 'bachelor'. And similar linguistic (or conceptual) priority claims have been made about weightier matters, such as whether truth is a substantive property, whether numbers are objects, whether possible worlds are concrete, and whether naturalism is correct. The conflict here is between those who approve of this approach to metaphysics ('the linguistic turn') and those who don't approve of it. Of the three grand divisions, this is the one that strikes me as the murkiest and the most in need of elucidation.

Clearly these debates, and the relationships between them, raise many more issues than can be covered in a single essay. So I'll be restricting myself to a small part of the terrain and even so will have to move through it with uncomfortable alacrity.

My plan is to begin with a recent proposal that ties those themes together: Huw Price's argument against naturalism on the basis of a combination of semantic deflationism and a linguistic conception of metaphysics. A review of his train of thought will lead us into a sceptical examination both of the grounds for this view of how metaphysical questions would have to be settled and of the possibility of implementing it. Finally I'll attempt to bolster that scepticism by offering an alternative route to the rejection of naturalism – one that contravenes Price's linguistic conception of the issue.

My principal goal in all of this will be to undermine that conception. I will be opposing the idea that there are apparently non-linguistic facts that are really matters of language and that there are apparently non-linguistic beliefs whose rationality depends on their inference from premises about language. In particular, I don't agree that the plausibility or implausibility of naturalism turns on whether or not it follows from linguistic facts.

---

[2] Like all philosophical 'ism' terms, 'naturalism' is used by philosophers for a confusing variety of different doctrines. For example, the above formulation is sometimes strengthened by adding (1) that all facts are *reducible* to the facts of basic physics, and perhaps (2) that no such basic facts can be *mental*. In addition, there's the epistemological doctrine that all genuine knowledge results from the scientific method. And the term is also used for the relatively uncontroversial idea ('anti-supernaturalism') that everything in the spatio-temporal, causal, empirical order is, in principle, explainable by science.

My own concluding argument against naturalism – although of some intrinsic interest I hope – will feature primarily as a test case. So it won't matter that my characterisation of the target position is imprecise, or (as was illustrated in footnote 2) that the philosophical literature contains various different ways of putting it. For not only will the argument apply, with appropriate modifications, to many versions of the doctrine but anyway the primary moral in the present context is not supposed to be the *result* of the argument but its *methodology*: namely, that – just like issues outside philosophy – the questions of naturalism can and should be addressed at the material level.

Also playing a relatively minor role is *semantic deflationism*. Its account of reference and truth is an assumption of Price's case against naturalism – but not of my own. More relevant to our main concern is that its Wittgensteinian view of different meanings as constituted by extremely different patterns of word-usage issues in a *conceptual* pluralism, which is itself correlated with the *metaphysical* pluralism that makes naturalism implausible. But although this correlation is indeed significant, it doesn't settle our main question, which concerns the *directions* of the epistemological and explanatory links that underlie it.

As for my definition of 'metaphysics', I'm afraid I don't have one. But nothing exact will be needed. We might well have in mind the vague Sellarsian idea that its aim is 'to understand how things in the broadest possible sense of the term hang together in the broadest possible sense of the term' – on the assumption that these 'broadest possible' types of 'thing' and of 'hanging together' are categories such as object, property, fact, event, exemplification, and constitution, whose central characteristics are open to *a priori* investigation. But nothing here will hinge on that idea, since what will be argued is that there are *no* apparently non-linguistic conclusions that must be inferred from linguistic premises (or whose truth is explained by linguistic facts). If this is right it will count against the linguistic conception of 'metaphysics', however that subject is defined.

A final statement of intent. Let it not be thought that my goal in opposing a linguistic approach to metaphysical questions is to defend traditional metaphysical investigations. On the contrary, I'm inclined to sympathise with Wittgenstein's anti-theoretical meta-philosophy. So, although I do believe that reflective attention to issues of language, concept-use, and rationality is of peculiar importance in philosophy (especially metaphysics), I think it is crucial to distinguish this sort of 'linguistic turn' from the above-defined 'linguistic conception of metaphysics'. It is one thing to denounce metaphysical theories for violating our norms of intelligibility or rationality and another to denounce them for failing to be derivable from linguistic premises.

2 PRICE'S CRITIQUE OF NATURALISM

Let's start with the intriguing anti-naturalist perspective being developed by Huw Price.[3] He does consider himself a naturalist of sorts – a 'subject naturalist' – for he holds that we human beings, together with all of our thinking, reasoning, meaning and communication, are natural phenomena. What he's questioning is the view that *everything* is natural. In fact, he's questioning the very coherence of that view (and of its negation).

Here's a sketch of what I take to be his main line of argument:

1. Metaphysical questions can be answered only in so far as they are transformations of more basic linguo-conceptual questions.[4] A case in point is the question of whether naturalism is correct, and of where – if it is correct – such peculiar things as numbers, values and possibilities are to be placed within the natural order. Issues concerning our use of words and our deployment of concepts are fundamental here, and the metaphysical issues of naturalism must be seen as deriving from them.
2. Any such jump from the linguistic level to the material level – from observations about words to conclusions about reality – would have to be mediated by principles specifying what the words in question stand for. In particular, it would be necessary to invoke the principle that the term 'X' refers to X itself.
3. But if *deflationism* provides the correct account of reference, then this strategy can't work. For, according to deflationism, there is no significant difference between talking about X itself and talking about the referent of the term 'X'. So the deflationist disquotational principle won't mediate a transition between distinct levels.
4. Therefore, the coherence of naturalism and of its various placement problems presupposes that reference is a *substantive* relation, i.e. that the deflationary account of reference is mistaken.

---

3 In his Descartes Lectures, delivered at the University of Tilburg in May 2008, and printed above. I will be concerned exclusively with Lecture 1 (Chapter 1 of this volume), previously published as Price (2004).

4 Following Price, I'll tend to call this a *linguistic* conception of metaphysics, dropping any explicit reference to *thought* or *concepts*. But this is merely for expository ease. The doctrine to which I'm alluding is always that of the exclusively linguistic or conceptual content of metaphysical issues.

5. However, deflationism is *not* mistaken. On the contrary, a scientific scrutiny of how the word 'true' is used provides compelling reason to endorse it.

6. Therefore, naturalism is in principle impossible to establish.

To summarise: the metaphysical doctrine of naturalism, together with any proposed solutions to its placement problems, would, according to Price, have to be verified (or refuted) through an investigation of linguo-conceptual phenomena. And the bridge between these domains would have to be provided by principles of reference. But, as deflationists have made plausible, such principles cannot serve that purpose. So it's undecidable whether or not naturalism is correct – a pseudo-issue; and the same goes for more specific questions of whether this or that particular sort of phenomenon is naturalistic.

3 FROM LANGUAGE TO REALITY?

It's worth distinguishing a variety of alternative strategies that might conceivably be employed to implement Price's fundamental assumption: namely, that an examination of linguistic or conceptual phenomena can be the only basis for deciding metaphysical questions, despite the fact that such questions do not on their face concern language or thought at all. Here's a list of nine such candidate strategies, divided into four categories. Let me first run quickly through them all and then return to consider each one in a little more detail.

1. *The peculiar need for clarification in metaphysics*

    (a) Disambiguation. The requirement to determine what is meant by the question – which particular metaphysical problem is being formulated.

    (b) The importance of reflecting on such matters as: (i) whether the problem has confused presuppositions; (ii) which approach to solving it should be taken; and (iii) where certain alternative lines of argument go wrong.

2. *The analyticity of metaphysics*

    (a) The general idea that 'p''s being an explicit or implicit definition entails *that p* – and that such entailments can ground both the explanation of metaphysical facts and our knowledge of them.

    (b) A modification of this idea, whereby what is entailed (and thereby explained) by 'p''s definitional status isn't the *truth* of 'p', but merely our justification for maintaining it.[5]

3. *Psychologistic reductionism in metaphysics*

    (a) Suggested by the 'construction' of normative facts from our (idealised) normative commitments. (See Rawls, Railton, Brandom, Street, et al.)

    (b) The reduction (a la Yablo) of metaphysical possibility to conceivability.

4. *The role of semantic descent in metaphysics*

    (a) The idea that metaphysical beliefs about worldly item, *X*, could be inferred from discoveries about *the referent of 'X'*. (This is the strategy emphasised and criticised by Price, as we've seen.)

    (b) Similarly, but without any appeal to explicit principles of reference, the bridge from language to metaphysics might be taken to be that our recognition of which of our sentences ('p') we accept implies commitments to the facts (*that p*) expressed by those sentences.

    (c) Or it might be supposed, in a neo-Fregean vein, that the basic metaphysical categories (object, property, fact, event, etc.) are defined in terms of linguistic categories (name, predicate, declarative sentence, gerundive nominal, etc.).

Each of these ideas deserves a more thorough scrutiny than will be possible in the context of this paper. For most of them, I'm afraid that all I can do is baldly state my own opinion of their prospects and hope that a fair number of readers will nod along if only for the sake of argument. So here goes.

    I regard the initial pair of clarification norms – (1a) and (1b) – as entirely uncontroversial. But they can't sustain Price's linguistic conception of metaphysics because, first, they apply to *any* inquiry, and, second, they don't offer a route from linguistic premises to non-linguistic conclusions.

---

[5] Paul Boghossian (1996) introduced the terms 'metaphysical analyticity' and 'epistemological analyticity' to mark the difference between 'true in virtue of meaning' and 'justified in virtue of meaning', which are the notions respectively deployed in (2a) and (2b). He himself argues against the former but is sympathetic to the latter. Williamson (2007: Chapters 3 and 4), criticises both strategies and goes on to argue more generally against the linguo-conceptual view of metaphysics. My own conclusions on these points are broadly in tune with his, although for the most part I come to them from quite different angles.

No matter what the domain of investigation may be, it's always a good idea, first, to make sure that one has fixed on a definite interpretation of the question as formulated and, second, to reflect on one's entrenched cognitive proclivities in order to check that each of the question's presuppositions, and each of the assumptions to be employed in settling it, is coherent and plausible. Thus it would seem that a responsible answering of *any* question involves *both* reasoning at the object level – with premises, suppositions, conjectures and inferences about the material world – *and* a meta-level critical scrutiny of that reasoning (alongside alternatives to it), applying norms of intelligibility and rationality.

Although the across-the-board value of semantic and normative self-scrutiny goes without saying, these desiderata have sometimes been combined with certain radical assumptions about the nature of meaning to yield the conclusion that any *metaphysical* pronouncement will inevitably be unmasked as *nonsense*. This was Wittgenstein's strategy in the *Tractatus* (1922), where it was presupposed (roughly speaking) that, in order to have any meaning at all, a sentence must reduce via conceptual analysis to a sentence whose components are either logical or observational. But, as he himself came to recognise (see the *Philosophical Investigations*, 1953), that requirement is absurdly restrictive. And although there may be more accurate views about meaning that would nonetheless undermine this or that metaphysical thesis, there's no reason to think that any of these better views would put the *whole* of metaphysics in jeopardy.

In particular, Wittgenstein's eventual identification of the meaning of a word with its use cannot threaten the intelligibility of metaphysics. On the contrary, given the use of terms in metaphysical theorising, that identification will entail that they *are* intelligible. Granted, he continued to oppose philosophical theorising. But, arguably, his later strategy was to reject it on the basis of *norms of rationality* rather than criteria of meaningfulness. Notice, however, that even if this idea can be vindicated (and I suspect that it can), the overall result is not a way of inferring metaphysical theories from broadly linguo-conceptual premises (including epistemic norms). What will be derived is the *irrationality* of metaphysical theorising.

Moving on to the pair of 'analyticity strategies', my sense is that these days, following Quine, they are generally regarded as defective, and rightly so.

Start with (2). How could the fact that sentence 'p' is a definition *ever* entail the fact that p? Consider 'The bachelors are the unmarried men', and let's suppose for the sake of argument that it provides the definition of 'bachelor'. What this supposition amounts to is that we treat that sentence in a special way: we regard it as certainly true, we aren't prepared to count anything as evidence against it, and we take it to hold in all *possible* scenarios. But there's no valid route from the fact that we do all these things with the sentence to the conclusion that it *is* true – and, thereby, via the disquotational truth schema, to the further conclusion that bachelors are unmarried men. Granted, we cannot do those things without being sure that bachelors are unmarried men. But such a conviction, no matter how strongly and rigidly it is maintained, could nonetheless be false – our being absolutely certain *that p* does not entail *that p*. Thus we don't arrive at our belief that the bachelors are the unmarried men by inference from the premise that 'The bachelors are the unmarried men' is a definition. Rather, this linguo-conceptual fact (*if* it is a fact) *incorporates* that belief.

Whilst agreeing with this point, quite a few philosophers have adopted a fall-back position: that we can be *justified in believing* a certain material fact because some of the concepts used in articulating it are *implicitly defined* by our having that belief. It might be thought, for example, that our commitment to the logical law, 'p or not p', helps to fix the meanings of 'not' and 'or', so that we cannot coherently deny it and are epistemically obliged to accept it. But a telling objection to this idea is that basic belief practices that conflict with our own are often judged to be irrational. We might feel that way about intuitionistic logic precisely for its renunciation of the above law. Perhaps, in any such case, we'll say that certain ingredient concepts are irrational (e.g., intuitionistic negation). Or perhaps it's better to suppose that important basic belief practices (such as logic and arithmetic) are never *merely* definitions: that, besides implicitly defining their concepts, they always involve additional *substantive* commitments, which are what we sometimes regard as irrational. For present purposes it doesn't matter which of these 'diagnoses' is preferred. The upshot either way is that important belief practices cannot be justified simply by virtue of being concept-constituting.

The third general strategy for trying to conjure up worldly facts out of linguo-conceptual materials is exemplified by the attempts of philosophers (focused on certain domains, such as ethics) to offer *reductive analyses* to those materials. (It might be suggested, for instance, that *the wrongness of lying* is constituted by *the fact that if one were epistemically coherent one would believe that lying is wrong*.) About this idea I can only say – but without of course expecting to convince its advocates – that such attempts are invariably contrived and implausible. This is because they are motivated by an extraneous philosophical agenda (e.g., the 'need' to preserve natural-ism) and not by an unbiased attempt to do no more than understand the target discourse.[6]

What about the fourth kind of rationale? Can't we employ general prin-ciples of *reference* – for example, that X is the referent of the word 'X' – in order to get from linguistic premises to our material conclusions? Well, as Price observes, deflationists about the truth-theoretic notions must say that no such bridge could be effective. The reason he gives is that, from a deflationary point of view, such principles are to be construed as claiming that 'the referent of "X"' means the same thing as 'X' – so they couldn't link genuinely different subject matters.

I myself have doubts about this particular ('redundancy') form of defla-tionism. Moreover, it's not clear to me why an advocate of the linguistic conception should resist the idea that metaphysical facts are at the same level as linguistic ones. But I won't quibble over these matters since I think Price's basic point is right. The deflationist takes the disquotation schema to implicitly *define* the concept of reference. But, in order for it to be able to do that, our material-level singular terms and predicates would have to be understood already. Thus, beliefs whose explicit subject matter is *the referent of 'X'* would have to be derived from beliefs about X itself, rather than the other way around. So, as Price says, we can't use principles of reference to go from linguistic premises to metaphysical conclusions.

Strategy (4b) provides a rather different disquotational suggestion – but no more effective. The idea is that when our acceptance of a (possibly conjunctive) sentence, '#f', involving our predicate 'f', implies something about the use and meaning of 'f' (hence about the concept F), then the fact to whose existence we are committing ourselves – the material fact that #f – implies some corresponding thing about the nature of f-ness itself. And this idea is quite right. But it entails no explanatory or inferential transition – no move from language to reality (or the other way around). All we have here is that our acceptance of a sentence is trivially the same thing as our commitment to a worldly fact.

---

[6] Such philosophers don't always start from the explicit premise that naturalism must be correct. But an implicit commitment to naturalism is typically in the background. For example, it is sometimes argued on the basis of epistemological principles deployed in naturalistic domains, but assumed to be *generally* valid, that ethical beliefs could not be justified unless ethical facts were naturalistic. (For further criticism of pro-naturalist strategies, see below).

Of course, our explicit *recognition* that we accept a certain sentence is indeed a further thing. But this *acknowledgement* of linguo-conceptual activity derives *from* the activity itself. Surely the awareness we have of our own beliefs is preceded, both explanatorily and epistemologically, by those beliefs themselves.

For example, our acceptance of the Peano axioms of arithmetic – that particular use of the words, 'zero', 'successor' and 'number' – constitutes our commitment to the arithmetical facts that specify the nature of zero, of the successor relation and of the property of being a number. And it's fairly obvious that these non-linguistic opinions (hence our appreciation of what the numbers are like) are prior to our explicit awareness that we have those opinions and that we express them as we do.

The final idea, (4c), is that metaphysical conclusions issue from linguo-conceptual premises because our conceptions of OBJECT, PROPERTY and FACT are nothing but 'projections' into material reality of the categories of singular term, predicate and declarative sentence. It might be suggested, for example, that our regarding five, if it exists, as an *object* derives from the fact that 'five' is a *name*.

The proposal, elaborated somewhat, is that the import of 'n' being a singular term is conveyed in our acceptance of the sentence, 'n (if it exists) is an object.' Similarly, the import of 'f''s being a predicate is contained in our accepting, 'k is f ↔ k has the property f-ness.' Thus, we are provided with *intra*-linguistic transitions from syntax to semantics. Words have been introduced ('object' and 'property') via meaning-constituting rules of use whose deployment presupposes little more than a mastery of syntactic categories.

The upshot is a slight extension of the conclusion we just reached about (4b). The facts about our linguistic activity that constitute material-level commitments also include *syntactic* facts. But we do *not* get any sort of *explanation* of the material phenomena themselves on the basis of those linguistic phenomena (or conversely). Nor do we get any sort of *epistemological* route from premises about language to conclusion about the world (or conversely).

4 APPRAISAL OF PRICE'S CRITIQUE

How do these general reflections bear on Price's reasoning of naturalism? As we saw, his argument rests on a pair of interlocking premises about metaphysics: (1) that any legitimate claim in that area would have to be derived from attention to our linguo-conceptual activity; and (2) that no such derivation can possibly be executed. Now, our scrutiny of the conceivable routes from language to metaphysics has vindicated the second of these theses. Indeed, it strengthens Price's own case for it – since he considers and criticises only one such putative route (the one based on principles of reference), and I have argued that none of the other prima-facie candidates will do either. However, this result can cast no doubt on the existence of metaphysical knowledge unless Price's first premise can also be justified: namely, that any reasonable metaphysical conclusion would *have* to be based on linguistic data. And it remains to be seen whether there is any good reason for agreeing that this is so.

A traditional rationale for it has been that in so far as metaphysics is *a priori* it must be entirely grounded in our use of language – its truths must be analytic. But there are many competing accounts of *a priori justification* in the philosophical literature. Amongst the candidates for what legitimises it or explains it are: (1) rational intuitions; (2) the reliability of certain belief-producing mechanisms; (3) considerations of coherence; or (4) what is *taken* to be *a priori* justified. And there's also the deflationary view that *a priori* justification has no theoretical basis. (The final idea here is that what are in practice treated as basic facts of *a priori* justification – e.g., that one ought to believe that dogs bark if and only if it's true that they do, that zero is a number, that a given red-looking thing is red, and that lying is wrong – are epistemologically and explanatorily *fundamental* [Horwich (2008)].) In light of this profusion of respectable alternative proposals, it can't be taken for granted that the *a priority* of metaphysics calls for a 'language first' conception of the subject.

Another candidate rationale for taking a 'linguistic turn' in philosophy resides in the Wittgensteinian idea (mentioned above) that metaphysical theorising is at best irrational and at worst incoherent. But, as we saw, such doctrines would motivate an *abandonment* of metaphysics. They don't at all suggest that reasonable metaphysical conclusions would have to be inferred from linguistic premises.

Anyway, neither of these two fairly familiar sorts of consideration provides Price's own principal reason for endorsing that conception of metaphysics. The reason that he emphasises is drawn from an examination of the debates over naturalism. He observes that in order to determine whether or not all facts are natural we must first be able to decide whether allegedly troublesome domains – such as ethics and arithmetic – have even so much as the *capacity* to harbour counter-examples. For example, could there conceivably be genuine *facts* as to what is right and wrong? Does ethics even purport to be in the fact-stating business? And that, he says, is surely a linguistic question. It's a matter of whether ethical sentences have the sort of meaning – i.e. the sort of usage – that enables them to express *propositions.*[7]

And this observation is eminently reasonable. But notice that the linguistic question is a mere preliminary and our settling it will take us only a little distance towards where we are supposed to be going. Questions about the material world often call for clarification and refinement: thus, linguo-conceptual considerations often enter into our attempts to answer them. But that's not enough to show that the questions are fundamentally about language. Such an inference is patently fallacious and would imply, absurdly, that *every* question concerns nothing but language.

In particular, a linguo-conceptual scrutiny of *normative* discourse might lead a philosopher to think that 'wrong' is not a *genuine* predicate (i.e. a predicate at the level of logical form) and therefore that the question whether 'wrongness is naturalistic' doesn't make sense. And this could indeed have considerable bearing on that philosopher's view of whether everything that exists is natural. It might well lead him to a revised sense of what must be done to settle the question of naturalism – a reduction of the number of material-level placement problems that he thinks need to be solved.

But many such problems will remain after such clarificatory preliminaries have been completed – problems concerning the placement of phenomena to whose existence we continue to be committed. Suppose *our* answer to the preliminary linguistic question is that 'wrong' *is* a genuine predicate and so 'stealing is wrong' *does* express a proposition, i.e. a conceivable fact. So, if stealing is wrong, then there *is* a fact to that effect. But how are we to determine whether or not naturalism is at all threatened by this conditional – whether it might contribute to committing us to the existence of a non-natural fact – unless we can establish whether stealing is wrong?

---

7 A second virtue of the 'linguistic conception' of placement problems, according to Price, is that it alone offers the prospect of a general argument in favour of naturalism. For one might reason to that conclusion from the suppositions, first, that each phenomenon is identified via the linguistic expressions of which it is the referent or truth-maker and, second, that reference and truth each have substantive natures. But against this alleged motivation we should note the following points: (1) It applies only to the case of naturalism and couldn't motivate a linguistic conception of any other metaphysical issue; (2) It can appeal only to those philosophers hoping to vindicate their pre-existing commitment to naturalism and cannot move those who are undecided or unsympathetic; (3) the premises of the argument are quite far-fetched – even less antecedently plausible than naturalism itself; and (4) we have been given no reason to think that it is the only possible pro-naturalist argument. On the contrary, a promising alternative will be considered in the next section, and there may well be others.

And we haven't been given the slightest reason to suppose that this can be done merely through an investigation of linguo-conceptual activity.

In addition, we're going to need a way of determining whether that fact, if it exists, would be *naturalistic*. Price might insist that this would have to be inferred from how we deploy the word, 'wrong' (or, equivalently, from how we deploy the concept it expresses). And there is indeed a plausible way such an inference might go. First, we might find that the word does not appear in any *causal/explanatory* sentences that we accept. Second, we might conclude (by definition) that this predicate thereby qualifies as 'non-naturalistic'. Third, we might invoke the above-mentioned neo-Fregean idea that properties are the material projections of predicates and so infer that a property is to count as naturalistic just in case a predicate expressing it is naturalistic. And, fourth, we'd then be able to conclude that wrongness is a non-natural property.

But, as I've emphasised, our use of a certain term in a certain way – that is, our acceptance of certain sentences containing it – goes hand in hand with our having certain worldly commitments. In particular, our accepting no causal/explanatory sentences involving the word 'wrong' goes hand in hand with our acknowledging no causal/explanatory facts about wrongness. Thus, the evidence relating to whether a given property is naturalistic can perfectly well be articulated in the material mode from the very beginning.

5 THE REAL CASE AGAINST NATURALISM

I have been suggesting, in reaction to Price's argument, that at least some metaphysical issues – in particular the question of whether naturalism is correct – are on a par with non-philosophical issues in that they call for reasoning from and to beliefs about the outside world and cannot be settled merely by an examination of language.

Now – and in conclusion – let me reinforce that suggestion by sketching what I myself take to be the case against naturalism.

1. Naturalism rests on the impression that non-natural facts would be intolerably weird.
2. That impression has three sources: first, the singular practical and explanatory importance of naturalistic facts; second, the very broad scope of the naturalistic order – the striking range and diversity of the facts that it demonstrably encompasses; and, third, the feeling that

reality must 'surely' be fundamentally uniform – so *all* facts must be naturalistic.

3. This third feeling is the crux of the matter, it seems to me. But I'd like to argue that it's based upon a misguided distortion of scientific norms, in particular, of the norm of theoretical simplicity.

4. Note, to start with, that it's *prima facie* extremely plausible that amongst the facts we recognise, some are *non*-natural – for example, that there are numbers, that it's good to care about the welfare of others, that if dogs bark then dogs bark, that the world could have been different from the way it is … An unbiased consideration of such facts will indicate that they aren't naturalistic. For it's as plain as day (to anyone not 'in the grip of a theory') that they aren't spatio-temporally located, aren't engendered by facts of physics and don't enter into causal/explanatory relations with other facts.[8]

5. However, it must be conceded that such anti-naturalistic considerations will be regarded by many philosophers as no more than *prima facie* reasonable and by no means obviously correct. After all, a committed naturalist will certainly argue against them. To deal with each such example, he will adopt one of the following pair of familiar strategies: either (a) propose some radical reductive analysis of the facts at issue – something that 'reveals' them to be naturalistic after all; or (b) deny that such facts exist, recommending either that we abandon the discourse that expresses our commitment to them, or – if that's too costly from a pragmatic point of view – that we adopt a 'fictionalist' stance of acting and talking *as if* we had those commitments, which we don't in fact have.

6. The committed naturalist will not be greatly perturbed by the accusation that these responses are ad hoc, contrived and intrinsically implausible. For he will reason that although such defects may indeed be present, and are indeed unwelcome in themselves, they are a price well worth paying for the wonderfully simple metaphysics that naturalism provides. And he will maintain that his background methodology – which tolerates local complexities for the sake of a global gain in simplicity – is intellectually impeccable: just what is done to admirable effect in the sciences.

---

[8] It's worth bearing in mind that Wittgenstein's critique of *a priori* philosophy (discussed above) is reserved for *theories* properly so-called – where these are distinguished from statements whose truth is potentially *obvious*. Thus it may be that naturalism, in so far as it is a conjectural generalisation, does qualify as a 'theory' (in his sense) – whereas its negation, if it can be established merely by drawing attention to certain obviously non-natural facts, does not qualify.

7. But this apology for naturalism is inaccurate in two related respects. In the first place, what is given up for its sake is *not* justly described as 'local theoretical simplicity'. For what must be denied are *data* – epistemologically basic convictions. It is blindingly obvious to us, as Frege observed, that Julius Caesar wasn't a number. Coming to accept that he in fact *was* a number would be much more difficult than tolerating a theory that is disappointingly complex. And no less obviously false are certain implications of every one of the sceptical 'error theories' (i.e. denials of existence) and strained reductive analyses aimed at safeguarding naturalism from the threats posed by numbers, values, possibilities and so on.

8. And, in the second place, the norm of simplicity, as it is deployed in science, is *not* in fact a licence to reject recalcitrant data – to conclude with no further ado that they must be wrong. A scientist is obliged to respect *all* relevant data, and when they don't conform to a simple pattern, that reality must be accepted. What can still be hoped for, of course, are simple laws at a deeper level. But that is not to say that the originally troublesome facts are now irrelevant or deemed non-existent. They still call for explanation. However, this is now to be done in terms of a combination of simple underlying laws and a messily variable spatio-temporal array of circumstances. The combined effects of these factors are superficial approximate regularities, with various exceptions.

9. But nothing like this happens when some of our basic *a priori* convictions about the properties of numbers, values, entailments, etc., are suppressed because of their conflict with a simple metaphysics. Nor, in this non-empirical domain, is there any prospect – as there is in science – of unearthing an *underlying* simplicity. For there *is* no underlying level; there is nothing corresponding to a complex spatio-temporal array of distorting circumstantial factors; and so there is no possibility of reconciling our messy data with simple fundamental principles.

10. Granted, scientists may discount observational beliefs when there is verifiable reason to think that they resulted from unreliable perceptual processes. And, granted, certain basic *a priori* convictions might also be discredited in some such way. This may well be the verdict on judgements made in circumstances that are notorious for interfering with good cognitive functioning – when the subject is, for example, tired, or drunk or distracted. However, the *a priori* intuitions cited above are obviously *not* tied to conditions like that. So the naturalist is left with nothing to say against them, except that their deliverances are inconsistent with his simplistic theory.

11. Thus, it is not true that the case for naturalism issues from the very norms that have earned respect from their fruitful role in science. In fact, those norms, if we aren't prepared to flout them, will lead an honest thinker to recognise a broad variety of *non*-natural phenomena.

These anti-naturalistic considerations included: (1) a clarification of the issue, in part to make sure we are not mislead by sub-questions (perhaps 'Is wrongness naturalistic?') that have no meaning; (2) a demonstration at the material non-linguistic level that certain objects, properties and facts are *not* natural; (3) an articulation of the standard material-level argument *in favour* of naturalism; and (4) an identification of methodological deficiencies in that argument.

Thus, my line of thought exemplifies a dialectical structure that is commonplace outside philosophy – one that combines preliminary clarification, evidence for a conclusion and objections to the usual case against it. So the general thrust of our earlier abstract reflections is reinforced: that metaphysical arguments and theses concern what they *seem* to concern: namely, facts that are not usually about us but about the external world. In so far as linguo-conceptual, and normative, and methodological self-consciousness play a significantly greater role in our field than in other areas of inquiry that is because confusion in philosophy is peculiarly rampant. So a certain kind of 'linguistic turn' was (and remains) extremely valuable. But the idea that metaphysical conclusions should (or could) be justified by facts emerging from these forms of self-scrutiny is another matter and appears to be simply wrong.[9]

---

9 I would like to thank Huw Price for the stimulus of his radical ideas and for his openness to their critical appraisal. Earlier versions of parts of this paper were presented at the London Institute for Philosophy (May 2010), the University of Durham (March 2011), the University of Zurich (May 2011) and the American University of Beirut (May 2011). I am grateful to the audiences on those occasions for helpful questions and suggestions.

CHAPTER 7

How pragmatists can be local expressivists

Michael Williams

I PRAGMATISM AND PLURALISM

Contemporary pragmatists – or perhaps that should be neo-pragmatists – are often sympathetic to expressivist accounts of vocabularies that have often been regarded as metaphysically problematic: moral and modal vocabulary, for example. Huw Price is one of the most prominent such philosophers. At the same time, as Price has been quick to recognise, there is a question of whether pragmatists such as himself have the right to such sympathy. The question circles round the issue of what James Dreier (2004) has called 'creeping minimalism'. I want to suggest an answer. But first I need to set up the problem.

Let me begin with a few words about the distinctive character of contemporary neo-pragmatism (which from now on I shall just call 'pragmatism'). According to David Macarthur and Huw Price, pragmatism is defined by two commitments.

Linguistic Priority. When dealing with metaphysical issues, don't start by asking about (say) the nature of values: examine what is distinctive about evaluative language.

Anti-representationalism. Representationalists explain the (proper) use of vocabulary items in terms of their meanings, and explain meaning (at least of non-logical vocabulary) in terms of semantic (word–world) relations, such as reference. By contrast, anti-representationalists eschew the use of semantic notions as explanatory primitives. All vocabularies – semantic vocabulary included – are to be characterized (or explained) functionally, in terms of their use properties. Oversimplifying a bit, meaning does not explain use: use explains meaning.

Macarthur and Price thus offer the following equation:

PRAGMATISM = LINGUISTIC PRIORITY + ANTI-REPRESENTATIONALISM.

There is a lot to be said for this account of pragmatism, though there is more to pragmatism than the equation allows.

The two components in pragmatism are not of equal weight. In practice, nearly all philosophers find themselves taking an interest in the distinctive characters of different vocabularies. The heart of pragmatism is anti-representationalism. Anti-representationalism links contemporary pragmatists with James and Dewey. James and Dewey think of belief in functionalist terms, as mediating (through inference) between perception and action. But, in contrast to contemporary pragmatists, they equate their anti-representationalist outlook with a view about *truth*.

James and Dewey treat anti-representationalism as implying the rejection of the correspondence theory of truth in favour of some kind of epistemic theory. Beliefs are worth having – 'true' – to the extent that they play their mediating role effectively, facilitating inference in ways that help us to cope with concrete problems (for example, by enabling us to anticipate experiences). On this instrumental view of truth, coping with problems replaces 'corresponding to the facts' as the criterion of truth: hence James' well-known claim that truth is whatever is 'good in the way of belief'.

By contrast, contemporary pragmatists are much more inclined to favour a *deflationary* or *minimalist* approach to truth, holding that the use of the truth predicate is fully captured by our commitment to the non-paradoxical instances of some appropriate equivalence schema: for example,

(DQT) 'P' is true if and only if P.

Deflationism allows them to concede to correspondence theorists that truth is a non-epistemic notion, without compromising a functional (use-based) approach to meaning. While retaining the anti-representationalist spirit of classical pragmatism, deflationism stays closer to our ordinary use of 'true' than do accounts such as James', which threaten to elide the distinction between truth and justification. This is a real step forward.

So much for pragmatism. Now for expressivism or 'non-cognitivism'. The basic expressivist thought is that although sentences involving certain vocabularies display the logical syntax of assertoric sentences – embedding in conditionals and so on – they remain *fundamentally non-descriptive*. Thus, free-standing moral judgements *express evaluative attitudes* and so are more intimately related to decision and action than to belief. Similarly, judgements of causal necessitation issue *inference tickets*: i.e. express commitment to the goodness of certain kinds of material inference. We understand moral and modal judgements through appreciating what we *do* with them rather than what we *say*. Strictly speaking, we don't say anything.

Price argues that the virtue of expressivist approaches to meaning – indeed, the virtue of use-theoretic approaches generally – is that they are *ontologically conservative*. Representationalist explanations of meaning tend to inherit the apparent ontological commitments of the vocabulary under review. A representationalist approach to moral predicates will tend to commit us *ab initio* to moral properties and thus (if we have naturalistic inclinations) to metaphysical worries about their character. By contrast, the only antecedent ontological commitments of use-theoretic approaches to meaning are to speakers, their utterances and so on: that is, to things that everyone is bound to recognise anyway. Expressivism's ontological conservatism gives it obvious attractions for philosophers with a naturalistic turn of mind. Values – or normative properties – enter the world through our taking on normative attitudes. They are not metaphysically problematic entities (or properties), waiting to be detected by some special faculty, distinct from our normal five senses. Further, the motivating aspect of value-judgements is built-in. If value-judgements express desires or preferences or decisions, there are no worries about whether we can recognise the to-be-doneness of an action without being motivated to act accordingly.

It should be no surprise that pragmatists are susceptible to expressivism's charms. Pragmatism is a naturalistic philosophy in several ways. Not least, pragmatists are anti-Platonist. They want to treat norms as human phenomena that we are responsible *to* but also responsible *for*. Granted, pragmatic naturalism is not reductive, say, in the manner of physicalism: this is one way in which pragmatism is anti-metaphysical. But pragmatism has no time for the *super*natural, another way in which pragmatism is anti-metaphysical. Pragmatists value anti-representationalism in part *because of* its anti-Platonist, anti-supernatural, potential. Anti-representationalists are excused from supposing that the meaningfulness of normative concepts depends on their referring to practice-independent normative properties, to which we must be presumed to stand in some kind of 'detective' relationship. Put more positively, anti-Platonism embodies what Robert Brandom calls 'pragmatism about norms': the view that normative *statuses* are instituted by our taking up normative *attitudes* (as is obviously the case with respect to the rules of games). Price shares this view, I think.

So far, so good. But now comes the problem. Standard expressivist views are strictly *local*. Thus, moral expressivists *contrast* the expressive character of moral vocabulary with the robustly representational character of scientific or other straightforwardly descriptive talk. They take this contrast between expressive and representational uses of language to be essential to their position. Local expressivism goes with local anti-representationalism. But pragmatists are anti-representationalists across the board. As semantic deflationists, they have no 'robust' notion of truth. If sentences are used in ways that respect the syntactic discipline of assertoric discourse, then they are used to make assertions and are as 'truth-apt' as sentences get to be. The apparently vital contrast between descriptive and expressive uses of language is erased.[1] Once it is erased, how is what remains of expressivism to be distinguished from the most extreme realism? As Dreier states the problem: 'Minimalism sucks the substance out of heavy-duty metaphysical concepts. If successful, it can help expressivists recapture the ordinary realist language of ethics. But in so doing, it also threatens to make irrealism indistinguishable from realism' (2004: 26).

Macarthur and Price deny that there is a problem here. Expressivists are right to trace metaphysical anxieties about, say, moral facts to representationalist prejudices. If we think that, to be significant, terms of moral appraisal must refer to moral properties, we will inevitably find ourselves trying to explain how such properties get a footing in the world around us. Expressivists are therefore also right to offer anti-representationalist accounts of moral talk. But they are *wrong* to suppose that, to make their point, they need to keep their anti-representationalism local. Pragmatists are *global anti-representationalists*, explaining *all* vocabularies along the anti-representationalist lines expressivists follow for particular cases. Far from

[1] Sellars does not face this problem, at least not immediately, since he is not a semantic deflationist. For deflationists, the conceptual content of 'true' is fixed by our primitive acceptance of the (non-paradoxical instances) of some equivalence schema, in the case of Paul Horwich's minimal theory: (MT) The proposition that P is true if and only if P. Sellars' claim is that these equivalences are not to be regarded as primitive but rather as 'following' from the 'definition' (the scare quotes are Sellars' own) of truth in that for a proposition to be true is for it to be … *correctly* assertible – assertible, that is, in accordance with the relevant semantical rules and on the basis of such additional – though unspecified, information as these rules may require. Truth is thus 'semantic assertibility'. However, since Sellarsian 'semantical rules' are rules of criticism, embodying inferential and other epistemic proprieties, semantical assertibility is a kind of idealised justification. This epistemic theory of truth allows for 'alethic pluralism'. Semantic assertibility defines the generic concept of truth: specific 'varieties of truth correspond to the relevant varieties of semantical rule'. So, for example, in mathematics truth is provability. But, notoriously, Sellars goes much farther. Basic factual discourse aims to *picture* the world. Picturing is a non-semantic form of representation involving a correspondence relation between 'natural linguistic objects' (utterances and inscriptions) and configurations of objects in the world. (Not *facts*: this is Sellars' emendation of this Tractarian idea.) The question of whether or not to try to find *anything* in this aspect of Sellars' philosophy is the main bone of contention between 'left wing' Sellarsians (such as Rorty and Brandom) and 'right wing', orthodox Sellarsians (such as Joanna Seibt and, with qualifications, Jay Rosenberg). But if we go with the left-wingers, we will be back to wondering what semantic minimalists should make of normative or modal expressivism. See Sellars (1968): Chapter 4 and Sellars (1962b).

conflicting with pragmatism, local expressivisms *support* it by providing templates for anti-representationalist approaches to meaning that invite generalisation.

Expressivists will not be impressed. Semantic deflationism, they will say, enforces a 'seamless' view of language, eliding essential distinctions. Not so, Price responds. Anti-representationalism leads to *metaphysical* quietism but not to *philosophical* quietism. Metaphysical quietism is compatible with functional pluralism. The relevant lines of demarcation can still be drawn, just *not in representationalist terms*. Charting the different functions that different forms of discourse fulfill is the (naturalistic) project of 'philosophical anthropology'.

I think that Price is exactly right. However, his response requires elaboration. There are lots of functionally different uses of words. Asserting is different from commanding or promising. What has to be shown is that pragmatists can draw lines more or less where expressivists want to draw them, for reasons bearing at least some relation to those that expressivists give, but without invoking the semantic distinctions that traditional expressivists rely on. Traditional expressivists will doubt that pragmatists can do any such thing. Radical quietists, such as Horwich, will agree, but on the grounds that there are no lines to be drawn. Of course, Horwich will deny that this erasing of boundaries makes his position indistinguishable from extreme, global realism. He will insist, fairly enough, that he has set *all* philosophical theses aside. In Price's terms, this radical quietism is both metaphysical *and* philosophical. But my sympathies are with Price. It would be more satisfying to show that global anti-representationalism is compatible with a form of functional pluralism that respects expressivist intuitions. However, perhaps unlike Price, I think that this is a non-trivial undertaking. The constraints imposed on pragmatists by semantic deflationism are severe. A semantic deflationist has no notion of fact beyond that of true proposition, and no notion of truth that can bear any explanatory weight.

Accordingly, it won't do to explain the functional difference between descriptive and normative discourse in terms of their expressing, respectively, beliefs and desires (or some other desire-like states) and then go on to explain the belief–desire distinction in terms of direction of fit (beliefs aiming to fit the world, desires aiming at getting the world to fit them). Such a strategy would bring in representationalist notions through the back door. It is all very well to talk about the 'different roles in our lives' that different vocabularies play. But how are these roles to be characterized, if the language of philosophical anthropology must *exclude any explanatory use of representationalist idioms*?[2]

If we are to recognize that there are insights to be retained from local expressivisms – moral or modal expressivism, say – while operating within the framework if a fully general anti-representationalism, we must draw lines in roughly the places that traditional local expressivists draw them and do so for reasons that bear some significant relation to those that motivate locally expressivist views. I think that this can be done. In what remains, I show how.

2 MEET THE EMU

To see whether pragmatism can accommodate expressivist insights, we have to ask what is involved in giving an explanation of meaning in terms of use (an EMU).

In offering to explain 'meaning' in terms of use, there are two explanatory goals we might have in mind. One is to explain *meaningfulness*: whatever distinguishes a linguistic item – a word or sentence – from a mere sound or scribble. Our goal, we might say, is to explain the *nature* of meaning. A second quite different goal is to explain the *meanings* of particular vocabulary items. This second task is not one that all philosophers associated with the pragmatist tradition take seriously. Some philosophers with pragmatist leanings (e.g., Quine and Davidson) are *sceptics about meanings*. However, scepticism about meanings comes in different grades.

1. There is no fact of the matter as to what a person's words mean. Accordingly, there is *nothing to explain*.
2. One can determine what someone's words mean, in the sense that there is a right thing to say in a particular interpretative- or speech-context. However, meaning is contextually sensitive and interest-relative. Accordingly, the conditions under which w means M cannot be specified in a *general, theoretically illuminating way*. Explanations of meaning are *incurably local*.

---

[2] I think that the tendency on the part of Price and Macarthur to downplay the problem of accommodating expressivist insights reflects their stripped-down view of pragmatism. The attractions of expressivism, for pragmatists, reflects pragmatism about norms, the flip side of pragmatic anti-Platonism. Pragmatism is 'anti-metaphysical' in its hostility to postulating supernatural entities to guide human practices. But if we take Price at his word and take metaphysical quietism to entail having *no* views about the nature of norms, pragmatism (in its most typical articulations) is not metaphysically quietist. But can it be expressivist? That is the question.

3. While compact and general explanations of the meanings of particular vocabulary items are not generally available, they can be given *in certain special cases.*

These distinctions will be important in our consideration of vocabulary-specific EMUs that are minimalist or deflationary.

Since we have a particular interest in minimalism, we can start with a case for which all neo-pragmatists are committed to giving a minimalist EMU: 'true' itself. I shall use this example to motivate a general meta-theoretical analysis of EMUs. I shall then exhibit the generality of the analysis by applying it to other cases: causal–modal vocabulary, observational vocabulary and deontic vocabulary. I shall show how the analysis provides for accommodating the insights of local expressivisms within the framework of global anti-representationalism.

I begin, then, with 'true'. As a concrete example of a deflationary account of truth, let us take Paul Horwich's minimal theory. (It should be clear that the general analysis of an EMU that I am going to present owes nothing to the details of Horwich's theory of truth. Any deflationary theory would have done as well.) Horwich holds that our use of 'true', hence the meaning of the truth predicate, is fully captured by our commitment to all (non-paradoxical) instances of the equivalence schema:

(MT) The proposition that P is true if and only if P.

Horwich is making three claims here. First, with respect to giving the meaning of 'true', the rule of use implicit in our acceptance of the instances of MT is *explanatorily* fundamental. Second, the instances themselves are *epistemologically* fundamental. That is, 'We do not arrive at them, or seek to justify them, on the basis of anything more obvious or more immediately known.' Third, accepting the instances of MT is 'the source of *everything else* we do with the truth predicate' (Horwich 2001: 149). This 'everything else' is the expressive function of the truth predicate, which is to endorse or repudiate claims that we do not or cannot specify. Truth talk is a useful generalising device.

Now, although the EMU for 'true' is deflationary – and so undoubtedly special in some ways – we can still treat it (following Horwich) as a paradigm for EMUs generally. Viewed this way, the template it offers breaks down into three components:

1. (I-T): A *material-inferential* (intra-linguistic) component. Excepting sentences that generate paradox, the inference from 'Snow is white' to 'It

is true that snow is white', and vice versa, is always good; the inference from 'Grass is green' to 'It is true that grass is green', and vice versa, is always good, and so on.

2. (E-T): An *epistemological* component. Such inferences are *primitively* acceptable (*a priori*). They are 'free' moves in the discursive game.

3. (F-T): A *functional* component. The truth predicate is important exclusively as a generalising device. It enables us to do things that we could not otherwise do: endorse or repudiate claims that we cannot explicitly state because we do not know what they are ('You can trust John: anything he tells you will be true') or because there are too many ('Every proposition of the form "p or not-p" is true').

This meta-theoretical analysis makes it clear that 'use-theoretic' explanations of meanings appeal to two distinct notions of use. The I- and E-clauses specify the inferential patterns that competent users of 'true' display (or the proprieties they respect) in their use of 'true'. This is use as *usage: how* a word is used. The usage-specifying clauses are fundamental in that they neither receive nor need any deeper *theoretical* explanation. They do, however, both invite and receive a *functional* explanation from the F-clause. After all, use patterns are ten a penny: you can make them up *ad libitum*. Why, then, do we have a concept that answers to the use patterns given by I-T and E-T? F-T tells us why. The F-clause appeals to use as expressive function: *what* a word is used to do, what it is useful *for*.

This distinction is vitally important. There is a sense in which Horwich is quite right to say that the rule of use indicated by MT is 'the source of *everything else* we do with the truth predicate'. The sense is this: the use properties given by I-T and E-T *enable* truth talk's functional role. But, as Horwich himself remarks, 'the truth-predicate exists solely for the sake of a certain logical need' (1998: 3). So there is an equally good sense in which *what we do with the truth-predicate* explains our possessing a concept determined by those use properties. The concept's function and utility point up its 'survival value'.

I now turn to the EMU's minimalist or deflationary character. The EMU for 'true' is minimalist in four distinct ways.

1. It is *compact*. The essential points about 'true' are briefly stated without anything vital being omitted.

2. It is *theoretically modest*. The analysis is given in terms of platitudes that virtually everyone would accept. Compared with, say, the view that truth depends on reference, which must in turn be identified with a complex causal relation, the minimalist account is *shallow*: more *phenomenological*

than *theoretical*. It is controversial *only* in claiming that nothing more need be said.

3. It is *ontologically conservative*. The use of 'true' is characterised without reference to the property of truth.

4. It is *functionally restrictive*. Truth talk plays a more limited role in our discursive practices than proponents of 'robust' theories imagine. In particular, truth is not a *theoretically significant concept*. It is in virtue of this last feature that the account can be thought of as *deflationary*.[3]

Items 1, 2 and 3 are aspects of theoretical minimalism. The fourth, functionally restrictive aspect of the account makes its theoretical minimalism plausible. With respect to the minimal theory's deflationary character, then, the key claim is that 'true' has no *explanatory* use. Indeed, it has no use beyond its generalising role. In this sense, truth is not a 'substantive' property.[4]

The results so far already suggest two possibilities. First, vocabulary items for which we can give minimalist or deflationary EMUs are the special cases that provide exceptions to Quinean scruples concerning compact meaning analyses. The second is that not all EMUs need be minimalist or deflationary, so there may be lines to be drawn. With these possibilities in mind, we look at the rest of our EMUs, beginning with Sellars' account of the causal modalities.[5]

Sellars treats causal statements (lawlike generalisations) as involving something like entailments. They embody, thus authorise, material inferences. Since Sellars thinks that natural-kind terms are richly dispositional, so that causal commitments are built into our concepts of ordinary things and substances, he holds that claims such as 'Salt dissolves in water' hold as a matter of conceptual necessity. In the form given by

---

3 The different ways of being 'minimalist' are only loosely related. In particular, it would be possible to claim a richer functional significance for truth talk without compromising the EMU's ontological conservatism. Price (1988, 2003) has a view of truth along these lines. Price thinks that truth talk has a distinctive normative flavour. In terms of my analysis, we should think of Price as espousing a less restrictive F-clause: adding a normative-expressive function to the generalising function stressed by Horwich and other strict deflationists. Whether we should follow Price in this is a question worthy of further discussion.

4 Paul Boghossian (1990) has argued that semantic deflationists fall into inconsistency when they say that truth is not a 'substantive' concept, since the distinction between substantive and non-substantive concepts implies a non-deflationary understanding of truth. But *pace* Boghossian, the substantive/non-substantive distinction is itself explicated in terms of use and does not presuppose the idea that predicates are (and others are not) 'robustly representational'.

5 Sellars (1957); see especially Sections 79–82, pp. 282–5. I have pieced the EMU together from various things Sellars says. He does not state his view in anything like the form in which I state it here.

my meta-theoretical analysis, a Sellarsian EMU for causal talk would go something like this:

1. (I-C):

   (a) Causal claims (lawlike statements) state physical necessities and involve material entailments (conceptual connections). (This is why causal claims 'support' counterfactual conditionals.) Causal claims constrain what is physically possible: thus, the inference from '$N_c(p \supset q)$' to '$\sim P_c(p \; \& \sim q)$' and vice versa, is always good.

   (b) Since there may be circumstances (that we cannot exhaustively specify) in which a given lawlike connection does not hold, entitlement to expect the effect, given the cause, is defeasible. The material inferences authorised by causal statements – or by the causal commitments embodied in natural-kind concepts – are non-monotonic.

2. (E-C): Causal claims (and/or lawlike statements) are open to repudiation and may require justification, on *empirical* grounds. This distinguishes causal from, for example, mathematical necessity (even if they conform to the same modal logic). Causal claims may be built into natural-kind concepts, but there can be *empirical grounds* for *conceptual change*.

3. (F-C): In advancing causal/lawlike claims, we are issuing inference tickets. We express commitment to inferring q from p, *ceteris paribus*.

In this case, the I-clause marks out lawlike connectedness as a kind of entailment (Sellars says 'physical' entailment); the E-clause distinguishes physical necessity from other kinds (e.g., mathematical) in terms of how entitlement to the entailments that express it is acquired or lost; and the F-clause gives the functional significance of concepts determined by such use properties. As with the EMU for 'true', the expressive aspect of the EMU for causal modality resides in the F-clause. And, as before, this clause is where the real explanation lies: the functional significance of causal talk explains our possessing a concept with the use characteristics captured by the I- and E-clauses.

Sellars' account of the causal modalities is fundamentally expressivist. For Sellars, causal talk is a special kind of normative (in fact deontic) talk: it issues inference tickets. The EMU quite obviously meets the criteria for being minimalist or deflationary: compactness, ontological conservatism, theoretical modesty and functional restriction. This brings me to my first thesis, which is that local-expressivist EMUs are minimalist EMUs with a particular kind of F-clause (one mentioning the expression of an evaluative or practical attitude). However, the tripartite template highlights a trap to avoid: the temptation to think of saying and doing (or expressing) as pointing to different *kinds* of meaning rather than as distinguishable *aspects* of meaning. Recall the EMU for 'true'. The F-clause says that truth talk is a generalising device: that's all. But we must not confuse the claim that truth is not useful for *explanatory* purposes with the claim that truth predications are not *descriptive*. Similarly, we should not think that the claim that causal laws issue inference tickets entails that they aren't used to say anything.

Let me reiterate the vital point made explicit by my meta-theoretical analysis. In any EMU, the I- and E-clauses, on the one hand, and the F-clause, on the other, are concerned with aspects of use that must not be confused and that must not be thought to compete. The inferential and epistemological properties (or proprieties) captured by the I- and E-clauses concern *how* certain vocabulary items are (to be) used, assertionally or inferentially, and so fix meaning in the sense of (or perhaps one sense of) *conceptual content*. They capture 'use' as *usage*. By contrast, the F-clauses capture what an item conforming to such proprieties can be used (is useful) *for*. They capture 'meaning' in the sense of *pragmatic (functional) significance*: expressive role and/or utility. If we fail to keep this distinction clearly in mind, or if we think that these different aspects of 'use' are in competition, we will be tempted to suppose that, when deploying certain vocabulary items susceptible of minimalist analysis, but having a distinctive expressive function, we aren't *really* saying anything but *only* doing something.

That the expressive function of a particular vocabulary item explains its assertional and inferential use proprieties, themselves specifiable in an ontologically conservative way, is the local expressivist's deep insight. The tendency to take this insight to imply that the vocabulary to which his analysis applies is not 'really' descriptive is his *ur*-mistake. The mistake occurs because the temptation to treat describing and expressing as alternatives that we must choose between is acute with respect to the standard candidates for expressivist treatment. This is so because these locutions have a *special* pragmatic significance beyond saying how things in some respects are: for example, by reporting on them. Focusing on this special pragmatic significance can encourage us to slip into thinking that use is at bottom *only* pragmatic significance, forgetting the use patterns that fix conceptual content. In this way, we will come to suppose that in deploying 'true' or 'cause', we aren't really ascribing a property – truth to a statement or causal power to an object – we are *merely* endorsing a claim (or set of claims) or expressing an inferential commitment.[6]

A question is likely to come up here. I suggested that the I- and E-clauses of an EMU explain conceptual content – what we are saying – whereas the (F) clauses explain what we are able to do by saying that. But *what* are we saying in the cases under review? *Pace* proponents of traditional meaning analyses, in which ways are suggested for translating statements of some problematic kind into complex statements belonging to some privileged kind, *there is no non-trivial answer to such questions.* By conforming to the use patterns/proprieties for 'true' or 'causes' – given by the material-inferential and epistemological clauses of the EMUs – we are able to say that P is true or that A causes B. End of story. Minimalist EMUs offer ontological conservatism without reduction or elimination.

3 NEED EMUs BE CONSERVATIVE?

The question is whether semantic minimalists can draw lines more or less where local expressivists want to draw them and for reasons that local expressivists can sympathise with. My suggestion that expressivist anal-yses are a particular kind of minimalist (or deflationary) EMU will help answer this question only if we can capture an appropriate contrast between minimalist and non-minimalist EMUs. So the next question is, are there non-minimalist or non-deflationary EMUs, and, if so, what makes them non-minimalist?

This brings me to a third EMU, extracted from Sellars' analysis of the observation term 'red'.[7] It too follows the tripartite template, though with a crucial complication.

---

[6] I think that Sellars was alive to this danger. This is why he says that 'the language of modal-ity is interpreted as a "transposed" language of norms' – see Sellars (1953), 21 (page references in this chapter are to the reprinted version). To stick with the case in hand, in making causal state-ments about things in the world, or even in deploying ordinary natural-kind terms, we express semantic (material-inferential) commitments, which are for Sellars a kind of normative commit-ment. As Sellars puts the point, we *convey* information (about our normative attitudes) that we do not *assert*. Indeed, since for Sellars the use rules given by the I- and E-clauses of an EMU concern *proprieties* of use, and not mere regularities, these clauses themselves have a prescriptive character and so an expressive function. This is why Sellars remarks, *a propos* of Carnap on rules for L-derivability, that the utterance 'ψ_a is L-derivable from ϕ_a' must be taken to *convey* what 'ψ_a is necessitates ϕ_a' conveys. Causal statements express rules, which in turn express inferen-tial commitments (Sellars 1953: 22). I am not sure whether endorsing Sellars' proposal sets me at odds with Robert Brandom's claim that inferential commitments are *made explicit* by modal vocabulary.

[7] See Sellars (1956): 35–8. Page references in this chapter are to the reprinted version.

1. (I-R): The inference from 'x is red' to 'x is not green', 'x is not yellow', etc., is always good. i.e. necessarily, if x is monochromatically red, x is not monochromatically green (yellow, etc.). Further inferential moves include those from 'crimson' to 'red', 'red' to 'coloured', etc.

2. (E-R):

   (a) The inferential moves specified by (I-R) are free.

   (b) To master 'red' in its reporting use, the speaker must have a reliable discriminative reporting disposition (RDRD), a disposition, given appropriate motivation and conditions, to report 'x is red' only in the presence of a red thing in his field of vision.

   (c) For a speaker fulfilling (b), a reporting move of 'x is red' is generally free but open to challenge, hence requiring justification, *in special circumstances*.

3. (F-R): In a reporting use, tokens of 'x is red' express reliable discriminative reactions to an environmental circumstance. In this way, they function as language entry transitions and thereby play a distinguished role in securing/undermining 'theoretical' entitlements. But, in themselves, they have no special *expressive* function. They are purely assertoric and *in this sense* 'merely descriptive'.

These clauses are of course illustrative rather than exhaustive. But they are enough to show that the EMU is *not* minimalist.

First, it is not mere laziness that deters me from attempting to state the EMU in a more complete form. Rather, I doubt that the inferential proprieties given in (I-R) *can* be exhaustively specified. I-R points towards the kind of inferences 'red' is involved in but does not fully display them. The EMU is thus not genuinely compact and so fails to be as uncompromisingly minimalist as that for 'true'.

While not minimalist with respect to 'red', the EMU can be seen as offering a non-metaphysical account *of observationality*. The EMU for 'red' stands to the EMU for a term's being an observation term rather as the EMU for, say, 'salt' stands to the EMU for the causally modal commitments that deployment of such a natural-kind term involves. On Sellars' account, the observation/theory distinction is *methodological*, not *ontological*. That is, the EMU for observationality does not postulate a privileged range of sensible qualities, intrinsically suited to be the objects of non-inferential reporting, nor a special mode of awareness tailored to the 'immediate' grasping of such qualities. (This is how it detaches the special epistemic weight attaching to observation reports from the myth of the given in its empiricist version.) The EMU is theoretically modest.

While not fully minimalist, then, the EMU for 'red' is still minimalist in spirit, or so we might suppose. And in some respects it is. But not in all. While theoretically modest, the EMU is *not ontologically conservative*. By (E-R), sub-clause (2b), observation reports are bound up with reliable discriminative reporting dispositions: this is what allows them to function as *language entry transitions*, making possible their distinctive role in the regulation of theory. But because of its appeal to such dispositions, the EMU for 'red', or any word with a reporting use, involves world–word relations essentially. To be sure, the world–word relations on which entry transitions depend are *causal*, not *semantic*. 'Red' does not refer to red things by virtue of this causal relation: the causal relation resides in the E-clause. Since the EMU attempts no reduction of reference to causal relatedness, it implies no representationalist backsliding. But this essential clarification does not affect the point that the EMU involves the *use*, and not merely the *mention*, of the term whose meaning it analyses. The avoidance by EMUs of semantic relations as explanatory primitives does guarantee ontological conservatism.

This point suggests a refinement in our understanding of the relations between the three types of clause in our template for an EMU. So far, I have been contrasting the I- and E-clauses with the F-clause, suggesting that the former determine conceptual (= assertional or descriptive) content. But we can see why Sellars is drawn to a narrow conception of 'conceptual content' in which such content is fixed by the (I) clauses alone. We can see why EMUs have three components; in particular why we should separate the material-inferential and epistemic clauses.

The prior fixing of conceptual content by the I-clause in an observation-term EMU saves the EMU from circularity. Because the E-clause for 'red' uses the word 'red' and does not merely mention it, the E-clause presupposes that 'red' has been given conceptual content independently of the application conditions that assure it a reporting use. Further, this prior fixing of conceptual content by the I-clause is what enables us to treat the observational/theoretical distinction as methodological rather than onto-logical. It is an essential feature of Sellars' account that a word introduced as a theoretical term can acquire an observational use – a new application – without change of meaning. The constant element is the conceptual content fixed by the I-clause.

In Sellars' view, though conceptual content is determined fundamentally by the I-clause, a language at large could not be about the world in which it is used unless it contained *some* observation terms. The presence of such terms is a condition on meaningfulness for *all* terms, even though mere causal relatedness to environmental circumstances does not fix the conceptual content of *any*. Still, meaning in the broadest sense involves all three components identified by my meta-theoretical analysis. Some terms build causal relations into their full EMUs and some don't. Observation terms do so directly. Theoretical terms do so indirectly, in that they are introduced in ways that involve essential relations to the observable facts that they explain.

Can we say that, in addition to giving a fundamental explanatory role to a special expressive function, 'expressivist' EMUs belong to the class of EMUs that don't involve world–word relations essentially? Yes, if we are careful enough.

To explain what I have in mind, let me turn to normative vocabulary, in particular to 'ought'. The EMU I want to consider combines ideas from Sellarsian analyses of causal modality and observationality. The EMU for 'ought' is a kind of mirror image of that for an observation term. The EMU for 'red' uses the idea of reliable discriminative responsiveness to capture the idea that, in acquiring information observationally, we react to our surroundings. In this way, observation reports function as 'language entry transitions'. But 'oughts' have motivational force: to decide what one ought (all things considered) to do is to decide what to do. As leading to action, 'oughts' are connected with what Sellars calls language *exit* transitions. So here (following Brandom following Sellars)[8] is a sketch of one form that an EMU for 'ought' might take:

1. (I-O): 'Ought' implies 'It is not permissible not to …', 'can', etc. (i.e. we are dealing with deontic *modality*).

2. (E-O): 'Oughts' are related to practical reasoning (of various kinds): reasoning to a conclusion ('I shall …') where the reasoner has a reliable disposition to act on his conclusion. (The modality is distinctively *deontic*.)

3. (F-O): 'Oughts' express endorsement (commitment to the soundness) of certain patterns of practical inferences. (Further refinement would distinguish different kinds of 'oughts': prudential, moral, etc.)

---

[8] See Sellars (1954); also Brandom (2000: Chapter 2).

This is crude but sufficient to make the point I need to make. This EMU, like that for 'red', involves a language–world relation. However, since in this case the language–world transitions are *exit* transitions, the EMU remains ontologically conservative. We get an analogue of representationalist talk of 'direction of fit' but without representationalism's theoretical baggage. The EMU for 'red' invokes responses to red things. In the EMU for 'ought', by contrast, deontic facts enter the characterisation of use only *via* deontic attitudes. The latter alone belong to the causal order. This is so both locally and globally. The EMU for 'ought' is minimalist in a way that the EMU for 'red' is not.

4 SUMMING UP

I distinguished three grades of scepticism about meaning. The least severe allowed that, while not generally available, compact EMUs for particular vocabulary items can be given in certain special cases. Vocabulary items susceptible of minimalist analysis are the special cases for which particularised EMUs can be given. We can't do this for items that stand for 'substantial' properties – paradigmatically natural-kind terms – because such terms find multifarious (and changing) explanatory uses: in other words, for all the reasons central to Quine's repudiation of the analytic–synthetic distinction. But in such cases we don't need an EMU because there is *nothing to explain* in a general, theoretical way. Sameness of meaning is a context-sensitive and interest-relative notion. The distinction between change of meaning and change of belief gets no purchase outside particular pedagogical or expository contexts. There are no 'meanings' to be captured. The same should probably be said of *thick* moral concepts. What we *can* deflate is their normative character.

Minimalist analyses of modal and deontic vocabulary accord with 'pragmatism about norms', the view that norms are instituted by – and enter into the causal order only by way of – normative attitudes. This non-reductively naturalist view contrasts with such supernaturalist views as Divine command theories of morality and what John McDowell calls 'Rampant Platonism', without being either 'subjectivist' or 'anti-realist' (1994: 77–8). The only sense in which norms do not belong to the 'natural' world involves the sense of 'nature' that contrasts nature with culture, not the sense that contrasts the natural with the supernatural or the non-natural. If there is a problem remaining to be solved it concerns the *emergence* of norms. But pragmatists know where to look for a solution: the evolution of cooperative behaviour (as explained by evolutionary game theory, perhaps).[9]

At the same time, pragmatists can draw lines that approximate those drawn by local expressivists. The key is to see local expressivisms as presenting minimalist or deflationary EMUs with a distinctive F-clause, while recognising that not all EMUs are minimalist. Minimalist EMUs are conservative at the *theoretical* level, the level where lines are drawn. But minimalism imposes no obligation to say that there is no property of truth, or that there are 'really no such things' as necessary connections or obligations. Quite the opposite: in a *plain* way we can and should talk about such things.

In sum, we get global anti-representationalism with functional pluralism, thus metaphysical quietism without philosophical quietism. And that is what we wanted.

[9] Sellars (1963b) thought that the puzzle of how we got into the normative dimension was 'the last refuge of special creation'. He also thought that an expressive account of the function of normative vocabulary, which went naturally with pragmatism about norms, told us to look to the evolution of co-operation for an answer.

PART III

Postscript and replies

CHAPTER 8

Prospects for global expressivism

Huw Price

In this chapter I want to try to bring into sharper focus the distinctive marks of the kind of pragmatist position advocated in three lectures in Chapters 1, 2 and 3 – *global* expressivism, as I called it in Lecture 2 – and its relation to various other pragmatist and expressivist positions on the one side, and certain self-avowedly 'realist' positions on the other. Aside from the possible benefits of some unanticipated temporal distance,[1] my main resource for this task lies in the challenges and insights of the four essays by Simon Blackburn, Michael Williams, Paul Horwich and Robert Brandom (to list them in the order in which I shall reply to them below), in Chapters 4, 7, 6 and 5, respectively. In this chapter I want to respond to some of those challenges and exploit some of these authors' insights.

I OVERVIEW

The chapter goes like this. The differences between my proposed 'global' expressivism and its 'local' ancestors turn mainly on my rejection, or modification, of the so-called *bifurcation thesis* – the claimed distinction between descriptive and non-descriptive uses of declarative utterances. In order to be able to highlight these differences, I shall begin with that thesis. I shall also re-emphasise the distinctively two-level character that I take to be one of the defining features of the kind of pragmatism I am recommending. This two-level character is certainly not unique to my version of pragmatism – on the contrary, as I emphasise both in the lectures and below, the two-level structure is certainly present, at least in some form, in the views of the pragmatists from whom I take inspiration (including, especially, both Brandom and Blackburn). To my knowledge, however, no one previously has called attention to its importance to the pragmatist picture, in the way

---

[1] For, with apologies to my patient editors at Cambridge University Press, I am writing this Postscript rather later than originally intended after the original lectures were delivered in Tilburg.

147

that I do. Against this background, and exploiting some useful taxonomy and terminology proposed in Blackburn's essay, I shall then take up the main issue on which my view seems to differ from his, viz., the question as to whether someone with our common philosophical inclinations is well advised to consider themselves a *global* pragmatist. (I shall argue, against Blackburn, that the answer is 'yes'.)

In the lectures I pointed out that my two-level structure brings with it the possibility of an irenic resolution of another (apparent) disagreement with Blackburn and other 'local' expressivists, about the status of the bifurcation thesis. This topic seems to me to deserve considerably more discussion than it received in the lectures, so here – after explaining once more how the irenic resolution proceeds – I take up the issue with respect to a writer who should ideally have figured here more, and sooner, namely Wilfrid Sellars. Sellars struggled with his own version of the bifurcation thesis, and I want to discuss, at least in a preliminary way, the relation between my proposal and his work on the topic. In particular, I want to try to sign Sellars up as a friend of the two-level picture, and of the distinction between two conceptions of representation with which it is associated. In other words, to put things in their proper order, I want to argue that my own view is rather Sellarsian, at this point.

This will lead me to Williams's essay, which frames related issues for my sort of global pragmatist in terms of what Jamie Dreier has called the challenge of 'creeping minimalism'. Williams also exploits Sellarsian resources, in a way that throws light not only on these issues of the nature of the diversity possible within a global pragmatism of the kind I advocate but also on the position's relation to previous forms of expressivism. I want to exploit Williams's discussion, in my turn, in order to clarify my account of the relation of my global expressivism to the various local expressivisms from which it claims descent.

As Williams notes, the challenge of creeping minimalism can also be seen as having a metaphysical dimension, in threatening to undermine distinctions between realism and various forms of irrealism. This metaphysical (or, perhaps better, *meta*metaphysical) turn brings me to Horwich's paper, which seeks to defend a space for anti-naturalist metaphysics in the face of my attempts to replace metaphysics with a kind of linguistic anthropology. In responding to Horwich I shall try to give a clearer sense of what I take to be at stake, and why I prefer to remain on the side of anthropology.

Finally, I turn to some issues raised by Brandom, in his contribution to this volume, about the relation between my two-level global pragmatism, on the one hand, and representationalism, anti-representationalism and especially *global* anti-representationalism, on the other. Brandom suggests that I go too far, in following Rorty in endorsing a strong version of the last position. While I agree with Brandom, I think, about all relevant points of detail, I want to identify a sense in which I still disagree – instead siding with Rorty – about the shape of the big picture. Indeed, I shall argue that Brandom, too, should stand with Rorty – in this respect, I think, he doesn't see clearly the implications of his own position. (Here, too, Sellars will prove a helpful ally.)

2 REVISITING THE BIFURCATION THESIS

The central idea of twentieth-century expressivism (often traced to Hume) was that some declarative uses of language were not really doing what philosophers had previously taken them to be doing; and that this fact had consequences for various traditional philosophical debates. By appreciating that moral claims are not genuinely factual claims, the early non-cognitivists told us, we avoid metaphysical puzzles about the nature of moral *facts* or *properties* – for the assumption that there are such things, for philosophy to concern itself with, rests on a mistake about the role of moral language.

Underlying this central idea was the view that there is a division, or 'bifurcation', between the bits of language of which this claim is true, and those of which it is not true. This 'bifurcation thesis' came in a bewildering array of forms, as Robert Kraut points out:

The bifurcationist often undertakes the task of determining which of our well-formed declarative sentences have truth conditions and which ones, though meaningful, are simply the manifestations of attitudes or the expressions of 'stances'. He wants to know which of our predicates get at real properties in the world, and which, in contrast, merely manifest aspects of our representational apparatus – 'projections borrowed from our internal sentiments'. On different occasions he articulates his task in different ways; but they all point to some variant of the *bifurcation thesis* … the thesis that some declarative sentences (call them the D sentences)

 – describe the world
 – ascribe real properties
 – are genuinely representational
 – are about 'what's really out there'
 – have determinate truth conditions
 – express matters of fact
 – limn the true structure of reality

whereas other declarative sentences (call them the E sentences)

- express commitments or attitudes
- manifest a 'stance' (praise, condemnation, endorsement, etc.)
- are expressive rather than descriptive
- do not 'picture' the world
- lack truth conditions, but possess 'acceptance conditions' or 'assertibility conditions'
- merely enable us to 'cope' with reality
- are true (or false) by convention
- do not express 'facts of the matter'. (Kraut 1990: 158–9)

To connect to some remarks in Lecture 2, I want to note that among these characteristics of what Kraut here calls E sentences, some are *negative* and some *positive* in character. E sentences 'lack truth conditions', 'do not picture the world', or 'do not express facts of the matter', for example – all those are *negative* claims. Instead, on the *positive* side, they do something else: 'express attitudes', 'manifest a stance', or whatever. Thus, non-cognitivism about an area of discourse was typically a combination of a *negative thesis* and a *positive thesis*, as I put it in Lecture 2.

If the non-cognitivist is right, why do our ethical claims take the form that they do? Why are they *claims* at all, at least superficially? These rather pressing issues were not given their due attention by some of the twentieth century's earlier expressivists, but, as we saw in Lecture 2, they provide the take-off point for Blackburn's quasi-realism. The quasi-realist's interest is in explaining how the folk come to 'talk the realist talk', without committing ourselves – qua theorists, now, given our interest in the explanatory project – to 'walking the metaphysical walk'.

Blackburn himself gives the following definition of the project:

QUASI-REALISM: a position holding that an expressivist or projectivist account of ethics can explain and make legitimate sense of the realist-sounding discourse within which we promote and debate moral views. This is in opposition to writers who think that if projectivism is correct then our ordinary ways of thinking in terms of a moral truth, or of knowledge, or the independence of ethical facts from our subjective sentiments, must all be in error, reflecting a mistaken realist metaphysics. The quasi-realist seeks to earn our right to talk in these terms on the slender, projective basis. (Blackburn 1994: 315)

Two comments about this definition, before we move on. First, the quasi-realist programme is not confined to meta-ethics, as Blackburn's formulation here suggests; and he himself elsewhere emphasises as much. Second, I think that this definition actually understates the importance of the quasi-realist project to expressivism (or projectivism, as Blackburn calls it here), in seeming to allow that there could be a version of the view that allowed that 'our ordinary ways of thinking in terms of a moral truth, or of knowledge' could 'all be in error'. In fact, however, such a concession would simply be a *reductio* of the expressivist claim, which is intended to be an *interpretation* of our ordinary ways of thinking and talking (and which must aim to make sense of them much as they are, in other words).[2]

So the relevant opponent is someone who says that the expressivist proposal is simply implausible, because it cannot make sense of the obvious fact that sentences of the disputed class *take the form* of ordinary factual claims. Such an opponent might be either a realist or an anti-realist (e.g., in the latter case, an error theorist or a fictionalist) themselves; either way, however, they maintain that the expressivist cannot make sense of the linguistic appearances, with respect to the utterances in question. The quasi-realist sets out to meet this challenge, in the way that Blackburn here describes.

In the quasi-realist's hands, expressivism thus becomes a more interesting doctrine, at least in the sense that it is making a serious attempt to respond to what otherwise seems a rather significant difficulty. Along the way, apparently, it has distanced itself from some of its own expressivist ancestors, in a manner reflected in some issues about the terminology in which it is best described. In particular, the term 'non-cognitivism' now seems inappropriate, given that quasi-realism is taking seriously the fact that we do, as Blackburn puts it, 'promote and debate moral views'; and in insisting that 'our ordinary ways of thinking in terms of ... [moral] knowledge' are *not* 'in error'.

By way of comparison at this point, and to introduce a figure whose views I wish to discuss further, I offer the following remarks from Wilfrid Sellars. They seem to me a rather apt summation of the viewpoint to which the quasi-realist is committed. It is not clear that Sellars himself does enough to explain how such an outcome may be achieved – more on his views on associated matters in section 5 below – but he seems to have the goal clearly in view: '[T]he core truth of "emotivism" is not only compatible with, but absurd without, *ungrudging* recognition of the fact, so properly stressed (if mis-assimilated to the model of describing) by "ethical rationalists," that ethical discourse as *ethical discourse* is a mode of rational discourse' (Sellars 1957: 285).

---

[2] I suspect that Blackburn has this *reductio* in mind, but it would be better expressed by saying that quasi-realism is in 'opposition to writers who think that if projectivism [*were*] correct then our ordinary ways of thinking in terms of a moral truth, or of knowledge, ... [*would*] all be in error [which, by assumption, they are not]'.

Sellars goes on to say that he takes the same to be true in the modal realm:

> It is my purpose to argue that the core truth of Hume's philosophy of causation is not only compatible with, but absurd without, *ungrudging* recognition of those features of causal discourse as a mode of rational discourse on which the 'metaphysical rationalists' laid such stress but also mis-assimilated to describing. (Sellars 1957: 285).

Sellars' view here seems close to Blackburn's in at least four respects. Three of these are, first, the acknowledgement that we find a 'core truth' in Hume on these matters; second, the recognition that this core truth is available in modal as well as moral cases; and third, most distinctively, the insistence that this insight be rendered compatible with the fact that moral and modal discourse presents itself in the clothing of a rational discourse. But my interest is in a fourth point of comparison: the fact that Sellars, like Blackburn, still takes for granted the bifurcation thesis – in other words, he still assumes a distinction between genuinely descriptive and genuinely non-descriptive (though perhaps quasi-descriptive) uses of declarative language. Both views are still *local* expressivist views, in other words.[3]

In Lecture 2 I challenged Blackburn's version of quasi-realism, questioning its entitlement to remain local. I argued that it faces pressure to become a *global* view – a view that takes the same explanatory stance towards what Blackburn calls the 'realist-sounding discourse within which we promote and debate [our] views' for *all* kinds of views, rather than for special cases (such as moral views). In other work (Macarthur and Price 2007, Price 2011a), where I have explored this challenge in more detail, I have suggested that this pressure comes from two sources: *externally*, from the attractions of semantic minimalism, which threatens to deflate the local quasi-realist's claim that some of our assertions are genuinely 'factual', or 'descriptive', in character; and *internally*, from within quasi-realism itself, in the sense that its own success in explaining the character of assertoric discourse in hard cases threatens to render redundant any other strategy in the easy cases.

However, in Lecture 2 I also held out an olive branch to local expressivism, suggesting that by exploiting the distinctively two-level character of the pragmatist view defended there – in particular the distinction between what I called e-representation and i-representation – this global

---

3 I set aside for the moment the question as to whether the term 'expressivism' is appropriate in Sellars' case.

view preserves a place for the bifurcationist intuitions: it allows that while all assertoric vocabularies are *i-representational*, some may be much more *e-representational* than others.

I now want to try to explore several aspects of this proposal in greater detail. In his essay in this volume, Blackburn resists my invitation to take up the flag of global pragmatism. I want to respond to Blackburn's comments on this issue, and – exploiting a helpful taxonomy of possible positions that he provides – to defend the most global option. After that, I'll return to Sellars: by looking at Sellars' attempts to make sense of the bifurcation thesis, I want to call attention to some affinities between his mature position and my two-level pragmatism. In particular, I want to argue that he has a version of the distinction between e-representation and i-representation. First, however, let me outline the two-level view itself once more, approached via the path of a globalised version of Blackburn's quasi-realism.

3 PRAGMATISM IN TWO STAGES

Suppose we do let quasi-realism 'go global', as I recommend. What does the resulting landscape look like? The crucial thing to stress, I think, is that it combines *uniformity* at one level with *diversity* at another. At both levels, the theoretical perspective is explanatory, or pragmatic – at neither does representationalism make an appearance, in its old form. The result is what we might call a two-level pragmatism, combining a *global* level and a *local* level.

Concerning the global level, recall that the thought behind the second version of the global challenge to quasi-realism is that whatever story the quasi-realist tells about the genealogy and functions of the 'factual' character of, say, moral language, the same story is likely to work for other cases, too. After all, the cases the quasi-realist thinks of as genuinely descriptive are simpler, prima facie. Whatever this story is, it will provide an account that is in one sense uniform, across a range of declarative vocabularies. For example, suppose that it begins with the plausible idea that putting expressions of affective attitudes into 'assertoric' form – subjecting them to community-wide norms of truth and assertibility – provides a powerful pressure towards alignment of such attitudes across a community, with long-run benefits. The thought behind the internal version of the global challenge is that this same explanation will work for expressions of other kinds of psychological states, too. In particular, it will explain our practice of 'expressing' in assertoric form the kind of behavioural dispositions the local expressivist thinks of initially as genuine, factual 'beliefs'. There, too, the challenge proposes, we should expect to be able to explain the 'factual' character of the language involved, without needing to rely in advance on the idea that it is 'genuinely descriptive'. (Our entitlement to call the behavioural dispositions in question 'beliefs' then emerges at the end, so to speak, in the same way that it does for moral 'beliefs'.)

The upshot would be a *uniform* story about the defining common characteristics of declarative speech acts – a common story about what assertion is *for*, as it were. In the simple version just mentioned, this story will say that assertions enable social creatures to express, revise and align behavioural commitments of various kinds. Note that the entire story is told in non-representational terms – after all, it is the same story that the quasi-realist tells for those vocabularies that he insisted are non-representational in the beginning.

As I noted in Lecture 2, a good place to look for a much less crude account of assertion with the same general features – being non-representational, being applicable to vocabularies with a range of expressive functions of their own, and yet, importantly, being uniform in character across this range of vocabularies – is in Brandom's (1994, 2000) account of 'the game of giving and asking for reasons'. Brandom is explicit that the raw materials of his programme are not representational. And while he says a great deal about the different expressive functions of various vocabularies, it is clear, nevertheless, that it is the same game of giving and asking for reasons in which vocabularies with these different expressive functions all participate.

In my terminology, then, Brandom is offering us an account of the uniformity of the *global* level. As this case already makes clear, and as I stressed in Lectures 2 and 3, this global uniformity is compatible with diversity at a *local* level. Brandom offers us a *diverse* story about the expressive functions of a range of different kinds of commitments, and ingredients of commitments, which are all capable of participating in the single, uniform 'assertion game'.

Switching back now to Blackburn's 'Humean' expressivism (and bracketing the question, tangential for present purposes, about the relation between this Humean expressivism and Brandom's inferential expressivism), the point is that my globalised quasi-realist is entitled to say almost everything that Blackburn himself says about the functional distinctions between different vocabularies – between moral and modal vocabularies, for example. The global quasi-realist, too, is allowed to say that moral and modal concepts are associated with projections of affective and epistemic states of distinctive kinds, playing characteristic roles in our agentive lives. What he is not entitled to do is to switch to the traditional (unbifurcated) representational idioms, to characterise the functions of some *other* vocabularies. In place of that, I have offered the concept of *e-representation*: itself explicitly a lower-level, functional notion, that may well be applicable in characterising the role of a local sub-class of assertoric vocabularies.

Thus, as I say, we have a two-level picture. At the top level, we seek an account of what assertoric vocabularies *have in common* – their common functions, both in the day-to-day sense and, if possible, in a genealogical sense.[4] At the lower level, we seek an account of what distinguishes one vocabulary from another. The picture puts our (*i-representational*) account of saying, asserting, judging and (propositional) thought in general at the higher, uniform, *global* level, and combines this with accounts of the various kinds of things we 'do' with this with this general resource, at the lower, diverse, *local* level. If we wanted a slogan for the two-level view, it might be 'think global, act local' – so long as we keep in mind that at the higher level, too, we have a kind of *doing,* or *acting:* a multipurpose doing, with application in a range of local cases.

4 IS THIS REALLY A *GLOBAL* PRAGMATISM?

In calling this two-level view a *global* expressivism, or *global* pragmatism, I have relied on the assumption that at neither level will we find ourselves resorting to an ontology of semantic properties and relations as an ingredient in our theoretical account. I will have more to say later about some terminological issues that arise here – in what sense is this 'expressivism', for example? But first to Simon Blackburn's essay, in which he resists my encouragement to become a global pragmatist (while considerably clarifying the issues at stake). I want to respond to some concerns he raises about the coherence and viability of the global project, relying on the map he himself provides of various local and global options. I shall argue that the position I recommend does indeed count as a global pragmatism, in his terms; and that by his own lights he should join me in that comparatively lonely corner of the landscape.

Blackburn characterises the pragmatic standpoint in what he describes as Carnapian terms. As he puts it:

The [Carnapian] external question is posed, about a piece of language or discourse of some identified kind, when we ask how to explain the fact that we have come

---

4 As I shall note below, one of the virtues of the EMUs Michael Williams offers us in his essay in this volume is the way in which they clarify this important distinction.

to think and talk like that: why do we go in for possible world talk, arithmetical talk, ethical or normative talk, and so on?' (Blackburn, this volume, 70–1)

To be a pragmatist is to offer a certain kind of answer to such a question:

> You will be a pragmatist about an area of discourse if you pose a Carnapian external question: how does it come about that we go in for this kind of discourse and thought? What is the explanation of this bit of our language game? And then you offer an account of what we are up to in going in for this discourse, and the account eschews any use of the referring expressions of the discourse; any appeal to anything that a Quinean would identify as the values of the bound variables if the discourse is regimented; or any semantic or ontological attempt to 'interpret' the discourse in a domain, to find referents for its terms, or truth-makers for its sentences. Instead, the explanation proceeds by talking in different terms of what is done by so talking. It offers a revelatory genealogy or anthropology or even a just-so story about how this mode of talking and thinking and practising might come about, given in terms of the functions it serves. ... It finds whatever plurality of functions it can lay its hands upon. (Blackburn, this volume, 75)

In terms of this Carnapian conception of the pragmatist project, Blackburn then proposes a four-way distinction, to clarify the options available on a spectrum from all-out representationalism, at one extreme, to global pragmatism, at the other.

> Returning to the characterisation of pragmatism given above, we should now see not a binary opposition, between pragmatism and some competitor called representationalism, but at least a fourfold division of alternatives. We could hold out for pragmatic stories *everywhere*. The opposition would be flat-footed representationalism *somewhere*. Or, we could hold out for pragmatic stories *somewhere,* and the opposition would be flat-footed representationalism *everywhere*. (Blackburn, this volume, 77)

Blackburn finds the last of these positions unattractive, of course:

> The last of these [options] is, I suppose, the position manifested by those conservative philosophers ... who automatically react to any pragmatic story by reaching for notions of truth, truth-condition, truth-makers, and their kin, and proclaiming that these lie beyond the pragmatist's grasp. I stand shoulder to shoulder with Price ... in finding that attitude reprehensible. Still, all that is needed to oppose it are *local* pragmatisms, for which, of course, I am more than happy to sign up. (Blackburn, this volume, 77)

Blackburn goes on to explain his concerns about going to the other extreme – 'pragmatic stories *everywhere*'. His first reservation turns on an objection raised by Robert Kraut:

On the other hand, I am much less certain about *global* pragmatism, the overall rout of the representationalists apparently promised by Rorty and perhaps by Robert Brandom. The reason is obvious enough. It is what Robert Kraut, investigating similar themes, calls the no-exit problem. It points out, blandly enough, that even genealogical and anthropological stories have to start somewhere. There are things that even pragmatists need to rely upon, as they produce what they regard as their better understandings of the functions of pieces of discourse. (Blackburn, this volume, 78)

Blackburn notes that this point 'is obvious when we think of the most successful strategies of the pragmatist's kind', and provides some examples:

A Humean genealogy of ... values ... talks of natural propensities to pain and pleasure, love and hate and an ability to take up a common point of view with others. It postulates a human nature in which some particle of the dove is kneaded together with the wolf and the serpent and provides a story of our evaluative practices on that basis. A broadly Fregean genealogical story of arithmetic and then mathematics more generally would start by placing us in a world of kinds of objects with distinct identity conditions, such as tigers and eggs and warriors and then a capacity to tally them, with there being an advantage to us in being able to rank pluralities of them by their magnitude ... And so on.

Such genealogical stories start with a common-sense background of us, and a world of physical objects, with distinct locations, changing only according to distinct regularities with a distinct speed limit. In the books in which he provides a genealogy of morals, Hume simply takes all that for granted, just as a Fregean account of arithmetic takes the tigers and eggs and warriors for granted. (Blackburn, this volume, 78)

But why, precisely, should a global pragmatism need an exit, of the kind Blackburn and Kraut have in mind? The view that it does so seems at least in part to be a legacy of the cases with which the expressivist began, such as that of ethics. There, it was important that the distinctive ontology of the ethical viewpoint – values, moral properties and the like – not be in view, from the pragmatist's external standpoint. By focusing on moral *talk*, rather than moral *properties*, the expressivist simply sidesteps the metaphysical condundrums that trouble her representationalist opponents, realists and anti-realists alike. ('Those are not my issues', she tells them.)

At least to the extent that the ethical conundrums arise from a commitment to naturalism, the case of science is different. There isn't a placement problem for scientific language, at least at first pass.[5] So there isn't any pressure to escape to a theoretical standpoint from which one doesn't need to

---

[5] More on the reasons for this qualification in a moment.

mention such things. However, the fact that pragmatism does not play the same metaphysics-evading role does not imply that it has nothing to say. On the contrary, as we shall see in a moment, it turns out to have plenty to say – provided we keep our mind on the fact that the pragmatist's external question is about the *talk,* not the *ontology.*

True, one can imagine perspectives from which the ontology of science does seem problematic – scepticism about the external world, or about theoretical entities, for example. Here, certainly, pragmatic reflection on the functions of scientific language may prove no help: 'You are simply assuming what I am worried about.' The necessary therapy needs to be found somewhere else – in Quine's or Carnap's denial of the external standpoint required by such metaphysics, perhaps. But the failure of pragmatism to deliver relief from *those* worries does not undercut the truth or interest of what the pragmatist has to say about scientific language – 'That wasn't the question I was addressing', the pragmatist will be entitled to say.

One can also imagine borderline cases, such as the language of modality. Here, we might have hoped for relief from metaphysics and looked to Humean expressivism to provide it. Do we get such relief if the language of science is unavoidably modal, as seems plausible? As we saw in Lecture 3, it is a tricky issue, but for present purposes we can short-circuit it by noting that it cannot be of any use to Blackburn, who is a card-carrying pragmatist about these modal cases. If the language of science is irreducibly modal, in other words, then Blackburn himself is in no position to appeal to the no-exit problem against more global opponents: he would simply be shooting himself in the foot.

This brings me to Blackburn's second reason for rejecting global pragmatism (which elaborates an argument I mentioned in Lecture 3):

If we ask the Carnapian external question about all *that* [i.e. about 'the tigers and eggs and warriors'], then we face a choice point. It may be that we take an Aristotelian, or perhaps Wittgensteinian, line on the priority of the everyday. There is simply no place for 'first philosophy' to stand behind the *endoxa*, the given in our common-sense situation. This attitude would be that of *quietism*, or the rejection altogether of at least some external questions. If we insisted instead on posing the Carnapian external-sounding question: how come that we go in for descriptions of the world in terms of surrounding middle-sized dry goods? – then the answer is only going to be the flat-footed stutter or self-pat on the back: **it is because we are indeed surrounded by middle-sized dry goods.** That answer, obviously, draws on the referential resources of the object language, and according to the account in front of us, **amounts to a victory for representationalism over pragmatism.** It is because it is no better than a stutter that I call it flat-footed representationalism.

A similar fate awaits us, in many people's view, if we pose a Carnapian external-sounding question about at least the coastal waters of science. How come we go in for descriptions of the world in terms of energies and currents? Because we have learned to become sensitive to, measure, predict and control, and describe and refer to, energies and currents. That is science's own view of how we have got where we are, and there is none better. (Blackburn, this volume, 78–9, emphasis in bold mine)

I want to make three responses here. The first focusses on the higher-level, global part of the two-level account sketched above. At this level, it is simply not true that there is 'nothing to say', from the pragmatist's point of view. For the pragmatist, *all* of the story told at that level – e.g., as it might be, Brandom's inferentialist account of the game of giving and asking for reasons – applies as much here as it does anywhere. If Brandom is right, or if the generalised quasi-realist's story about the functions of representationalist 'talk' is right, this is still something substantial to say, *and it is all said in pragmatist terms*. To think otherwise is just to take one's eye off the ball when it comes to explaining the language we use in talking about everyday things – to regard that language as explanatorily 'transparent', as it were. As Blackburn posed it above, the Carnapian question was 'How come that we go in for descriptions of the world in terms of surrounding middle-sized dry goods?' But how could the pragmatist's answer to the more general question 'How come that we go in for descriptions *at all*?' be any less relevant, less applicable, here, than it is in other cases?[6]

The second response turns to the lower, local level. Even at this level it is still not true that we are simply being flat-footed representationalists, if we have the notion of e-representation on the table. On the contrary, we will be drawing interesting parallels between scientific language and much more primitive kinds of e-representations – nothing flat-footed about that! (Recall that e-representation, unlike deflated semantic notions of representation, remains a substantial theoretical notion, by my pragmatist's lights.)

Combining these two responses, we get a sense of how Blackburn seems to be misled by the assumption that the pragmatist needs a standpoint *outside* any vocabulary on which she wants to turn her gaze. 'The aim will be to see reference to everyday objects as an instrument for coping with

---

[6] The thought that it is less relevant is surely a legacy of the traditional expressivist's assumption that everything was already in order, well understood in representational terms, in the cases on one side of the old bifurcation.

something else' [this volume, 79, emphasis added], as Blackburn puts it, when he tries to make sense of pragmatism about the language of coastal science or everyday objects. But why something *else*? The point of my first two responses here is that there is plenty for the pragmatist to say, both in i-representational and in e-representational terms, about the practical foundations of our ordinary ways of talking and thinking about, and hence coping with, the everyday objects themselves. (Once again, a failure to appreciate this point seems to be a legacy of old-style local expressivism, that took for granted that representationalism was all in order, on the descriptive side of the old bifurcation thesis.)

The third response picks up on a point we noted earlier. If we agree that modal talk is indispensable, even within the coastal waters of science, and agree, too, that an expressivist account (in my terms, a lower-level account) is appropriate for *that*; then again we have lower-level pragmatist work that needs to be done everywhere (and is flat-footed representational nowhere). Note that this need not be in tension with the previous response. The claim that scientific language is more e-representational than, say, moral language is compatible with the discovery that scientific language (unlike, no doubt, more primitive forms of e-representation) is necessarily *also* party to the functions of modal language. A traditional bifurcationist expects a sharper divide, of course, but there is no reason for my pragmatist to do so.[7]

I conclude that at neither level is it true that the pragmatist, characterised in Blackburn's Carnapian terms, has nothing to say about the discourse of the everyday world – about the language of the coastal waters of science, for example. Pragmatists can expect to do better, everywhere, than flat-footed representationalism and hence claim entitlement to a *global* view, in Blackburn's own terms.

5 SELLARS ON THE DESCRIPTIVE AND THE FACTUAL

Now to Sellars. As I noted above, Sellars is clear that Humean insights about the functions of certain vocabularies should be seen as compatible with the observation that these vocabularies are also, as he puts it, *rational* discourses – they participate in our conceptual, cognitive and inferential lives on equal terms with those assertoric vocabularies (such as those of science, perhaps) from which the Humean insight emphasises that they are distinct. (They are properly called true or false, for example. As Sellars puts it elsewhere [Sellars and Chisholm 1957: 531], 'it is just as proper to say of

---

7 As I noted in Lecture 3, this point can be reinforced by appeal to the lessons of the rule-following considerations, and the ubiquity in language of the kind of generality on which they depend.

statements of the form "Jones ought to do A" that they are true, as it is to say this of mathematical, geographical or semantical statements'.)

In this respect, then, Sellars is not an old-fashioned non-cognitivist. Yet, as the passages above indicate, he also relies on the bifurcation thesis – he wants to say that evaluative and modal discourse is not properly 'assimilated to describing'. However, he seems to have seen that there is potential trouble here and that it is by no means easy to say what 'describing' means. In his contribution to the Carnap volume of *The Library of Living Philosophers* (written in 1956), he notes the problem, and proposes a tentative solution:[8]

> [T]he concept of a descriptive term is … by no means intuitively clear. It is easier to specify kinds of terms which are *not* descriptive than to single out what it is that descriptive terms have in common. Thus, I think it would be generally agreed that the class of non-descriptive terms includes, besides logical terms in a suitably narrow sense, *prescriptive* terms, and the logical and causal modalities …
>
> It might be thought that, in the last analysis, a descriptive term is one that is used, in its typical sentences, to describe. But what is to describe? Must one be describing an object if one says something about it that is either true or false? Scarcely, for modals and even prescriptive statements (e.g., 'Jones ought to make amends') can be correctly said to be either true or false. Perhaps to describe an object is to specify some of its qualities and/or relations. Unfortunately, the terms 'quality' and 'relation' raise parallel difficulties. Is it absurd to speak of goodness as a *prescriptive quality?* Indeed, one use of the terms 'property' and 'relation' is such that it is correct to say of any meaningful expression which has the grammatical characteristics of a predicate that it means a quality or relation. And in this usage it is correct to say the 'good' means a quality. On the other hand, there is a usage which ties the term 'quality' and 'relation' to *describing* as opposed to *prescribing*.
>
> We are back with the question, What is it to describe? In my opinion, the key to the answer is the realization that describing is internally related to *explaining,* in that sense of 'explanation' which comes to full flower in scientific explanation – in short, causal explanation. A descriptive term is one which, in its basic use, properly replaces one of the variables in the dialogue schema
>
> What brought it about that x is ϕ? The fact that y is ψ.
>
> where what is requested is a causal explanation. I say 'in its basic use' to exclude the use of a term in mentalistic and semantical contexts. For since it is proper to ask 'What brought it about that Jones believes he ought to go downtown?' and 'What brought it about that the German word "gut" means good?' even prescriptive terms would be descriptive, on the above account, were we to admit these contexts. (Sellars 1963a: 450–1)

[8] I am very much indebted here to Lionel Shapiro, who pointed me in the direction of many of the passages from Sellars that I discuss below.

A little later, however – in correspondence with Roderick Chisholm from 1957 – Sellars expresses doubts about this proposal. He and Chisholm are discussing the significance of meaning ascriptions, and Sellars proposes that they, too, are not descriptive: 'My solution is that "'...' means - - -" is the core of the unique mode of discourse which is as distinct from the *description* and *explanation* of empirical fact, as is the language of *prescription* and *justification*' (Sellars and Chisholm 1957: 527). Quoting this passage, Chisholm replies:

I am more skeptical than you are about the content of such 'solutions' as the one you propose ... I am inclined to feel that the technical philosophical term 'descriptive' is one which is very much over used, and I am not sure I can attach much meaning to it. Indeed I would be inclined to say that if the locution 'Such and such a sentence is not descriptive' means anything at all, it means that the sentence in question (like 'Do not cross the street' and 'Would that the roses were blooming') is neither true nor false. But the sentence '"Hund" means dog in German' is a sentence which is true. (Sellars and Chisholm 1957: 529)

To this, Sellars responds:

The most important thing that needs to be said is that I not only admit, I have never questioned that '"Hund" means *dog* in German' is true in what, for our purposes, is exactly the same sense as 'Berlin is part of Warsaw' would be if the facts of geography were somewhat different.
    '"Hund" means dog in German' is true ≡ 'Hund' means dog in German just as 'Berlin is part of Warsaw' is true ≡ Berlin is part of Warsaw.
    There is just no issue between us on this point. When I have said that semantical statements *convey* descriptive information but do not *assert* it, I have not meant to imply that semantical statements *only* convey and do not assert. They make semantical assertions. Nor is 'convey', as I have used it, a synonym for 'evince' or 'express' as emotivists have used this term. I have certainly not wished to assimilate semantical statements to ejaculations or symptoms.
    It might be worth noting at this point that, as I see it, it is just as proper to say of statements of the form 'Jones ought to do A' that they are *true*, as it is to say this of mathematical, geographical or semantical statements. This, of course, does not preclude me from calling attention to important differences in the 'logics' of these statements.
    I quite agree, then, that it is no more a solution of our problem simply to say that semantical statements are 'unique,' than it would be a solution of the corresponding problems in ethics simply to say that prescriptive statements are 'unique.' What is needed is a painstaking exploration of statements belonging to various (prima

facie) families, with a view to discovering *specific* similarities and differences in the ways in which they behave. Only *after* this has been done can the claim that a certain family of statements is, in a certain respect, unique, be anything more than a promissory note …

I also agree that the term 'descriptive' is of little help. Once the 'journeyman' task (to use Ayer's expression) is well under way, it may be possible to give a precise meaning to this technical term. (Presumably this technical use would show some measure of continuity with our ordinary use of 'describe'.) I made an attempt along this line in my Carnap paper, though I am not very proud of it. On the other hand, as philosophers use the term today, it means little that is definite apart from the logician's contrast of 'descriptive expression' with 'logical expression' (on this use 'ought' would be a descriptive term!) and the moral philosopher's contrast of 'descriptive' with 'prescriptive'. According to both these uses, 'S means p' would be a descriptive statement. (Sellars and Chisholm 1957: 531)

By the mid-1960s, however, Sellars seems to have thought that he was making some progress on the matter. As a direct result, he adds an additional chapter to his six John Locke Lectures, to make up the published volume, *Science and Metaphysics* (1968). In the Introduction to that volume he describes the role of this chapter as follows:

[This new] chapter is … the heart of the enterprise. In it I attempt to spell out the specific differences of matter-of-factual truth. Levels of 'factual' discourse are distinguished and shown to presuppose a basic level in which conceptual items such as items *in rerum natura* 'represent' or 'picture' (in a sense carefully to be distinguished from the semantical concepts of reference and [predication]) the way things are. (Sellars 1968: ix)

Later, at the beginning of the chapter in question, he characterises the project like this:

My concern in this chapter will be with what might initially be called 'factual truth'. This phrase is intended to cover both the truth of propositions at the perceptual and introspective level, and the truth of those propositions which, though 'empirical' in the broad sense that their authority ultimately rests on perceptual experience, involve the complex techniques of concept formation and confirmation characteristic of theoretical science.

Since the term 'fact' is properly used as a synonym for 'truth' even in its most generic sense, so that we can speak of mathematical and even ethical facts, 'factual', in the more specific sense indicated above, should be thought of as short for 'matter-of-factual', and as equivalent to Leibniz' technical term *verité de fait*. (Sellars 1968: 116)

Since, as Sellars puts it here, 'the term "fact" is properly used as a synonym for "truth" even in its most generic sense', it should come as no surprise

that this distinction between 'generic' and 'more specific' notions of fact
goes hand in hand with a corresponding distinction at the level of *truth*. As
James O'Shea puts the point, 'truth for Sellars involves both a normative
dimension and an underlying naturalistic or causal dimension' (2007: 144).
O'Shea goes on to note that the normative notion is also a *general* notion, in
the sense that it has global scope in assertoric language: 'In the normative
and most general sense, Sellars contends that the truth of all kinds of
propositions, whether they are empirical, mathematical, or moral claims,
consists in their being what he calls *correctly semantically assertible*' (2007:
144). This is Sellars' own account of this general notion:

[F]or a proposition to be true is for it to be assertible, where this means not *capable*
of being asserted (which it must be to be a proposition at all) but *correctly* assertible;
assertible, that is, in accordance with the relevant semantical rules, and on the basis
of such additional, though unspecified, information as these rules may require ...
'True', then, means *semantically* assertible ('S-assertible') and the varieties of truth
correspond to the relevant varieties of semantical rule. (Sellars 1968: 101)

However, as O'Shea puts it, 'Sellars also argues that [in addition to this
generic notion] there is a further "correspondence" dimension to truth in
the specific case of what he calls *basic matter-of-factual truths*' (2007: 144).
This correspondence dimension involves 'a carefully qualified descendant
of Wittgenstein's "picture theory" in the *Tractatus:* basic matter-of-factual
propositions in some sense form *pictures,* or "cognitive maps," or "representations" of how objects or events in the world are related and characterized.'
(O'Shea 2007: 144).

I shall not attempt here to give a gloss of Sellars' complex account of
this 'picturing' relation,[9] but merely stress a few features of Sellars' view
of its relation to other matters. For one thing, as Willem deVries notes,
Sellars sees it as continuous, in some sense, with simpler notions of animal
representation:

[I]t is clear that Sellars believes our linguistic representations are themselves built
upon a primitive animal representational system that more or less systematically
maps the immediate environment of the organism, although the map in such an
animal representational system is not a *linguistic* map. The mapping function,
however, is essential to any empirically useful representational system and will
therefore also be performed within the linguistic representational system that is
the peculiar possession of human beings. (deVries 2005: 53)

---

9 For that, I recommend the works of O'Shea (2007) and deVries (2005) on which I am relying in this
   section.

Even more relevantly for my present purposes, deVries also notes that this aspect of Sellars' work is both similar to and yet distinct from some contemporary positions:

Sellars clearly makes contact with work in both cognitive science and contemporary philosophy of mind that seeks to explain important mental phenomena by reference to systematic relations between the internal states of organisms and the conditions in the world they represent … Sellars' notion of picturing is similar to such attempts to naturalize meaning and the mental. But the dissimilarity cannot be ignored: Sellars does not identify picturing and meaning and does not attempt a reductive naturalization of meaning or intentionality. The naturalistic core provided by picturing is a necessary but not sufficient condition of using an empirically meaningful language. Nevertheless, Sellars claims that the picturing relation is 'a mode of "correspondence" *other than truth* that accompanies truth in the case of [elementary] empirical statements' (Sellars 1962b: 54) (deVries 2005: 53–4)

The remark from Sellars that deVries quotes here occurs in a passage in which Sellars is raising and rejecting an objection to his own view, to the effect that picturing might be just truth after all:

For, it might be argued, even if it were made to work, [picturing] could not do what I want it to do. For, surely, I have at best indicated how a structure of natural-linguistic objects might correspond, by virtue of certain 'rules of projection' to a structure of nonlinguistic objects. But to say that a manifold of linguistic objects *correctly* pictures a manifold of nonlinguistic objects is no longer to consider them as mere 'natural-linguistic objects' – to use your term – but to consider them as linguistic objects proper, and to say that they are *true*. Thus, instead of finding a mode of 'correspondence' *other than truth* that accompanies truth in the case of empirical statements, your 'correspondence,' is simply truth all over again.

So the objection. I reply that to say that a linguistic object *correctly* pictures a nonlinguistic object in the manner described above is not to say that the linguistic object is *true*, save in that metaphorical sense of 'true' in which one geometrical figure can be said to be a 'true' projection of another if it is drawn by correctly following the appropriate method of projection. (Sellars 1962b: 54)

Later, in *Science and Metaphysics,* Sellars puts it like this: 'Picturing is a complex matter-of-factual relation and, as such, belongs in quite a different box from the concepts of denotation and truth.' (Sellars 1968: 136). Why 'quite a different box'? Because, as Sellars often stresses, his view is that the generic notion of truth does not stand for such a relation. He explains this point in terms related to now-familiar deflationary approaches to truth that focus on the role of the so-called equivalence principle:

[W]e see that what we have here is the principle of inference:
   That snow is white is true entails and is entailed by that snow is white which governs such inferences as

That snow is white is true.

So, Snow is white.

But if the word 'true' gets its sense from this type of inference, we must say that, instead of standing for a relation or relational property of statements (or, for that matter, of thoughts), 'true' is a sign *that something is to be done* – for inferring is a doing. (Sellars 1962b: 38)

Elsewhere, Sellars emphasises the need to

grasp the difference between the *primary* concept of factual truth (truth as correct picture) ... and the *generic* concept of truth as S-assertibility, which involves the quite different mode of correspondence ... in terms of which the 'correspondence' statement (i.e. equivalence statement)

That 2 plus 2 = 4 is true $\leftrightarrow$ 2 plus 2 = 4

is to be understood. (Sellars 1968: 119)

5.1 My diagnosis

It seems to me that Sellars' remarks on these matters illustrate a pattern that pervades the issues we have been discussing. What is happening, in Sellars' work as in the debates I have been discussing in the lectures, is that a cluster of notions – what we might loosely call the *semantic* notions – are being pulled in two directions, one inclusive and one exclusive. In these passages, we have seen Sellars making this point with respect to the notions of 'descriptive', 'fact', 'proposition' and 'true' itself. In all these cases, he ends up saying, there's a *generic* notion application to declarative statements of all kinds and a *local* notion applicable much more narrowly – to the matter-of-factual, as Sellars puts it.

My response to this fundamental terminological tension has been to see it as reflecting the fact that all these notions are trying to serve two quite different masters. I have suggested we get a much clearer view of the landscape by making this explicit – by recognising that we have two quite distinct notions or clusters of notions in play, misleadingly being forced together by our failure to recognise the distinction and to modify our terminology accordingly. My terms *e-representation* and *i-representation* were my attempt to mark this distinction.

This recommendation seems to accord very closely with Sellars' own conclusions – in particular, with the remarks I have just quoted about the distinction between two notions of truth. Hence it is very natural, from my point of view, to regard Sellars' account of picturing as an attempt to spell out a particular kind of *e-representation*, and to regard his account of truth as

S-assertibility as a contribution to an understanding of an important kind of *i-representation.* I see Sellars' strenuous efforts to insist that these notions of truth are distinct, and 'belong in different boxes', as of a piece with my insistence that e-representation and i-representation are not different attempts to get at the same thing but different attempts to get at *different* things (each perhaps important in its own right, depending on the details of the case).

Sellars puts the difference in terms of the idea that picturing is a natural relation between *objects* – linguistic items considered as objects, on one side, and objects in our environment, on the other – whereas truth in the generic sense is a 'pseudo-relation', to be understood in terms of its inference-supporting role within the language game. I think we can emphasise this distinction even further, as I did in Lecture 2, by noting the different theoretical stance we employ in each case.

In the case of the generic notion, we are interested in a notion we find in use in ordinary language. To the extent – the very great extent, in my view – that the explanatory, pragmatist approach recommends itself in such a case, our theoretical focus will be on the use of the notion. We will be asking, in effect, 'What are creatures like us *doing* when they use this notion? Why do they have it in their language in the first place?'

In the case of picturing, however, our focus, as Sellars himself always stresses, is first-order, matter-of-factual and highly theoretical.[10] There is no reason whatsoever to imagine that the notion we find ourselves investigating will be in play in folk usage. And our theoretical interest is in the relation *in the world,* not in the use of certain terms in ordinary *language.*

I will return to these distinctions later, for they are relevant to what I want to say in response to Robert Brandom's essay. For the moment, I want to close these reflections about Sellars by considering the implications of his conception of what is right about the bifurcation thesis for certain traditional jobs that that thesis was supposed to do. (I want to find another respect in which Sellars' view is more like mine than it is like that of some of my traditional expressivist opponents.)

5.2 Sellars, bifurcation and object naturalism

I have suggested that Sellars' proposal about the distinctive feature of 'matter-of-factual' truth – that is, the notion of 'picturing' – can be seen

---

[10] I mean that our stance in employing the notion is highly theoretical. The language to which we take this highly theoretical notion to be relevant is itself some of the most basic and least theoretical, in Sellars' view.

as an example of e-representation, in my terms. As I noted in Lecture 2, the notion of e-representation offers an olive branch to proponents of the bifurcation thesis, in the face of global pragmatism: it does provide a notion of 'keeping track' such that some declarative vocabularies are arguably distinctive, in being 'for' – having the function of[11] – keeping track of our physical environment, in this sense.

I now want to ask how much weight this olive branch will bear, in the following sense. One job a traditional bifurcationatist might want the bifurcation thesis to do is to support what in Lecture 1 I called *object naturalism*: the view that 'all the facts there are' are the kind of facts discovered and discussed by natural science – that all genuine knowledge is scientific knowledge. It is easy to imagine how such an appeal to the bifurcation thesis would proceed. With a criterion for being a genuinely factual use of language in hand, we examine declarative uses of language as a whole and discover (the object naturalist hopes) that only scientific language passes the test. (Think of logical positivism at this point, as a framework within which this move was often explicit.)

Does Sellars' account of matter-of-factual truth, or mine of e-representation, support this kind of argument for object naturalism? The answer is 'no', because it is a matter of *stipulation*, not *discovery*, that it is claims about the natural world that pass this test. In effect, Sellars has proposed a distinctive functional role occupied by *some* declarative uses of language and has chosen to call these the matter-of-factual uses. At this point it is no surprise (of course!) that other declarative uses of language do not count as matter-of-factual, but this tautology is no use at all to the object naturalist (who takes herself to be articulating a significant metaphysical truth, not a mere triviality). It is worse than useless, in fact, if we bear in mind how Sellars comes to this point, having given up on the idea that there is any other interesting account of descriptive language to be had – any account, that is, that might do the positivists' work of vindicating the thought that only scientific language is genuinely factual. (Recall Sellars' own insistence [1957: 282] that 'once the tautology "The world is described by descriptive concepts" is freed from the idea that the business of all non-logical concepts is to describe, the way is clear to an *ungrudging* recognition that many expressions which empiricists have relegated to second-class citizenship in discourse are not *inferior,* just *different'*.)

---

[11] These notions are helpfully clarified in Michael Williams's essay, as I shall note below.

I conclude that although the irenic move of Lecture 2 does preserve a space for the traditional (local) expressivist's intuition that there is a useful distinction to be drawn between those claims that are, and those that are not, in the business of 'tracking our physical environments', it does not thereby resuscitate object naturalism, by relegating other uses of assertoric language to 'second-class citizenship', to use Sellars' phrase.

What has happened here is that for *fact*, as for other semantic notions, we have had to recognise that the notion has an inclusive sense and an exclusive sense. In the exclusive or narrow sense, it is a matter of stipulation that all the facts there are natural facts. In the inclusive or broad sense, it is immediate – not quite a matter of stipulation, perhaps, but an observation easily made about our language, once the question is in front of us – that this is not the case. Either way, then, there is no interesting *metaphysical* thesis in the offing – be it for object *naturalism* or object *non-naturalism* – despite the availability of the bifurcation.

In Lecture 3 I expressed this idea as the claim that we need a bifurcation in the notion of the *world,* to match our distinction between inclusive and exclusive senses of these various semantic notions. So far as I know, there is no corresponding move to be found in Sellars, at least not in an explicit form.[12] My impression is that Sellars is in a sense shielded from it by his insistence that facts lie on the language side of a language–world divide.

We have seen, however, that 'nonlinguistic facts' in the sense of facts about non-linguistic entities are *in another sense* themselves *linguistic* entities and that their connection with the nonlinguistic order is something done or to be done rather than a relation. It is the inferring from 'that-p is true' to 'p'. And as long as picturing is construed as a relationship between *facts* about linguistic objects and *facts* about nonlinguistic objects, nothing more can be said. (Sellars 1962a: 43–4)

Thus, Sellars retains a conception of the world as a domain of *objects* and *properties,* not of *facts.* Yet, as he also recognises at some points, these notions, too, come under the same kind of pressure to 'go generic':

Is it absurd to speak of goodness as a *prescriptive quality*? Indeed, one use of the terms 'property' and 'relation' is such that it is correct to say of any meaningful expression which has the grammatical characteristics of a predicate that it means a

---

12 As Lionel Shapiro pointed out to me, there is perhaps a hint of it in a distinction Sellars makes in passing in Sellars (1962a) between the 'world of fact in that narrow sense which tractarians like Professor Bergmann and myself find illuminating' (1962a: 25), on the one hand, and 'that broad sense in which the "world" includes linguistic norms and roles viewed … from the standpoint of a fellow participant' (1962a: 7), on the other.

quality or relation. And in this usage it is correct to say the 'good' means a quality. (Sellars 1963a: 450)

So the shield seems unlikely to protect Sellars for very long, even by his own lights.

Once again, my diagnosis is that we need inclusive and exclusive notions of *world*, just as we do for *fact* and the other notions we have mentioned. And for *world*, as for *fact*, it becomes a trivial matter that the world is the natural world, or a trivial matter that it is not, depending on which of the two senses we have in mind – so there is no space here for substantial metaphysical naturalism or metaphysical non-naturalism, of the old varieties.

For me, these conclusions follow from the recognition that we need to separate the content assumption from the correspondence assumption, as I put it in the lectures – in other words, that we need to abandon the presupposition at the core of orthodox naturalistic Representationalism, that *propositional content* and *word–natural-world correspondence* live in the same box (to borrow Sellars' metaphor). It seems uncontroversial that Sellars *has* abandoned that presupposition: sentences in the vocabularies he describes as 'not *inferior,* just *different*' clearly possess propositional content, in his view, *without* 'picturing' the natural world. And my claim is that we can't stop there. As I would put it, paraphrasing Sellars, 'The way is [now] clear to an *ungrudging* recognition that many [*facts, objects* and *properties*] which [naturalists] have relegated to second-class citizenship … are not *inferior,* just *different.*'

But can Sellars, too, take this further step, or would it be in tension with his own brand of naturalism? I leave that question on the table at this point, though I shall return to related issues about the fate of metaphysics in my reply to Paul Horwich, below.

6 WILLIAMS ON CREEPING MINIMALISM

Michael Williams is concerned with the question as to whether neo-pragmatists of the kind I claim to be are really entitled to present themselves as fellow travellers of traditional expressivists:

Contemporary pragmatists – or perhaps that should be neo-pragmatists – are often sympathetic to expressivist accounts of vocabularies that have often been regarded as metaphysically problematic: moral and modal vocabulary, for example … At the same time, as Price has been quick to recognise, there is a question of whether pragmatists like himself have the right to such sympathy. (Williams, this volume, 128)

The problem, as Williams sees it, is the one that Jamie Dreier (2004) has called the threat of creeping minimalism. Williams puts it like this:

[P]ragmatists are anti-representationalists across the board. As semantic deflation-ists, they have no 'robust' notion of truth. If sentences are used in ways that respect the syntactic discipline of assertoric discourse, then they are used to make asser-tions and are as 'truth-apt' as sentences get to be. The apparently vital contrast between descriptive and expressive uses of language is erased. Once it is erased, how is what remains of expressivism to be distinguished from the most extreme realism? (Williams, this volume, 131)

I shall return to the last issue Williams raises here – the threat of extreme realism, as it were – somewhat later, in discussing a related issue in my response to Paul Horwich's essay. For present purposes I want to focus on the underlying issue: the threat of the loss of the 'apparently vital contrast between descriptive and expressive uses of language', as Williams puts it.

Williams himself gives the following account of the challenge:

What has to be shown is that pragmatists can draw lines more or less where expressivists want to draw them, for reasons bearing at least some relation to those that expressivists give, but without invoking the semantic distinctions that traditional expressivists rely on. (Williams, this volume, 132)

Williams agrees with me – against more radical quietists, of whom he sees Horwich as an example – that this goal is achievable, and worthwhile. But he thinks I may underestimate the task:

[P]erhaps unlike Price, I think that this is a non-trivial undertaking … It is all very well to talk about the 'different roles in our lives' that different vocabularies play. But how are these roles to be characterised, if the language of philosophical anthro-pology must *exclude any explanatory use of representationalist idioms?* (Williams, this volume, 132–3)

While I'm puzzled how I gave the impression that I thought that this would be a trivial undertaking, I agree, of course, that there is much more to be said than I have said myself. I agree, too, with Williams' account of the source of the problem:

The constraints imposed on pragmatists by semantic deflationism are severe. A semantic deflationist has no notion of fact beyond that of true proposition, and no notion of truth that can bear any explanatory weight.
    Accordingly, it won't do to explain the functional difference between descrip-tive and normative discourse in terms of their expressing, respectively, beliefs

and desires (or some other desire-like states) and then go on to explain the belief–desire distinction in terms of direction of fit (beliefs aiming to fit the world, desires aiming at getting the world to fit them). (Williams, this volume, 132)

I am also sympathetic with the sentiments Williams goes on to express, in framing the project of his paper:

If we are to recognise that there are insights to be retained from local expressivisms – moral or modal expressivism, say – while operating within the framework of a fully general anti-representationalism, we must draw lines in roughly the places that traditional local expressivists draw them and do so for reasons that bear some significant relation to those that motivate locally expressivist views. I think that this can be done. In what remains, I show how. (Williams, this volume, 133)

Williams' proposed solution turns on an approach to the study of meaning he takes from Sellars. As he puts it, 'To see whether pragmatism can accommodate expressivist insights, we have to ask what is involved in giving an explanation of meaning in terms of use (an EMU)' (Williams, this volume, 133). The bulk of the remainder of his essay consists of some detailed and illuminating comparisons between the kind of EMUs appropriate for various particular vocabularies. I found little, if anything, to disagree with in this material, which I found immensely useful. I would simply like to call attention to one passage that seems to me especially helpful – it makes a point to which I have already appealed above – before returning to the more general issues of creeping minimalism and bifurcation.

The passage in question concerns a distinction between two notions of use. Following Sellars, Williams takes his EMUs to involve three kinds of clauses: intra-linguistic *inferential* (I) clauses, epistemological (E) clauses and functional (F) clauses. He emphasises that between the I- and E-clauses, on one side, and the F clauses, on the other, there is a crucial conceptual divide:

Let me reiterate the vital point made explicit by my meta-theoretical analysis. In any EMU, the I- and E-clauses, on the one hand, and the F-clause, on the other, are concerned with aspects of use that must not be confused and which must not be thought to compete. The inferential and epistemological properties (or proprieties) captured by the I- and E-clauses concern *how* certain vocabulary items are (to be) used, assertionally or inferentially, and so fix meaning in the sense of (or perhaps one sense of) *conceptual content*. They capture 'use' as *usage*. By contrast, the F-clauses capture what an item conforming to such proprieties can be used (is useful) *for*. They capture 'meaning' in the sense of *pragmatic (functional) significance*: expressive role and/or utility. If we fail to keep this distinction clearly in mind, or if we think that these different aspects of 'use' are in competition, we will be tempted to suppose that, when deploying certain vocabulary items susceptible of minimalist analysis, but having a distinctive expressive function, we aren't *really* saying anything but only *doing* something. (Williams, this volume, 138)

Clashing terminology aside, I believe that the distinction Williams draws here aligns very nicely with (and very helpfully elucidates) my own distinction between the top level, *i-representational*, aspect of my two-level pragmatism, and the lower level (and in some but not all cases *e-representational*) aspect.

6.1 Creeping minimalism and its egalitarian cousins

In order to get a clearer sense of what Williams' Sellarsian machinery can deliver, let's return to the issue of creeping minimalism, where Williams himself begins. I think we can usefully distinguish several different concerns, in the same general vicinity.

6.1.1 Losing a metaphysical distinction?
Dreier's own opening paragraph makes it sound initially as if the problem is about metaphysics, or perhaps *meta*-metaphysics (in the domain of ethics – Dreier himself mentions, but does not explore, the likelihood that similar concerns will arise in other domains, for much the same reasons):

This is a paper about the problem of realism in meta-ethics (and, I hope, also in other areas, but that hope is so far pretty speculative). But it is not about the problem of whether realism is true. It is about the problem of what realism *is*. More specifically, it is about the question of what divides meta-ethical realists from irrealists. (Dreier 2004: 22)

Read in this metaphysical (or meta-metaphysical) vein, the threat is that minimalism abolishes a distinction many have thought important, between two possible metaphysical positions (or clusters of positions, perhaps) in meta-ethics: realism and irrealism. And if that's the problem, then while it might be construed, as Williams suggests, as a problem for the expressivist – '[W]hat remains of expressivism to be distinguished from the most extreme realism?', as Williams puts it – we could follow Dreier himself at this point in replying that this is equally a problem for the would-be extreme realist: both sides in the traditional debate should be embarrassed, surely, by the lack of the distinction on which they both rely. So to the extent that creeping minimalism raises a *metaphysical* concern, it seems best to see it as the demarcation issue rather than as a specific threat to one side or other.

I want to put this concern to one side for now and to come back to it later in the context of Horwich's remarks about metaphysics.

6.1.2 'Soothing away of distinctions'
A related but different concern – different because its focus is not necessarily on any *metaphysical* issue – is the one often aired by Blackburn, that minimalism has (or is thought to have) the effect of homogenising our conception of language, by removing distinctions:

There is a contemporary river that sometimes calls itself pragmatism, although other titles are probably better. At any rate it is the denial of differences, the celebration of the seamless web of language, the soothing away of distinctions, whether of primary *versus* secondary, fact *versus* value, description *versus* expression, or of any other significant kind. What is left is a smooth, undifferentiated view of language, sometimes a nuanced kind of anthropomorphism or 'internal' realism, sometimes the view that no view is possible: minimalism, deflationism, quietism. (Blackburn 1998b: 157)

Blackburn himself thinks that this concern is entirely misplaced, and I think it is clear that Williams' EMUs have the resources to explain why this is so. Williams' model easily shows how to avoid the danger of homogenisation, in allowing us to draw many distinctions between individual vocabularies. Whether they do so in a way that provides comfort to would-be local expressivists is another matter (to which I shall turn in a moment); but they cannot be accused of relentless homogeneity.

6.1.3 Making sense of local expressivism?
A third concern that we might have, with Williams, is that of making sense of the intuitions driving traditional *local* expressivists in the moral and modal cases. This concern itself seems to split into two elements, however:

1. Making sense of the *descriptive* side of the contrast – the idea that some vocabularies are genuinely *factual*, that they are in the business of *keeping track of the world* (to borrow some of the ways of cashing this idea that we have encountered above).
2. Making sense of the *expressive* side – of local expressivists' appeal to the notions of 'expressing', or 'projecting'.

It seems to me that Williams' EMUs have the potential to speak to both of these motivations and also to illustrate how they come apart in a significant way. However, I think that Williams doesn't quite make the right use of his own framework at this point. To explain this, let me take these points in turn.

The first task is that of making sense of the intuition that some vocabularies are 'descriptive'. Here Williams' proposal is on exactly the right lines, in my view, and his discussion illustrates how his Sellarsian framework can help to draw some of the distinctions we have noted earlier. In the case of the EMU for 'red', the E-clauses and F-clauses invoke the notion of a 'reliable discriminative reporting disposition (RDRD): a disposition, given appropriate motivation and conditions, to report "x is red" only in the presence of a red thing in [one's] field of vision' (Williams, this volume, 140). This puts the account into the territory of *e-representation,* in my terms. As Williams stresses, it also makes the EMU ontologically non-conservative, thus bolstering the realist intuitions that are such a typical component of the local expressivist's picture, on the 'descriptive' side of the line. (As I say, more on these metaphysical issues later.)

The second task is that of making sense of the intuition that some vocabularies are (merely) 'expressive'. In this case, I feel, Williams uses the term 'express' a little bit more loosely than is helpful. Concerning the EMU for 'red', he offers the following account of the F-clause:

(F-R): In a reporting use, tokens of 'x is red' **express** reliable discriminative reactions to an environmental circumstance. In this way, they function as language entry transitions and thereby play a distinguished role in securing/undermining 'theoretical' entitlements. **But in themselves, they have no special *expressive* function.** They are purely assertoric and *in this sense* 'merely descriptive'. (Williams, this volume, 140, emphasis in bold mine)

There is an evident tension here between the two uses of the notion of expression. It is the latter that should go, in my view. It would be better to rely on the factors already noted to spell out the sense in which tokens of 'x is red' are 'descriptive' and then to allow that they *do* have a special expressive function. As Williams himself puts it, they do 'express' a special kind of mental state, viz., 'reliable discriminative reactions'. We can then make sense of the local expressivists' intuition that other cases (e.g., ethical and modal cases) are different in terms of the idea that in *those* cases the psychological states expressed don't have this 'descriptive' face. What's distinctively 'expressive' about those cases isn't the 'expression' as such, in other words, but the fact that the states expressed do not have a 'descriptive' character, in the sense just elaborated.

Williams himself seems close to this way of putting things at other points: 'This brings me to my first thesis, which is that local-expressivist EMUs are minimalist EMUs with a particular kind of F-clause (one mentioning the expression of an evaluative or practical attitude)' (Williams, this volume, 137–8). What needs adding, I've suggested, is that what makes such an F-clause distinctive is not the expression by itself but that the attitude expressed does not have a 'descriptive' face (something in any case guaranteed by minimalism, in Williams' framework, if I understand it correctly). The term 'expressivism' is thus a little misleading. We have expression on both sides of the line, in so far as there still is a line. But this is hardly new news – on the contrary, it has been part of the view since infancy. The traditional non-cognitivist idea was that whereas descriptive claims *express* beliefs, evaluative claims *express* desires.

Seen in these terms, Williams' framework serves to illustrate how the traditional local expressivists' terminology is unhelpful in another way, too. For, as Williams' account of the EMU for 'true' makes clear, there are cases that don't meet the criteria for having a 'descriptive' face but which are nevertheless not expressive, in the sense that there is no distinctive psychological state mentioned in their F-clause.[13]

So to the extent that EMUs really do make sense of traditional local expressivist intuitions, it is not in the end the notion of *expression* that draws the useful boundary: not only do we have expression on the descriptive side of the line, too (in so far as the descriptive/non-descriptive line can still be drawn, at any rate), but we need not have it on the non-descriptive side.

This means that the terms 'expressivism' and 'global expressivism' are to some extent unhappy. My use of them derives from that of Humean 'expressivists' such as Blackburn and Gibbard and – separately but, as I've argued, wholly consistently – from Brandom's inferentialist 'expressivism'. The justification for this use, if any be needed, turns both on this ancestry and on the lack of any ready alternatives. 'Non-representationalism' would be an option, but it is clumsy and would in any case call for precisification in terms of this 'expressivist' ancestry. 'Pragmatism' is also an option, of course, but here the need for precisification would be even greater. So for the moment, foregrounding respect for my philosophical ancestors, 'expressivism' and 'global expressivism' seem the best of a bad bunch.[14]

---

[13] Williams obscures this point a little, by saying when he introduces the notion of the F-clause that the F-clause appeals to 'what an item conforming to such proprieties can be used (is useful) *for* ... [its] expressive role and/or utility'. (Williams, this volume, 138). This seems clearly a different use of 'expressive' than that involved when in saying that local-expressivist EMUs have an F-clause mentioning the *expression* of an evaluative or practical attitude.

[14] If Williams' terminology catches on, perhaps I shall take to calling myself a global EMU-theorist.

6.2 Local expressivism in hindsight

With the above clarifications, I think that Williams' framework allows us to say something useful about why local (Humean) expressivism was in fact most popular, initially, in cases with certain distinctive features. They turn out to be cases in which we can give an interesting functional description of a state of mind (apparently closely associated with the making of assertions in some class) that is not a matter of saying, blandly, that the state in question is that of believing that P. (That would hardly count as interesting, of course!) In other words, they are cases in which there is an interesting *non-representational* functional characterisation of a mental state to hand – a passion, pro-attitude, credence, inferential disposition, or whatever.

In this way, we can see why certain cases stood out – the peaks illuminated first, as light dawned over the pragmatist landscape, so to speak. They are the cases which, plausibly, do involve 'giving voice' to a state characterisable in terms other than belief. The prominence of these peaks then perhaps obscured the fact that there were other cases, like deflationary accounts of 'true', that fitted the pragmatist model, without this distinctively expressive element – i.e. cases in which there was no such independently characterisable associated mental state to be found.

There are two paths forward from this point, once these peaks are in view. The one actually followed, in most cases, was to say that the distinctive states in question were not beliefs and that the claims that expressed them were not genuine assertions, or not genuinely descriptive. This path turns out to lead into a swamp from which the subject as a whole has yet to extract itself. (I think it is fair to say that the majority of victims, both expressivists and their would-be opponents, have yet to appreciate their predicament.) Williams characterises the mistake rather nicely, I think:

That the expressive function of a particular vocabulary explains its assertional and inferential use proprieties, themselves specifiable in an ontologically conservative way, is the local expressivist's deep insight. The tendency to take this insight to imply that the vocabulary to which his analysis applies is not 'really' descriptive is his *ur*-mistake. The mistake occurs because the temptation to treat describing and expressing as alternatives that we must choose between is acute with respect to the standard candidates for expressivist treatment. This is so because these locutions have a *special* pragmatic significance beyond saying how things in some respects are. Focusing on this special pragmatic significance can encourage us to slip into thinking that use is at bottom only pragmatic significance, forgetting the use patterns that fix conceptual content. In this way, we will come to suppose that in deploying 'true' or 'cause', we aren't really ascribing a property – truth to a statement or causal power to an object – we are *merely* endorsing a claim (or set of claims) or expressing an inferential commitment. (Williams, this volume, 138–9)

Like Williams and Sellars, then, I recommend the second path. This interprets the local expressivists' peaks as involving rather interesting *special kinds of beliefs*: viz., beliefs with respect to which we observe that something unusually interesting and distinctive is taking place at an underlying functional level – at the F-level, in the applicable EMU, to put it in Williams' terms. What makes them beliefs, what gives them conceptual content, what makes them i-representations in my terms, is what happens at the I- and E-levels. But what made them show up on the local expressivists' radar is what's true of them at the F-level.

This diagnosis makes Williams' project of 'respect[ing] expressivist intuitions' (Williams, this volume, 132) a little delicate. It is as if we wanted to respect the lemmings' intuition that a change of scenery would do them a lot of good, without signing up for their *ur*-mistake, the plunging off a cliff that their change of scenery turned out to involve in practice. It requires some careful choice of words, and if we're speaking to the lemmings themselves, we shouldn't expect them to like everything they hear.

Like Williams, however, I think we can find some way to make sense of the original local expressivist intuitions, on both sides of the lines that they themselves drew: on what they thought of as the belief side, we can say that some beliefs in the inclusive sense are more in the e-representational business than others (Williams' ontological test picks this up, more or less); on what they thought of as the other side, we can say that some beliefs do have F-roles associated with psychological states with distinctive roles in our cognitive architecture. (We just need to avoid the trap of thinking that everything that isn't world-tracking has to be like this instead – again, think of 'true'.)

7 THE WORLD REVISITED

Like me, Paul Horwich sees himself as an opponent of what I call object naturalism – in his terms, the view that all that exists is

a vast, unified network of objects, properties and facts that bear spatial, temporal, causal and explanatory relations to one another – a network incorporating observable phenomena, the elementary particles, fields, strings, etc., of physics for which those phenomena provide evidence, and all the macroscopic objects and events built out of such elements. (Horwich, this volume, 112)

Our paths to this common opposition to object naturalism are somewhat different, however. Horwich takes me to subscribe to some version of the view that 'questions of metaphysics – most of which appear superficially to be about the non-linguistic, non-cognitive world – can be answered only, and merely, by attention to our linguistic and conceptual practices' (Horwich, this volume, 113). Horwich rejects this view. As he puts it, his principal goal lies in 'opposing the idea that there are apparently non-linguistic facts that are really matters of language' (Horwich, this volume, 113).

These are very interesting issues, from my point of view, both for their content and their personal context.[15] While I feel that Horwich misconstrues my argument, to some extent – more on this in a moment – I think that a substantial difference of opinion still remains, when those misconstruals are corrected. I shall try to explain and defend my position in contrast to Horwich's and thereby clarify the question of the relevance of my conclusions to the metaphysical issues he has in mind.

7.1 Clarifications

First, then, to the points that concern the structure of my argument in Lecture 1. In outlining what he takes that structure to be, Horwich gives the following gloss of what he calls my 'fundamental assumption':

Metaphysical questions can be answered only in so far as they are transformations of more basic linguo-conceptual questions. A case in point is the question of whether naturalism is correct and of where – if it is correct – such peculiar things as numbers, values and possibilities are to be placed within the natural order. Issues concerning our use of words and our deployment of concepts are fundamental here; and the metaphysical issues of naturalism must be seen as deriving from them. (Horwich, this volume, 115)

Horwich then goes on to explain how I argue that if this assumption is granted, the object naturalist gets back to her intended metaphysical or material issues only by invoking a substantial semantic 'bridge' (from words to things, as it were); and that such a bridge is simply unavailable, if deflationists are right about semantic notions such as reference and truth. Next, he takes me to rely on the claim that 'deflationism is *not* mistaken' – that 'on the contrary, a scientific scrutiny of how the word, "true" is used

---

[15] I have found myself in agreement with Horwich about so many issues, over so many years, that our few significant disagreements – such as this at least *appears* to be – have a particular fascination.

provides compelling reason to endorse it.' And he says that I conclude that object naturalism 'is in principle impossible to establish'.

My concerns about this gloss of my argument arise at three points: with the stated conclusion, with the claimed role and force of my appeal to deflationism and with the status of what Horwich calls my 'fundamental assumption'. Taking my conclusion first, the theses I actually defend in Lecture 1 are as follows:

Priority Thesis   Subject naturalism is theoretically prior to object naturalism, because the latter depends on validation from a subject naturalist perspective.

Invalidity Thesis   There are strong reasons for doubting whether object naturalism deserves to be 'validated' – whether its presuppositions do survive subject naturalist scrutiny.

Strictly speaking, then, I don't argue that object naturalism 'is in principle impossible to establish', but only that it is properly seen as on the table for subject naturalist scrutiny (the priority thesis); and that there are significant reasons for doubting whether it survives scrutiny (the invalidity thesis).

Moreover, while semantic deflationism plays a role at both stages, neither stage rests on it to the extent that Horwich suggests. On the contrary, the priority thesis requires only that deflationism be seen to be a live option, and properly assessed from a subject naturalist standpoint – after all, the priority thesis itself is entirely compatible with a vindication of object naturalism, via a (subject) naturalistic vindication of Representationalism. While for its part, the invalidity thesis claims only that there are 'strong reasons for doubting whether object naturalism deserves to be "validated"'. I offer three such reasons, one of them the attractions of deflationism, and thus remain two steps short of a need to make an all-out commitment to deflationism: I'm only looking for 'strong reasons', and I have two other strings to my bow.

Finally, I think Horwich misconstrues the role of my fundamental assumption, as he terms it. In Lecture 1, the context for this assumption, or my version of it, is provided by the question as to how placement problems arise in philosophy. I note that there are two possible views on this matter:

On one possible view, the starting point is the object itself. We are simply acquainted with X, and hence – in the light of a commitment to object naturalism – come to wonder how this thing-with-which-we-are-acquainted could be the kind of thing studied by science. On the other possible view, the starting point lies in human linguistic practices, broadly construed. Roughly, we note that humans (ourselves or others) employ the term 'X' in language, or the concept X, in thought. In the light of a commitment to object naturalism, again, we come to wonder how what these speakers are thereby talking or thinking *about* could be the kind of thing studied by science. (Chapter 1, 7–8)

Dubbing these two views the material conception and the linguistic conception, respectively, I go on to describe my strategy:

> I'm going to proceed as follows. For the moment, I'll simply assume that the linguistic conception is correct and explore its consequences for object naturalism. (I'll remind readers at several points that my conclusions depend on this assumption.) At the end of the chapter I'll come back to the question whether the assumption is compulsory – whether object naturalism can evade my critical conclusions by adopting the material conception. I'll argue, albeit somewhat tentatively, that this is not a live option and hence that my earlier conclusions cannot be side-stepped in this way. (Chapter 1, 8)

The assumption is thus both less sweeping and more tentative than Horwich suggests: less sweeping, because it concerns only the question as to where placement problems originate, and more tentative, because I am explicitly open to the possibility that it might be challenged (but go on to argue that such a challenge seems unlikely to help my object naturalist opponents).

Horwich responds to the latter arguments – the reasons I give for thinking that my object naturalist opponents cannot retreat to the material conception – and I turn to those responses in a moment. First, I want to acknowledge that there is an important sense in which my own commitment to the kind of 'language-first' view with which Horwich disagrees is more thoroughgoing than the dialectic of Lecture 1 actually requires. As I put it elsewhere, I take it that the kind of global expressivism I want to defend 'isn't a way of doing metaphysics in a pragmatist key' – 'it is a way of doing something like anthropology' (Price 2010: §5). As such, it has its eyes on questions about human thought and linguistic usage (about moral or modal topics, for example), not on the matters a metaphysical approach would take such usage to be *about*.

I would not myself describe this view, as Horwich does, as 'the idea that there are apparently non-linguistic facts that are really matters of language'. In my view, the shift I recommend is not a matter of *recasting* metaphysical issues as issues about language but of *abandoning* the metaphysical questions altogether, in favour of the anthropological questions (though thereby scratching the same fundamental itch, at least in some sense, so long as that itch can be regarded as disquiet about 'what's going on' in a certain region of our practice). But this is little more than a terminological matter. Horwich is quite right that there seems to be a difference between us, in that he wants to continue to take seriously some material-mode metaphysical issues – e.g., to use his own example, this question: 'Is *everything* located within [the] network [of spatio-temporally located objects and relations], as naturalism dictates? Or do certain perfectly real features of the world lie outside it – perhaps numbers, or possibilities, or values, or meanings?' (Horwich, this volume, 112–13) – whereas I think there is little or no non-trivial place for such metaphysical questions, once the anthropological alternative is properly in view. So Horwich and I agree that *if* this question needs to be asked, the object naturalist answer is the wrong one. But we disagree about whether it needs to be asked. Let us now consider Horwich's defence of material-mode metaphysics, in the light of that understanding of the disagreement.

7.2 Anthropology or metaphysics?

As I noted a moment ago, Horwich considers the two arguments I offer in Lecture 1 for not abandoning a linguistic conception of the origin of placement problems. One of these arguments turns on the idea that substantial semantic relations have become, as I put it, 'part of the toolkit of contemporary metaphysics'. I go on to argue that object naturalists face a dilemma, in this respect:

If they appeal to substantial semantic relations, they have some prospect of an argument for naturalism, couched in terms of those relations – for example, an argument that all truths have natural truth-makers. In this case, however, they are implicitly committed to a linguistic conception of the 'raw data' for these investigations ... If they don't appeal to substantial semantic relations, they avoid these difficulties, but lose the theoretical resources with which to formulate a general argument for naturalism, conceived on the object naturalist model. (Chapter 1, 19)

To this Horwich objects that there may be other candidates for a general argument for naturalism, besides the semantic-relation-based version of a Jackson–Lewis argument that I had considered. He offers some examples, but then goes on to say that he doesn't think that they cut much ice, so we do not seem far apart, on this point. In any case, for present purposes a more relevant point is that Horwich notes, quite rightly, that this argument of mine need have no force against a non-naturalist (who won't be looking for such a general argument for naturalism, of course).

For present purposes, then, this leaves my second argument – the fact that 'the cat is out of the bag', as I put it:

The linguistic conception of the placement issue is already in play ... [T]o treat non-cognitivism as an option in these debates is to commit oneself to a linguistic conception of the origin of the problem. The threat to object naturalism takes off from this point, noting that the representationalist assumption is non-compulsory – that there are other possible theoretical approaches to language, in which semantic notions play no significant role. We have thus been offered the prospect of a (subject) naturalistic account of the relevant aspects of human talk and thought, from the perspective of which the material question ('What are Xs?') simply doesn't arise. (Chapter 1, 16)

Horwich responds to this argument, but his characterisation of the argument, and hence his response to it, seems from my point of view to be insufficiently sensitive to the respects in which I want to distance myself from my local expressivist ancestors. Horwich puts it like this:

Price's own principal reason for endorsing that [linguistic] conception of metaphysics … is drawn from an examination of the debates over naturalism. He observes that in order to determine whether or not all facts are natural we must first be able to decide whether allegedly troublesome domains – such as ethics and arithmetic – have even so much as the *capacity* to harbour counterexamples. For example: could there conceivably be genuine *facts* as to what is right and wrong? Does ethics even purport to be in the fact-stating business? And that, he says, is surely a linguistic question. It's a matter of whether ethical sentences have the sort of meaning – i.e. the sort of usage – that enables them to express *propositions*. (Horwich, this volume, 122–3)

Horwich goes on to agree with my point, as he has characterised it, but to argue that it won't get me very far:

[Price's] observation is eminently reasonable. But notice that the linguistic question is a mere preliminary and our settling it will take us only a little distance towards where we are supposed to be going. Questions about the material world often call for clarification and refinement …

In particular, a linguo-conceptual scrutiny of *normative* discourse might lead a philosopher to think that 'wrong' is not a *genuine* predicate (i.e. a predicate at the level of logical form) and therefore that the question whether 'wrongness is naturalistic' doesn't make sense. And this could indeed have considerable bearing on that philosopher's view of whether everything that exists is natural. It might well lead him to a revised sense of what must be done to settle the question of naturalism – a reduction of the number of material-level placement problems that he thinks need to be solved.

But many such problems will remain after such clarificatory preliminaries have been completed – problems concerning the placement of phenomena to whose existence we continue to be committed. Suppose *our* answer to the preliminary linguistic question is that 'wrong' *is* a genuine predicate and so 'stealing is wrong' does express a proposition, i.e. a conceivable fact. So if stealing is wrong, then there *is* a fact to that effect … [W]e're going to need a way of determining whether that fact, if it exists, would be *naturalistic*. (Horwich, this volume, 122–3)

How do I claim to avoid these material-level issues? Certainly not by say-ing 'no', in all the relevant cases, to the traditional questions that Horwich here allows at the linguistic level: 'Could there conceivably be genuine facts as to what is right and wrong? Does ethics even purport to be in the fact-stating business?' On the contrary, as I have emphasised, I want to deflate notions such as *fact* and *proposition*, giving up entirely the *negative*, seman-tic side of traditional non-cognitivism – the view that statements in some disputed class are not genuinely factual, descriptive or truth-evaluable.

In a sense, then, I have already welded shut the escape hatch from metaphysics that Horwich here allows me. But I have no need of it, in my view, because I have in mind a different escape route. My linguistic cat, though freed from its bag by traditional non-cognitivists, now seeks its fortune in the company of descendants of those original expressivists who differ in crucial ways.

With Williams' help, in fact, the cat now gorges itself on a diet of Sellarsian EMUs. The crucial question, as the EMUs so elegantly reveal, is whether the story we tell about the *use* of the terms and vocabulary in question – 'wrong', to use Horwich's example – is itself ontologically committed to some corresponding domain of facts or properties. If so, then anthropology leads us back to the material questions, though in such a way that the issue of the naturalistic status of the properties in question is already settled, in my view – they have turned out to be needed in an explanation of our natural practice, after all.[16] But if not, then it does not.

Suppose that the latter option turns out to be the right one, for 'wrong' and its normative cousins. I want to say that the puzzle of the 'placement' of normative facts and properties is now resolved, in the light of the fact that we now take it that we understand 'what's going on' when we and our fellow speakers use these normative terms and concepts. What may have presented as a 'puzzling plurality' at the material level – at the level of *properties* – has been explained in terms of a non-puzzling 'natural plurality of kinds of talk', as I put it in Lecture 1.

At this point, is there any content or interest in the question that Horwich offers as the kind of metaphysical issue that I overlook (or wrongly try to render linguistic), namely, the question as to whether, if we were to agree that there is a fact to the effect that stealing is wrong, 'that fact ... would be

---

[16] Some Representationalists will get off the boat at this point, I think. They will claim to have a notion of representational function such that an EMU can tell us that the F-role of a vocabulary is to keep track of items in some platonic, nonnatural realm. In my view they thus render themselves vulnerable to the considerations that underlie my invalidity thesis, in the dialectic of Lecture 1.

naturalistic'? My inclination is to say that we can reply to this question by saying either that it is ill posed, or that it has a trivial (negative) answer – relying, in either case, on what the relevant EMU has told us about nature and function of normative discourse – and that it doesn't matter much which answer we choose. Either way, there's no place left for a non-trivial metaphysical investigation. Someone who persists in pressing a *metaphysical* question – 'Is wrongness a natural property?', say – when the relevant linguistic considerations are in view is like someone who wants to ask 'But is rhubarb *really* a fruit?', when it has been explained that 'fruit' can mean two different things and that rhubarb is a fruit in the culinary sense but not in the botanical sense. We are tempted to say that they haven't understood what they have just been told.

In my view, then, the combination of the linguistic cat and Williams' EMUs leaves little place for Horwich's kind of *metaphysical* non-naturalism. The first job of the cat, as personified by the early non-cognitivists, was to make us sensitive to the issue as to what we are doing with language – to encourage us to question the 'transparency' of language, in Russell's metaphor. Once this issue has been raised, once we have learnt to make the sideways, anthropological glance at our own ways of speaking, then the option of handling placement problems entirely at the linguistic level is on the table. At this point, there's no going back: the cat is out of the bag. What it takes to return us to metaphysics is a particular kind of answer to what is first and foremost an anthropological question: it takes the right sort of EMU, an ontologically non-conservative EMU (which my subject naturalist expressivist takes to be nowhere in sight, in the cases in question).[17]

The traditional non-cognitivists' mistake was to fail to exploit the full potential of the cat, by making the mistake of invoking the traditional birfucation thesis to characterise the relevant options. As Williams puts it, in a passage I quoted above, the non-cognitivists' 'deep insight' was that 'the expressive function of a particular vocabulary explains its assertional and inferential use proprieties, themselves specifiable in an ontologically conservative way'. Their 'ur-mistake' was the 'tendency to take this insight to imply that the vocabulary to which his analysis applies is not "really" descriptive'. It seems to me that Horwich may still be to some extent in the

---

[17] I am not sure whether Horwich would disagree at this point. As I noted above, my own view (presupposing subject naturalism) is that there is very little room for non-naturalist metaphysics to gain any traction here – little room, in other words, for an ontologically non-conservative EMU to make appeal to *nonnatural* ontology or states of affairs.

grip of this *ur*-mistake and that that may explain his lingering attachment
to the metaphysical questions. If so, then by my lights, he hasn't fully
appreciated how in letting the cat out of the bag we also let the fly out of
that particular fly bottle.

8 BRANDOM ON ANTI-REPRESENTATIONALISM

Finally, then, to Robert Brandom, whose characteristically incisive essay
discusses the view in advocacy of which I align myself with Rorty, namely, a
thoroughgoing global anti-representationalism. While sympathetic to some
of the motivations for such a position, Brandom concludes that Rorty and
I go too far:

> Rorty and Price agree that the evils representationalism is prey to require, or
> at least make advisable, global anti-representationalism. The sort of expressivist,
> deflationary, pragmatic account of what one is doing in using representational
> vocabulary that I am advocating suggests that this response is an overreaction. I have
> tried in this essay to assemble some analytic materials that might help us towards
> a more nuanced conclusion. ... [R]epresentational vocabulary can be understood
> as performing an important, indeed essential, expressive role in making explicit
> a discursive representational dimension of semantic content that necessarily helps
> articulate every autonomous discursive practice. (Brandom, this volume, 109)

In one sense, I find it easy to agree with Brandom at this point. Indeed,
in Lecture 2, I characterised myself as shifting from 'nihilism' to 'dualism'
about representation – saying that far from rejecting representation, as
Rorty does, I now recognised not one but *two* varieties of it!

However, I also noted that that somewhat tongue-in-cheek concession
did not imply that I did not remain a Rortyean anti-representationalist in
a deeper sense. My faithfulness to Rorty turns on the fact that neither of
my two notions of representation (i-representation and e-representation) is
what traditional representationalist had in mind – on the contrary, I think,
the traditional view rests on confusing them.

In my remarks here, I want to enlist Sellars as an ally (drawing on points
emphasised above), in order to argue that Brandom, too, fails to see the
importance of distinguishing these different senses of 'representation' (and
associated terms) and hence misses a sense in which the position he recommends remains entirely compatible with a global anti-representationalism,
of the kind I recommend. Accordingly, while I agree with Brandom on
most points, I feel that he does not appreciate the extent to which the

position we share (at least in most respects) is indeed a vindication of the radical Rortyean viewpoint.[18]

8.1 Representational vocabularies

Brandom offers the following characterisation of his own account of the expressive function of representational vocabulary in ordinary usage:

What I am advocating is a *soft* global semantic representationalism. It is an account of the *expressive* role of representational vocabulary that shows the same expressive function that makes it ubiquitously available to express a crucial dimension of conceptual contentfulness also *dis*qualifies it from playing a fundamental *explanatory* role in an account of the semantics of at least some discursive practices. For the expressive role characteristic of representational vocabulary (like that of logical, modal and normative vocabulary) can itself be fully specified in a social, normative, inferential pragmatic metavocabulary that does *not* itself employ representational vocabulary. (Brandom, this volume, 106–7)

As he himself notes, the kind of representational vocabulary that he has in mind at this point is best thought of as i-representation, in my terms:

I offer the story I am gesturing at here (and have told elsewhere), about why what is expressed by *de re* ascriptions of propositional attitudes is present wherever propositional contents in the inferential-functional sense are in play as a way of redeeming the promissory note that Price has issued under the rubric of 'i-representation'. (Brandom, this volume, 106)

From my point of view, in other words, it is natural (and very congenial) to read Brandom as offering an account of at least one important facet of what I have called the Level 1 aspect of my two-level pragmatist picture – in other words, of what *unifies* the various assertoric vocabularies. And as we have just seen, Brandom himself notes that this aspect of his view is global in scope, explaining the point as follows:

The account has the consequence … that [this] representational dimension turns out to be ubiquitous. *Every* vocabulary can be used in expressing commitments that can be both attributed and acknowledged. Every vocabulary can figure in *de re* ascriptions, and so be talked about in representational vocabulary. (In fact, the vocabulary of *de re* ascriptions can itself be used to ascribe such ascriptions *de re*.) So representational vocabulary makes explicit an essential and ubiquitous

---

[18] As in a previous piece (Price 2010), I am arguing, in effect, that Brandom is further to the left than he himself believes.

dimension of conceptual content. This is a kind of global semantic representationalism, underwritten by a *local* expressivism about representational vocabulary
itself. (Brandom, this volume, 105)

In a moment I shall want to stress that although I agree that this is '*a* kind
of global semantic representationalism', it is nevertheless very different
from the view to which Rorty and I have been opposed. That point aside,
however, I am in complete agreement with Brandom at this stage.

Brandom continues:

What I am doing, I think, is just filling in Price's notion of i-representation.
At least, I want to offer this account of what is expressed by *de re* ascriptions
of propositional attitudes for that purpose. But I also want to emphasise how
serious the need for such a filling-in is. For, as things stand at the end of his
Descartes Lectures, I think the notion of i-representation is a mere placeholder
– the mark of an aspiration rather than the specification of a serviceable concept. My reasons for saying that will emerge if we ask what makes the notion
of i-representation a notion of a kind or sense of 'representation'. If, as Price
recommends, we look for it horizontally, at the relations states and locutions
stand in to other states and locutions, to the functional role they play in a system of others, rather than vertically, to their mapping or tracking relations to
something outside the system, what is it about such roles that justifies us in treating them as *representations* in *any* sense? Price likes the idea – at the core of my
own thought – that a decisive line is crossed when we become entitled to think
of the relations they stand in to one another as *inferential* relations. Indeed, I
think we then become entitled to think of them (for the first time) as expressing
propositional contents. For me, such contents are just what can play the role of
premises and conclusions of inferences – what can both serve as and stand in need
of *reasons*. But what results from that view is at least to begin with a notion of
i-*expression*, not i-*representation*. For what does expressing propositional contents
in this sense have to do with representation? Here it looks as though Price is seeking
to procure by terminological fiat what can legitimately be secured only by honest
toil. (Brandom, this volume, 105–6)

The point is a good one, even if I could reply that my interest in distinguishing i-representation and e-representation was more in *taxonomy* – in
the project of distinguishing two importantly *different* notions (or clusters
of notions) that are often assimilated and confused with one another – than
in defending the right of either notion to bear the label 'representation'. For
even in this modest form, my claim needs some explanation of the fact that
these notions could plausibly have been thought of as 'representational'
in the first place. I am happy to accept that Brandom's account of *de re*

ascriptions of propositional attitudes provides at least a significant part of this explanation, in the case of i-representations.[19]

Brandom then turns to the question of the implications of this sort of pragmatic account of representational vocabulary.

> The question remains: just how deflationary is it to provide this sort of non-representational pragmatic metavocabulary? It opens up a space for a view that *is* deflationary, according to which this sort of account in terms of pragmatic metavocabulary is all there is to say about the vocabulary in question. No further semantic questions should be asked or could be answered. Price might be tempted by such a view. But it also seems compatible with acknowledging that at least in some cases an orthodox representational semantic metavocabulary might *also* be available. That is, we can ask, does this sort of deflationary *explanatory* anti-representationalism about what representational vocabulary expresses entail a global explanatory anti-representationalism? (Brandom, this volume, 107)

'I do not see that it does', Brandom replies.

> For it might well be that although representational vocabulary need not be used in specifying the use of **representational** vocabulary itself (because its expressive role can be fully specified in a non-representational, social-normative-inferential pragmatic metavocabulary) nonetheless in order to specify the proprieties governing the use of ordinary empirical descriptive vocabulary, its distinctive expressive role requires specification with the help of a **representational** semantic metavocabulary. I have talked so far only about *discursive* representational vocabulary. But this is not the only candidate for a representational semantic metavocabulary. In addition there are at least three others: those that express *mapping* relations (static), those that express *tracking* processes (dynamic) and those that express the *practical* intentional directedness of goal-seeking systems. I think the expressive role characteristic of each of these kinds of representational vocabulary can also be made fully explicit in an *inferential*, itself non-representational pragmatic metavocabulary. Understanding (practically taking or treating) something as a representation in the mapping sense is exercising the ability to make inferences from map facts to mapped facts. Tracking is updating a map in that sense so as to keep the map inferences good as the mapped facts change. Taking or treating something as a practical intentional system is understanding its behavior in terms of sample pieces of practical reasoning. Here, too, the possibility of an adequate non-representational pragmatic metavocabulary for these varieties of representational vocabulary would not seem to rule out their playing fundamental roles in a semantic metavocabulary for some other vocabulary – quite possibly, empirical descriptive vocabulary. (Brandom, this volume, 107–8, emphasis in bold mine)

[19] If I have reservations, it is on the grounds that *representation* is a cluster concept (in fact, if I am right, a two-cluster concept), and that we need to say something about other elements in the relevant cluster, too, such as notions of truth, tracking and the like.

Three comments on this passage: first, I am not disagreeing that *mapping*, *tracking* and *practical intentional directedness* are useful notions to have in one's theoretical repertoire for characterising the roles of some vocabularies. On the contrary, I take the first two, at least, to count as examples of e-representation, in my terms – indeed, I think the notion of e-representation is very usefully elaborated by the distinctions Brandom draws at this point. So I take Brandom's remarks to be fully compatible with my own picture (though not, as I'll explain in a moment, in tension with my residual Rortyian anti-representationalism).

Second, I suspect that Brandom's own formal machinery may be leading him slightly astray here, in leading to a confusion between (1) the first-order question as to what practical ability properly counts as mapping – Brandom's answer: 'Exercising the ability to make inferences from map facts to mapped facts' – and (2) a meta-level question about the 'expressive role characteristic of [the use of a] representational vocabulary' that includes the term 'mapping'. Why are these issues distinct? Simply because a creature *engaged in mapping behaviour* need not have the *theoretical vocabulary* required to *say* that this is what it is doing, or even the *practical abilities* it would be the role of such a *saying* to express. (Argument: think about bees.)[20] Of these two questions, (1) seems to me the more important one. While I would be the first to agree that we *can* legitimately ask questions about the expressive role of our scientific vocabulary, that option should not blind us to the possibility of simply *using* that vocabulary – in this case vocabulary ascribing e-representational relations between words and our physical environments – in describing the distinctive character of those vocabularies that do stand in such relations.

Third, in referring both to *de re* ascriptions and to these new examples (talk of mapping, tracking and the like) as cases of 'representational semantic vocabularies', Brandom seems to me to be missing the opportunities provided by the recognition that *representation* is not a usefully univocal notion. Much better, in my view, to insist that these new examples are just *different* – to recognise an important *change of subject matter* between the two uses of 'representational' I have emphasised in bold in the passage above – than to try to pretend they are further examples of some usefully unified class. As noted earlier, moreover, I think I can enlist Sellars as an ally at this point. Here he is, carefully distinguishing his (as I would

---

[20] Brandom is thinking about examples of linguistic creatures, but similar examples can be found there – there's much that we *do* that we don't have the theoretical vocabulary to *describe*.

put it, *e-representational*) notion of *picturing* from other familiar semantic notions: 'The concept of a linguistic picture is meta-linguistic in a sense which must be carefully distinguished from meta-linguistic statements in the Carnap–Tarski sense.' Sellars goes on to say that the former concept concerns 'correlations [that] involve the complex machinery of language entry transitions (noticings), intra-linguistic moves (inference, identification by means of criteria) and language departure transitions (volitions pertaining to epistemic activity), and [that] must not be confused with the pseudo-relation of *standing for* or *denoting*' (Sellars 1968: 136).

I take Sellars' point here to be analogous to the one I made in Lecture 2, in saying that we need to distinguish the notion of keeping track as something that we do within the assertoric language game – a notion constituted, within the game, by the fact that the normative structures always hold open the possibility that one's present commitments will be challenged, so that 'correctness' is always in principle beyond the present reach of any individual player – from a notion that we might employ from outside the game, in saying that in at least some of its versions its function is to aid the players in keeping track of their physical environment. As I put it there, there's a temptation to call both kinds of external constraint 'truth', but we shouldn't make the mistake of thinking that we're dealing with two aspects or sub-species *of a single notion of truth*. Both notions may be useful, for various theoretical purposes, but we shouldn't confuse them, and we should keep in mind that they present themselves as objects of enquiry in quite different ways: the in-game notion presents itself (like *de re* ascriptions) as a feature of our linguistic practice that we want to *explain* – the term 'true' is part of a linguistic *explanandum*. The other notion is a relation we postulate in the world, as part of a theoretical *explanans*. As Sellars puts the analogous point, once again, in his framework: 'Picturing is a complex matter-of-factual relation and, as such, belongs in quite a different box from the concepts of denotation and truth' (1968: 136).

8.2 *Sticking up for Rorty*

Thus my main complaint about Brandom's essay could be put by saying that I take him to be insufficiently Sellarsian, in failing to take the opportunity to draw some important distinctions among the various things he lumps together as 'representational' vocabularies. These distinctions are needed, I have urged, if we are to avoid some old mistakes and temptations.

In particular, these distinctions are crucial to explaining in what sense – despite acknowledging that there are not one but two clusters of 'representational' vocabularies of considerable importance and theoretical interest – I remain a card-carrying Rortyian anti-representationalist. For in my view the bad kind of representationalism – the kind I join Rorty in opposing – depends precisely on failing to notice the distinction between two harmless, in fact useful, kinds of representation (loosely so-called, at least). In Lecture 2, I expressed this in terms of the need to prise apart the (i-representational) content assumption, from the (e-representational) correspondence assumption. Here is Brandom himself, on the picture that I take prising these assumptions apart to enable us to avoid:

> A popular idea is that what sentences represent in the sense of designate is a special kind of thing: states of affairs. The thought is that what *true* sentences designate is *facts*, and some states of affairs are merely *possible* facts, designated by false sentences. This model inevitably leads to metaphysical extravagance. For there are lots of different kinds of sentences, because there are many different ways of using sentences (things one can do with them). Pretty soon one must worry about logical facts and states of affairs (including negative and conditional ones), modal facts and states of affairs, probabilistic ones, normative ones, semantic and intentional ones, and so on, and corresponding kinds of properties to articulate each of them. One of the motivations for various local expressivisms is precisely to avoid such extravagance. (Brandom, this volume, 98)

I take it that so long as we prise apart the content assumption and the correspondence assumption – so long as we distinguish i-representation from e-representation – it is easy to avoid such metaphysical extravagance, while retaining much of the intuitive picture of which it is otherwise a consequence. So long as we understand that *designation* belongs at the i-representational level (in Sellars' terms, like 'the pseudo-relation of *standing for* or *denoting*') and think of states of affairs, correspondingly, as mere projections of sentences – and so long as we thereby distinguish designation of states of affairs from the various 'complex matter-of-factual relation[s]' that our utterances bear, in various ways and to various degrees, to items in our natural environments – then we can free ourselves of this temptation to generate puzzles of metaphysical extravagance from mere linguistic pluralities.

To solve the problem in this way, we have to give up the idea that there is a single kind of relation of which two things are true: first, that it is the relation that sentences in general bear to the states of affairs that they are 'about'; and second, that it is a relation that some sentences, at least (the 'genuinely factual' ones) stand in to items in our physical environment. That is, we have to give up the idea that semantic 'aboutness', in the general sense, is a relation of correlation or correspondence between sentences (or thoughts) conceived as items in the world, on the one hand, and other items in the world, on the other. This is the traditional representationalist picture that we need to abandon, and I take it that it is at least closely related to the one that Rorty recommends that we abandon. (As I have said, I think that Sellars also saw that we need to abandon it.)

8.3 Rortyian enough for Rorty?

My disagreement with Brandom here does not go very deep, I think. It is about the right way to characterise the position in the landscape of a viewpoint that we both share, in all important respects. More precisely, it is about how best to characterise the shift involved in moving to that viewpoint, from more popular positions in the landscape. I have argued that the shift does involve a global rejection of a certain representationalist conception and hence, to that extent, amounts to a defence of Rorty's anti-representationalism.

To finish, however, I want to qualify this claim in one important respect. I don't mean to suggest that Rorty would have felt that my view – my global expressivism, with its bifurcated notions of representation – was sufficiently Rortyian for his own tastes. On the contrary, I think: Rorty was famously a critic (see Rorty [1988], for example) of Sellars' invocation of the notion of 'picturing' and would presumably have objected to my e-representations in the same way. Nor would he have liked my i-representations. Responding to an ancestor of some of the material in Lecture 2, which invoked what I described as an 'internal' notion of representation, corresponding to what I later called i-representation, Rorty said the following:

> [A]s you might have expected, my doubts are all about whether you are radical enough. I am not sure that it is worthwhile retaining lower-case representationalism by means of your notion of 'internal representations', just as I am unsure whether it was good strategy for Brandom to try to revivify representationalist notions within the bosom of his inferentialism. (Rorty, email communication, 19 May 2006)

(As he goes on to say, 'My strategy is more slash-burn-uproot-sow-with-salt than yours.')

Thus I may be somewhere between Rorty and Brandom – though if so, I think, then not very far from either. Rorty is perhaps more dismissive of representational notions, Brandom more inclined to retain them by explaining them (and hence making them respectable by subject-naturalist lights). My contribution (following Sellars, as I now see it) is to urge that we draw some distinctions before making up our minds – that we recognise that the representational vocabulary at loose in the contemporary landscape is not of a single logical category, much less of a single genus. Once we understand that, I think, then we may well want to slash-and-burn-uproot-sow-with-salt in some places, gently explain and deflate in other places and theorise as anthropologists in yet further places. So, as Brandom urges, a very 'nuanced conclusion'. But these distinctions are a necessary part of the nuance, in my view. In so far as neither Brandom nor Rorty seems to me sufficiently sensitive to them, I may be closer to Sellars than to either.

Bibliography

Armour-Garb, B. P. and Beall, J. C. (eds.). 2005. *Deflationary Truth*. Chicago, IL: Open Court.

Armstrong, D. M. 1993. 'A world of states of affairs', *Philosophical Perspectives*, 7: 429–40.

Auxier, R. and Hahn, L. (eds.). 2010. *The Philosophy of Richard Rorty*. Chicago, IL: Open Court.

Black, M. (ed.). 1950. *Philosophical Analysis*. Ithaca, NY: Cornell University Press.

Blackburn, S. 1980. 'Truth, realism, and the regulation of theory', *Midwest Studies in Philosophy*, 5: 353–72. Reprinted in Blackburn (1993), pp. 15–34. Page references in the text are to the latter version.

1984. *Spreading the Word*. Oxford University Press.

1993. *Essays in Quasi-Realism*. Oxford University Press.

1994. *The Oxford Dictionary of Philosophy*. Oxford University Press.

1998a. *Ruling Passions: A Theory of Practical Reasoning*. Oxford University Press.

1998b. 'Wittgenstein, Wright, Rorty and minimalism', *Mind*, 107: 157–82.

2005. *Truth: A Guide for the Perplexed*. London: Penguin Books.

2007. 'Pragmatism: all or some', conference paper delivered at *Expressivism, Pragmatism and Representationalism,* Centre for Time, University of Sydney, 29 August.

Boghossian, P. 1989. 'The rule-following considerations', *Mind*, 98: 507–49.

1990. 'The status of content', *Philosophical Review*, 99: 157–84.

1996. 'Analyticity reconsidered', *Noûs*, 30: 360–91.

Braddon-Mitchell, D. and Nola, R. (eds.). 2009. *Conceptual Analysis and Philosophical Naturalism*. Cambridge, MA: MIT Press.

Brandom, R. 1994. *Making It Explicit: Reasoning, Representing, and Discursive Commitment*. Cambridge, MA: Harvard University Press.

2000. *Articulating Reasons: An Introduction to Inferentialism*. Cambridge, MA: Harvard University Press.

2002a. 'Expressive vs. explanatory deflationism about truth', in Schantz (2002), pp. 103–19. Reprinted in Armour-Garb and Beall (2005), pp. 237–57.

2002b. *Tales of the Mighty Dead: Historical Essays in the Metaphysics of Intentionality*. Cambridge, MA: Harvard University Press.

2004. 'Hermeneutic practices and theories of meaning', *SATS – Nordic Journal of Philosophy*, 5: 5–26.

2008. *Between Saying and Doing: Towards an Analytic Pragmatism*. Oxford University Press.

2009. *Reason in Philosophy: Animating Ideas*. Cambridge, MA: Harvard University Press.

Cartwright, N. 1999. *The Dappled World: A Study of the Boundaries of Science*. Cambridge University Press.

Chalmers, D. 1996. *The Conscious Mind: In Search of a Fundamental Theory*. Oxford University Press.

Davidson, D. 1974. 'On the very idea of a conceptual scheme', *Proceedings and Addresses of the American Philosophical Association*, 47: 5–20. Reprinted in Davidson (2001), pp. 183–98.

1983. 'A coherence theory of truth and knowledge', in Henrich (1983), pp. 423–38. Reprinted in Davidson (2001b), pp. 135–57. Page references in the text are to the latter version.

1986. 'Empirical content', in LePore (1986), pp. 320–32.

2001a. *Inquiries into Truth and Interpretation*. Oxford University Press.

2001b. *Subjective, Intersubjective, Objective*. Oxford University Press.

De Caro, M. and Macarthur, D. (eds.). 2004. *Naturalism in Question*. Cambridge, MA: Harvard University Press.

deVries, W. A. 2005. *Wilfrid Sellars*. Durham: Acumen.

Dreier, J. 2004. 'Meta-ethics and the problem of creeping minimalism', *Philosophical Perspectives*, 18: 23–44.

Dupré, J. 1993. *The Disorder of Things: Metaphysical Foundations of the Disunity of Science*. Cambridge, MA: Harvard University Press.

Feigl, H., Maxwell, G. and Scriven, M. (eds.). 1957. *Minnesota Studies in the Philosophy of Science*, vol. II. Minneapolis, MN: University of Minnesota Press.

Feigl, H. and Scriven, M. (eds.). 1956. *Minnesota Studies in the Philosophy of Science*, vol. I. Minneapolis, MN: University of Minnesota Press.

Field, H. 1994. 'Deflationist views of meaning and content', *Mind*, 103: 249–84.

Hegel, G. W. F. 1931. *The Phenomenology of Mind*. New York: Dover Publications.

Henrich, D. (ed.). 1983. *Kant oder Hegel*. Stuttgart: Klett-Cotta.

Horwich, P. 1998. *Truth*, 2nd edn. Oxford University Press.

2001. 'A defense of minimalism', *Synthese*, 126: 149–65.

2008. 'Ungrounded reason', *Journal of Philosophy*, 105: 453–71. Reprinted with revision as Chapter 10 of Horwich (2010).

2010. *Truth – Meaning – Reality*. Oxford University Press.

Hume, D. 1902. *Enquiry Concerning the Principles of Morals*, 2nd edn. Oxford University Press.

Jackson, F. 1997. 'Naturalism and the fate of the M-worlds', *Proceedings of the Aristotelian Society, Supplementary Volume*, 71: 269–82.

1998. *From Metaphysics to Ethics*. Oxford: Clarendon Press.

Jackson, F. and Pettit, P. 1998. 'A problem for expressivism', *Analysis*, 58: 239–51.

Jeffrey, R. C. (ed.). 1980. *Studies in Inductive Logic and Probability*, vol. ii. Berkeley, CA: University of California Press.

Knell, S. 2004. *Propositionaler Gehalt und diskursive Kontoführung: Eine Untersuchung zur Begrundung der Sprachabhangigkeit Intentionaler Zustande bei Brandom*. Berlin: Walter De Gruyter.

Knowles, J. and Rydenfelt, H. (eds.). 2011. *Pragmatism, Science and Naturalism*. Frankfurt am Main: Peter Lang.

Kraut, R. 1990. 'Varieties of pragmatism', *Mind*, 99: 157–83.

LePore, E. (ed.). 1986. *Truth and Interpretation: Perspectives on the Philosophy of Donald Davidson*. Oxford: Blackwell.

Lewis, D. 1966. 'An argument for the identity theory', *Journal of Philosophy*, 63: 17–25.

1970. 'How to define theoretical terms', *Journal of Philosophy*, 67: 427–46.

1972. 'Psychophysical and theoretical identifications', *Australasian Journal of Philosophy*, 50: 249–58.

1979. 'Attitudes de dicto and de se', *Philosophical Review*, 88: 513–43.

1980. 'A subjectivist's guide to objective chance', in Jeffrey (1980), pp. 183–200. Reprinted with added postscripts in Lewis (1986), pp. 83–132.

1986. *Philosophical Papers*, vol. ii. Oxford University Press.

Macarthur, D. and Price, H. 2007. 'Pragmatism, quasi-realism and the global challenge', in Misak (2007), pp. 91–120.

McDowell, J. 1980. 'Quotation and saying that', in Platts (1980), pp. 206–37.

1994. *Mind and World*. Cambridge, MA: Harvard University Press.

Mellor, D. H. (ed.). 1990. *Philosophical Papers*. Cambridge University Press.

Menand, L. 2001. *The Metaphysical Club: A Story of Ideas in America*. New York: Farrar, Strauss & Giroux.

Menzies, P. and Price, H. 2009. 'Is semantics in the plan?', in Braddon-Mitchell and Nola (2009), pp. 183–200.

Millikan, R. G. 1984. *Language, Thought, and Other Biological Categories*. Cambridge, MA: MIT Press.

Misak, C. (ed.). 2007. *The New Pragmatists*. Oxford University Press.

Moore, G. E. 1903. *Principia Ethica*. Cambridge University Press.

O'Shea, J. R. 2007. *Wilfrid Sellars: Naturalism with a Normative Turn*. Cambridge: Polity Press.

Perry, J. 1979. 'The problem of the essential indexical', *Noûs*, 13: 3–21.

Platts, M. (ed.). 1980. *Reference, Truth and Reality: Essays on the Philosophy of Language*. London: Routledge & Kegan Paul.

Price, H. 1988. *Facts and the Function of Truth*. Oxford: Blackwell.

1991. 'Agency and probabilistic causality', *British Journal for the Philosophy of Science*, 42: 157–76.

1992. 'Metaphysical pluralism', *Journal of Philosophy*, 89: 387–409. Reprinted in Price (2011b), pp. 34–53.

1997. 'Naturalism and the fate of the M-worlds', *Proceedings of the Aristotelian Society, Supplementary Volume*, 71: 247–67. Reprinted in Price (2011), pp. 132–47.

1998. 'Two paths to pragmatism', *European Review of Philosophy*, 3: 109–47. Reprinted in Price (2011b), pp. 80–111.

2003. 'Truth as convenient friction', *Journal of Philosophy*, 100: 167–90. Reprinted in Price (2011b), pp. 163–83.

2004. 'Naturalism without representationalism', in De Caro and Macarthur (2004), pp. 71–88. Reprinted in Price (2011b), pp. 184–99.

2006. 'Blackburn and the war on error', *Australasian Journal of Philosophy*, 84: 603–14.

2007. 'Quining naturalism', *Journal of Philosophy*, 104: 375–405.

2008. 'Brandom and Hume on the genealogy of modals', *Philosophical Topics*, 36: 87–97.

2009. 'The semantic foundations of metaphysics', in Ravenscroft (2009), pp. 111–40. Reprinted in Price (2011b), pp. 253–78.

2010. 'One cheer for representationalism?', in Auxier and Hahn (2010), pp. 269–89. Reprinted in Price (2011b), pp. 304–22.

2011a. 'Expressivism for two voices', in Knowles and Rydenfelt (2011), pp. 87–113.

2011b. *Naturalism Without Mirrors*. Oxford University Press.

2012. 'Causation, chance and the rational significance of supernatural evidence', *Philosophical Review*, 121: 483–538.

Putnam, H. (ed.). 1978. *Meaning and the Moral Sciences*. London: Routledge & Kegan Paul.

1981. *Reason, Truth and History*. Cambridge University Press.

Quine, W. V. 1951. 'Two dogmas of empiricism', *Philosophical Review*, 60: 20–43.

1970. *Philosophy of Logic*. Englewood Cliffs, NJ: Prentice-Hall.

Ramsey, F. P. 1990. 'General propositions and causality', in Mellor (1990), pp. 145–63.

Ravenscroft, I. (ed.). 2009. *Minds, Worlds and Conditionals: Essays in Honour of Frank Jackson*. Oxford University Press.

Rorty, R. 1980. *Philosophy and the Mirror of Nature*. Cambridge University Press.

1988. 'Representation, social practice, and truth', *Philosophical Studies*, 54: 215–28.

1989. *Contingency, Irony, and Solidarity*. Cambridge University Press.

Ryle, G. 1950. '"If", "So", and "Because"', in Black (1950), pp. 323–40.

Schantz, R. (ed.). 2002. *What Is Truth?* Berlin: Hawthorne de Gruyter.

Scharp, K. and Brandom, R. (eds.). 2007. *In the Space of Reasons: Selected Essays of Wilfrid Sellars*. Cambridge, MA: Harvard University Press.

Schiller, F. C. 1907. *Studies in Humanism*. London: Macmillan.

Schilpp, P. A. (ed.). 1963. *The Philosophy of Rudolph Carnap*. Chicago, IL: Open Court.

Sellars, W. 1953. 'Inference and meaning', *Mind*, 62: 313–38. Reprinted in Scharp and Brandom (2007), Chapter 1.

1954. 'Some reflections on language games', *Philosophy of Science*, 21: 204–28. Reprinted in Scharp and Brandom (2007), Chapter 2.

1956. 'Empiricism and the philosophy of mind', in Feigl and Scriven (1956), pp. 253–329. Reprinted in Sellars (1963c), pp. 127–96.

1957. 'Counterfactuals, dispositions, and the causal modalities', in Feigl et al. (1957), pp. 225–308.

1962a. 'Naming and saying', *Philosophy of Science*, 29: 7–26.

1962b. 'Truth and "correspondence"', *Journal of Philosophy*, 59: 29–56. Reprinted in Sellars (1963c), pp. 197–224.

1963a. 'Empiricism and abstract entities', in Schilpp (1963), pp. 431–68.

1963b. 'Philosophy and the scientific image of man', in Sellars (1963c), pp. 1–40. Reprinted in Scharp and Brandom (2007), Chapter 14.

1963c. *Science, Perception and Reality*. New York: The Humanities Press.

1968. *Science and Metaphysics: Variations on Kantian themes*. London: Routledge & Kegan Paul.

Sellars, W. and Chisholm, R. M. 1957. 'Intentionality and the mental', in Feigl et al. (1957), pp. 507–39.

Smith, M. 1994. *The Moral Problem*. Oxford: Blackwell.

Stich, S. 1996. *Deconstructing the Mind*. Oxford University Press.

Strawson, P. F. 1950. 'Truth', *Proceedings of the Aristotelian Society, Supplementary Volume*, 24: 129–56.

1992. *Individuals: An Essay in Descriptive Metaphysics*. London: Methuen.

Wanderer, J. 2008. *Robert Brandom*. Montreal: McGill-Queens University Press.

Williams, M. 1977. *Groundless Belief*. New Haven, CT: Yale University Press.

Williamson, T. 2007. *The Philosophy of Philosophy*. Oxford: Blackwell.

Wittgenstein, L. 1922. *Tractatus Logico-Philosophicus*. London: Routledge & Kegan Paul.

1953. *Philosophical Investigations*. Oxford University Press.

Wright, C. 1992. *Truth and Objectivity*. Cambridge, MA: Harvard University Press.

Index